The Coastal Chronicles

Volume III

by
Jack E. Fryar, Jr.

Dram Tree Books

First Edition 2022.
Published in the United States of America by Dram Tree Books

Publisher's Cataloging-in-Publication Data
(Provided by DRT Press)

Names: Fryar, Jack E., Jr., author.
Title: The coastal chronicles, volume III / by Jack E. Fryar, Jr.
Description: Includes bibliographical references. | Wilmington, NC: Dram Tree Books, 2022.
Identifiers: ISBN 9780984490097
Subjects: LCSH Atlantic Coast (N.C.)--History. | North Carolina--History. | North Carolina--Atlantic Coast. | North Carolina--History--Colonial period, ca. 1600-1775. | North Carolina--History--Civil War, 1861-1865. | North Carolina--History--20th century. | North Carolina--History--21st century. | BISAC HISTORY / United States / State & Local / South (AL, AR, FL, GA, KY, LA, MS, NC, SC, TN, VA, WV)
Classification: LCC F262.A84 F79 2022 | DDC 975.6--dc23

Dram Tree Books
P.O. Box 7183
Wilmington, N.C. 28406
www.dramtreebooks.weebly.com
dramtreebooks@gmail.com
(910) 538-4076
(Call for bulk discounts!)

These stories are dedicated to Alejandra, Alexa, Bart, Maddi, Dylan, Arabeny, Sarah, Ethan, Olivia, Kailee, Mynnie, Evea, Victor, Lilian, and all of the other students it has been my privilege to teach. Introducing you to the complexities and importance of history may just be the most valuable thing I have done in my life, and I thank you for the opportunity. I have no doubt you will all be good stewards of our future.

The Coastal Chronicles Volume III

Contents

Coastal Cousins...2

Having A Voice:
Black Political Activity In Post-Civil War Wilmington...18

Fighting The Good Fight in France and at Home:
North Carolina Doughboys in World War I...28

"Per Mare, Per Terra:"
The Confederate Marines and Navy on the Cape Fear...62

Showboat:
The James Adams Floating Theater...86

They Had Their Reasons:
Loyalism In Revolutionary North Carolina...96

The Lords Proprietors, Charles Town, and Neglect:
A Matter of Priorities...118

The King's Americans:
The Colonial Regiment at Cartagena During the War of Jenkins' Ear...124

Running to Beat the Devil:
Blockade Running and the Port at Wilmington...138

Hardscrabble Lives:
North Carolina's SharecroppersBefore and During the Great Depression...158

Fort Dobbs and the Fight for Empire...182

The Sinking of the *John D. Gill*...196

Wilmington and the Spanish Lady...204

Good Ships and True:
Shipbuiding on the Cape Fear River...212

Robley D. Evans Account of the Fall of Fort Fisher...220

The General Goes Down To Georgia...238

Nicholas Shapley's map of the Cape Fear River, based on Hilton's explorations, is the earliest known map of the region.

Coastal Cousins:
The Connections Between the Cape Fear and Charleston, S.C.

by
Jack E. Fryar, Jr.

A scant three years separated the end of the first English settlement on North Carolina's Cape Fear River from the beginning of a similar effort on the Ashley River in South Carolina. For the next two and a half centuries, the communities that sprang from those humble beginnings continued to mirror each other in a host of ways, with ties that have made the history of the two places inextricably linked.

In 1627, eighty English settlers crossed the Atlantic Ocean to colonize the westernmost island of the Lesser Antilles, a place they called Barbados. Thirteen years later sugar arrived with Portuguese Jews from Brazil, and all other cash crops on the island fell by the wayside. Within just a few short years, Barbadian small holders saw their lands being bought up by wealthier planters, and every square inch of arable land on the small island was put under cultivation. Sugar was king, and turned a struggling colony in a vast ocean into England's wealthiest New World jewel. But for those displaced small farmers, and the sons of the great planters themselves, the close confines of Barbados soon proved to be a place of few prospects.

On the North American mainland, English attempts at settlement below Virginia had seen mixed results. Settlers from the Chesapeake had begun migrating south, into the Albemarle region of what would eventually become North Carolina, but immigration was muted by fears of Spanish interdiction from Florida and a leadership crisis in England. While Oliver Cromwell's Interregnum put a hold on serious attempts to colonize Carolina, circumstances on Barbados and the restoration of the English monarchy in the person of King Charles II made it a priority by 1662.

That same year, mariner William Hilton was contracted to explore the Carolina coast for suitable places where English colonists might plant the King's standard. The original interest in Carolina came from Puritan New England, where some settlers were beginning to chafe at the restrictions placed on them by the dominant church hierarchy. Hilton sailed from Massachusetts to explore the waters of the Cape Fear River aboard his sloop, the *Adventure*. He returned with a glowing account of a land well suited to provide for the needs of Englishmen looking to make new lives for themselves. Months later, Hilton shepherded a shipload of the New Englanders to the river to establish a colony, but the settlement never took root. The Puritans remained on the Cape Fear only long enough to refill their water casks and release their livestock to forage in the woods lining the river, before leaving Carolina to return to New England or Barbados.

A year later, Hilton returned carrying Barbadians led by John Vassall. The Barbadian effort was sponsored by a group of influential and enterprising planters that formed the Corporation of Barbadian Adventurers. The Vassall group had hired Hilton to reprise his investigation of Cape Fear a year after the Massachusetts venture failed, this time in more detail. Hilton explored tributaries on both sides of the river, to include the numerous creeks. Before returning to Speightstown to report, he bought a large swath of the lands bounding the river from local Indians.

Based on the glowing report filed by Hilton, Vassall and company loaded their ships and sailed for Carolina. Unfortunately for them,

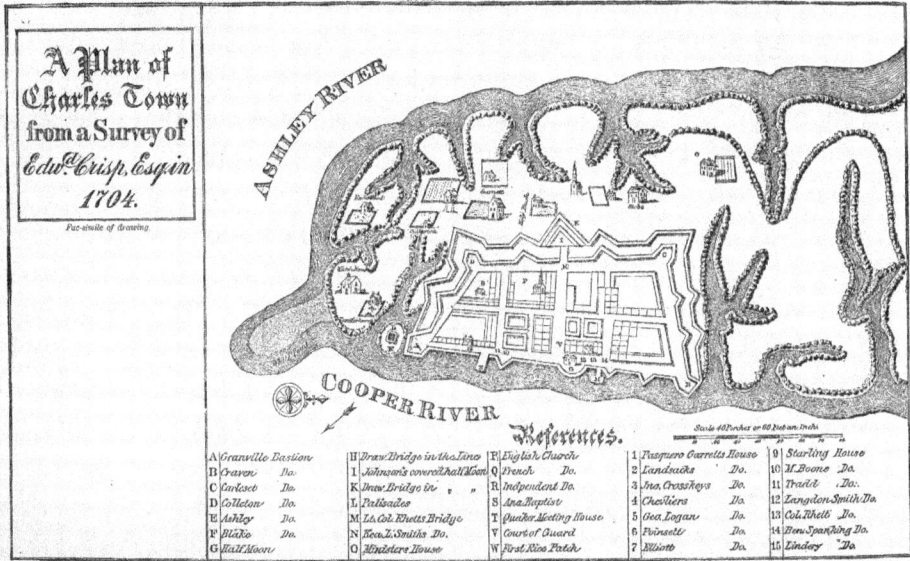

A Plan of Charles Town from a Survey of Edwd Crisp, Esqr in 1704.

Fac-simile of drawing.

ASHLEY RIVER

COOPER RIVER

References.

Scale 40 Inches or 60 Foot an Inch.

A	Granville Bastion	H	Draw Bridge in the Line
B	Craven Do.	I	Johnson's covered Half Moon
C	Carteret Do.	K	Draw Bridge in , ,
D	Colleton Do.	L	Palisades
E	Ashley Do.	M	Lt Col. Rhetts Bridge
F	Blake Do.	N	Rev L. Smiths Do.
G	Half Moon	O	Ministers House

P	English Church
Q	French Do.
R	Independent Do.
S	Ana. Baptist
T	Quaker Meeting House
V	Court of Guard
W	First Rice Patch

1	Pasquere Garretts House
2	Landmarks Do.
3	Jno. Crosskeys Do.
4	Chevliers Do.
5	Geo. Logan Do.
6	Poinsett Do.
7	Elliott Do.

9	Starling House
10	M. Boone Do.
11	Tradd Do.
12	Langdon Smith Do.
13	Col. Rhett Do.
14	Bens Sparking Do.
15	Lindsey Do.

Charles Town in 1704. The settlement moved inland tot he junction of the Ashley and Cooper Rivers after originally settling closer to the sea at Port Royal.

they lacked permission from the Lords Proprietors for the venture. John Vassall had assumed securing a patent from the proprietors would be a mere formality, but a competing group of settlers under Sir John Yeamans and Thomas Modyford made the more convincing argument before the Lords. Whereas the petition presented by Vassall's cousin Henry sought concessions that were contrary to the newly completed Carolina Charter, the Yeamans group readily accepted the Lords Proprietors' terms. Among them was a preference for establishing a colony further south, nearer Cape Romain, at Port Royal.

When Hilton dropped off the Vassall colony at Cape Fear, he sailed south to explore the waters of what would come to be known as the Ashley and Cooper Rivers. His good opinion of the lands contributed to the Lords' favoring the more southern option. Meanwhile John Yeamans was made governor of the Carolina enterprise, and Vassall had to settle for becoming Deputy Governor. Yeamans' one and only trip to the Vassall enclave at the mouth of the Cape Fear's Town Creek came in 1665, when a wrecked flyboat carrying supplies for the settlement left the governor stranded until arrangements could be made to get him to the preferred settlement at Port Royal. Shortly after arriving there, Yeamans claimed illness and returned to Barbados, never to set foot in the colony again.

The Vassall effort ran afoul of neglect by the Lords Proprietors and Governor Yeamans, Indian troubles, and a Proprietor-imposed quit rent system that would have charged settlers for fallow lands unsuitable to cultivation along the Cape Fear. By 1667, Vassall lamented that if he could have gotten just twenty men to stay with him, he would have continued to try and make a go of the Cape Fear settlement that had been dubbed Charles Town. Instead, the remaining settlers on the Cape Fear who had not already done so left for either Virginia, Barbados, or joined the Yeamans colony. By 1680, that colony took the name Charles Town, replacing the defunct settlement of the same name on the Cape Fear. The new Charles Town evolved to become one of the premiere cities of the South. So while the famous Charles Town (Charleston, these days) is in South Carolina, the first Charles Town was on the Cape Fear River. The similarities and connections between the two places are many.

During the Golden Age of Piracy, the Carolina coastline was a magnet for high seas rogues who plundered merchant shipping and, on occasion, coastal towns themselves. The nearly six hundred miles of combined North and South Carolina coastlines seemed tailor made for sea robbers, full of coves, bays, rivers, and inlets ideal for hiding a pirate ship. Combined with the sparse population of the Carolinas, and the weakness of the government (especially in North Carolina, where Gov.

Pirate Stede Bonnet was captured on the Cape Fear River in the Battle of the Sandbars in 1718.

Charles Eden was widely suspected of being in league with the pirates), the Carolinas became a favorite haunt of buccaneers likes Edward Teach, *a.k.a.* Blackbeard, and Stede Bonnet. In May 1718, Teach blockaded the harbor of Charles Town, holding local dignitaries hostage until a collection of medicines was gathered ashore to secure their release. On the Cape Fear, Bonnet used Fiddler's Creek to careen his ship, *Royal James*, for repairs that same year. While the Cape Fear had no organized settlement at the time, it was not totally free of prying eyes. Someone saw the pirate ship and got word to South Carolina Governor Robert Johnson in Charles Town. The governor dispatched William Rhett with two sloops-of-war to

Stede Bonnet and his crew were hanged at Charlestown's White Point.

corral Bonnet. After a running gun battle down the Cape Fear, Bonnet was taken off Bald Head Island. He and his crew were transported to Charles Town and hung by Judge Nicholas Trott. Bonnet's death in December 1718, a month after the demise of Blackbeard at Ocracoke Inlet, signaled the end of major piracy along the Carolina coast.

Forty-four years after the last colonist left the Charles Town settlement on the Cape Fear River, the Tuscarora Indian War, around New Bern, North Carolina, saw South Carolina militia dispatched to help quell the violence that threatened to wipe out Baron Christopher DeGraffenreid's colony at the mouth of the Neuse and Trent Rivers. South Carolina Governor James Moore sent sons Nathaniel, Roger, and Maurice to lead the expedition. When the conflict ended, the Moore brothers took notice of the potential of lands around the Cape Fear. The land was attractive to them because at home, around Charles Town and nearby Goose Creek, all of the good coastal lands had already been claimed by previous generations. But on the Cape Fear, there was easy access to the Atlantic Ocean, plentiful natural resources, and lots of land to be had. The Moore brothers returned to Goose Creek and pitched the idea of moving to the Cape Fear to their young cousins and friends. Ten years later, in 1725, Brunswick was chartered as the official port of entry for the North Carolina colony on the Cape Fear River.

During the colonial period, ties between the towns on the Cape Fear (Brunswick and Wilmington), and Charles Town, were especially strong. The shallow Cape Fear River allowed no vessels bigger than small brigs to call on the ports there, so cargos of naval stores, indigo, and – later – rice, had to be shipped first to either Charles Town, Norfolk, or Boston to be loaded on the deep draft ships that would take it to England and other places. The Carolina Low Country, stretching from Georgetown to a northern terminus marked by the Cape Fear River, became famous for the quality and quantity of its rice production. Plantations lining the Cape Fear marked the northernmost boundary of rice cultivation in the United States until after the Civil War.

Rice is a very labor-intensive crop to grow, and longleaf pine trees do not harvest themselves. As a result, another shared aspect of Charles Town and the Cape Fear was the importance of African slaves. Even during earliest attempts at settlement in both the Cape Fear region and at Port Royal, slaves were a crucial component of the enterprise. The influence of black Caribbean and African cultures on the Carolinas can be seen in their blending with white culture to give birth to the Gullah peoples of the Low Country. The pidgin language that resulted eventually evolved to become native to the region from the Cape Fear to Georgetown.

The tidal nature of rivers in both the Cape Fear and round Charlestown, S.C. made rice cultivation possible. Slavery was a key element of the plantation system that developed, as growing rice (and later, cotton) was a labor intensive proposition. The Cape Fear River marked the northernmos boundary of Lowcountry rice cultivation.

On the Cape Fear, slaves were considered an integral part of economic success for would-be planters. When the Moores moved part and parcel to North Carolina, they brought a number of their family slaves with them. Charles Town became the chief source of slaves who ended up working the rice fields and forests of the Cape Fear, and assumed that role early on. The blacks' knowledge of rice made them well suited to labors on the Cape Fear.

The Revolutionary War highlighted links between the port towns of the Cape Fear and Charles Town on both the micro and macro levels. Tactically, both places were population centers that had both loyalists and Whig rebels among their populations. Controlling the Cape Fear and Charles Town would rob the rebellion of valuable resources, and provide the British with a solid base of loyalist support for operations in the interior. Strategically, possessing Charles Town and Wilmington offered secure logistical bases to supply bread and bullets to redcoats in the field.

N.C. royal governor Josiah Martin

In 1776, North Carolina Royal Governor Josiah Martin conceived a plan to raise loyalist Highlanders in the colony, march them to the coast at Brunswick, and link them with British regulars to sweep through the North Carolina interior, reclaiming the rebellious colony for the crown. The plan went awry at Moores Creek Bridge in modern Pender County, when militia under Alexander Lillington and Richard Caswell defeated the Highland force in a fierce but brief battle that was the first victory for Patriot forces in the Southern theater of the war.

By March 1776, twenty British warships and troop transports lay anchored in the Cape Fear River, waiting to meet up with a Highlander force that had already been vanquished weeks before. The number of British hulls would swell to thirty-four within a month, all under the command of Admiral Sir Peter Parker. The British spent several weeks causing havoc among the Whig plantations lining the west side of the river between Wilmington and Old Inlet, and sacked the sleepy old port town at Brunswick. Finally it became apparent the loyalists were not coming, so Parker and General Sir Henry Clinton set their sites on Charles Town.

As British warships tested the mouth of Charleston Harbor in June 1776, palmetto-shrouded Patriot gun batteries under the direction of Col. William Moultrie barked a challenge from the sand walls of the Patriot fort. The ferocious battle ended in defeat for the British, who were unsuccessful in their attempts to reduce Moultrie's defenses on Sullivan's Island. Those attempts included landing British troops on nearby Long Island, but those soldiers were unable to wade across a deep channel separating the them from Moultrie's men. The British took severe damage to several of their ships, including the *Actaeon*, which they had to fire to keep it out of rebel hands.

Maj. John D. Hedrick

Four years later, British ships returned to Charleston. This time Continental forces under Gen. Benjamin Lincoln were surrounded and placed under siege until forced to surrender on May 12, 1780. With Charleston and Savannah in their hands, British commanders once again sought to tap into what they believed were many loyalists in the Carolina countryside just waiting for a redcoat army to provide them a king's standard to rally to. Gen Charles Lord Cornwallis devised his Southern Strategy to wrest the Carolinas back for the king, and eventually squash Washington's army between two British ones hitting him from the north and the south. To do that, he dispatched Major James Henry Craig with the 82nd Regiment of Foot to Wilmington to provide a logistics base for his army that would be leaving from Charleston and cutting a swath through the Carolina backcountry. The strategy ultimately failed when Nathaniel Greene met the British at Guilford Courthouse, which led to Cornwallis getting trapped on the Yorktown Peninsula. Craig eventually evacuated Wilmington and returned to Charleston when American forces under Griffith Rutherford closed around the town to push the British out. Soon the fighting part of the war ended everywhere. America was a free nation.

History generally credits P.G.T. Beauregard's shots at Major Robert Anderson's undermanned garrison at Fort Sumter with starting the Civil War, but weeks earlier, men in the Cape Fear got a jump on even the most ardent secessionists in Charleston. As the movement to leave the Union gained momentum, Cape Fear men feared Forts Johnston and Caswell at the mouth of the river could be occupied by Federal troops, effectively closing the river to outside traffic and choking off a vital lifeline for the nascent Confederacy. To prevent that, Major John D. Hedrick and the Cape Fear Minute Men took steps to secure the installations. On January 9, 1861, Ordnance Sergeant James Reilly was forced to turn over the keys to Fort Johnston in Smithville to an armed band of men under Hedrick's command. The same thing happened at Fort Caswell on Oak Island shortly afterwards. But as the war had not officially started (hence North Carolina was still officially a part of the Union), Gov. John Ellis made Hedrick return the forts to Federal control. After the guns of Charleston's Battery opened the war by firing on Fort Sumter the following April, President Abraham Lincoln called for North Carolina to contribute 75,000 men to put down the rebellion. At that point, North Carolina joined her sister states in secession, and Hedrick was given the go ahead to reclaim Forts Johnston and Caswell.

Those forts would prove vital to the South's war efforts, as would Sumter and the installations protecting Charleston's harbor. When hostilities seemed imminent, Union war planners recognized that the South did not have the industrial base to support a long-term conflict. The things the Confederacy would need to sustain the fight – bullets, cloth, medicines, foodstuffs, manufactured goods, and more – would have to come from outside the South. To stop that flow of supplies, Lieutenant General Winfield Scott, the old warhorse who had been in a U.S. Army uniform since the War of 1812, conceived of a plan to blockade Southern ports. His "Anaconda Plan" would starve the Southerners' ability to prosecute the war by literally starving them of the raw materials to field an army or even feed their people.

Southerners could read a map, too. They realized that access to the oceans, and the fast ships willing to brave the Union blockade to bring in the supplies the South would desperately need, was of paramount importance. To that end, Confederate planners began building a series of eleven forts and batteries from the mouth of the Cape Fear River all the way to the port at Wilmington. The anchor of this massive system of riverine fortifications was Fort Fisher, the largest fort in the South and one that compared favorably with Russia's Sevastopol. Its forty-seven big guns, including five rifled Whitworth breech-loading cannon, provided a protective umbrella that made Wilmington a favorite destination for block-ade-runners.

Charleston attempted similar measures to shore up its harbor defenses, but geography conspired to thwart Confederate efforts. Access to Charleston's harbor is by way of a wide bay where the Ashley and Cooper Rivers empty out into the Atlantic. But that width, and the concentration of Federal warships to close off the seat of the rebellion, made the days of access for blockade-runners to Charleston numbered. As the port at Charleston was closed, the blockade running firms closed their offices in the city and shifted operations to Wilmington, where blockade-runners could still reach Confederate docks.

Wilmington, on the other hand, was geographically blessed. If Confederate planners had been given the chance to design a port for blockade running, they could hardly have improved on what nature already provided. The Cape Fear River was accessible by two inlets. The first, between Bald Head Island and Oak Island, was Old Inlet, the traditional entrance to the river dating back to the first explorations of the region. The second, at the southern tip of Confederate Point (the pre-war Federal Point), was New Inlet. Between the two, running for twenty-eight miles into the Atlantic Ocean from the southeastern tip of Bald Head Island, was Frying Pan Shoals, which had been wrecking ships for centuries. Both inlets were heavily fortified by Confederate guns at Forts Campbell, Caswell, Holmes, Fisher, and by a gun battery on Zeke's Island. The practical result of this geographical gift was that to close off the port at Wilmington, the U.S. Navy would require essentially two fleets: one for New Inlet, one for Old Inlet. Eventually Wilmington became the last open port of the Confederacy, through which literally everything the South needed to fight an increasingly desperate war flowed. It stayed open until Fort Fisher fell in January 1865.

Connections between Charleston and the Cape Fear exist in the humanitarian realm as well. In 1862, an epidemic of yellow fever made Wilmington into a ghost town. Soldiers from Confederate forts nearby were forbidden to venture into the city. People died in such great numbers that an acres-wide mass grave in the city's Oakdale Cemetery was used to inter their remains. Whole families perished, and did so at such a frighteningly fast rate that no one was left to record their passing. Only three physicians remained in Wilmington to tend to the sick and dying, and two of them perished from the disease, too. Wilmington Mayor John Dawson sent out a desperate plea for help, and Charleston answered.

Confederate headquarters in Charleston responded by dispatching a physician and some nurses to Wilmington. As well, Charleston's Sisters of Charity of Our Lady of Mercy sent a contingent of nuns to succor the sick and dying in Wilmington.

The similarities between the evolution of the Cape Fear and Charleston are striking. Both regions developed out of the adventurous spirit of Barbadians during the colonial period when the Carolina coast was literally the frontier in the most literal sense. The same people who attempted settlement on the Cape Fear later contributed to the settlement of Port Royal. Fifty years later, their descendants returned to build the first permanent settlement on the Cape Fear River at Brunswick.

Economically, the people of the Cape Fear depended on the deep-water port at Charleston to provide a means of getting their trade goods to a wider, global market. At the same time, those same ships brought in the fine things that adorned the great houses of the Cape Fear and their owners. Slaves from Charleston sweat in both Low Country and Cape Fear fields. The two places were linked socially, economically, and to a large degree politically for most of the years prior to Reconstruction.

It has been a long time since American land was the stage on which wars were fought, but when it was, Charleston and the Cape Fear shared a proximity that made them likely to feel the brunt of war's hammer equally. Through Indian wars, revolution, and secession, Charleston and the Cape Fear have battled together, fighting both common enemies and terrible diseases. These shared commonalities, of culture and hardship, triumphs and defeats, have in many cases mirrored each other over the course of centuries. The end result is that the Cape Fear and Charleston are truly cousins, in that shared pedigrees and lineage have created irrevocable links between the two places.

Endnotes

[1] Though it should be noted that at the time, neither North nor South Carolina existed as separate entities. In the seventeenth century, the lands below Virginia and above Spanish Florida were simply known as Carolina (or Carolana, depending on which map you were reading).

[2] L.H. Roper. Conceiving Carolina: Proprietors, Planters, and Plots, 1662-1729. New York: Palgrave Macmillan, 2004. Hereafter cited as Roper. The introduction of sugar

planting and processing techniques is generally accepted to have come with Jewish émi-grés from Portuguese colonies in Brazil, where anti-Semitism forced them to seek homes elsewhere. Other accounts say that Danes brought sugar to the island. While the exact origins of sugar's arrival in Barbados is obscure now, the fact remains that it transformed Barbadian society.

[3] J.H. Parry. A Short History of the West Indies. New York: St. Martin's Press, 1987. Hereafter cited as Parry. Barbadian settlers had attempted to grow tobacco, but the island strain was woefully inferior to that being cultivated in Virginia.

[4] Roper. Conceiving Carolina: Proprietors, Planters, and Plots, 1662-1729. New York: Palgrave Macmillan, 2004. Sugar was so profitable that it was actually cheaper to import foodstuffs than to use any of Barbados' precious land for growing anything other than sugar cane.

[5] Parry. As small landholders sold out to wealthier sugar planters, they worked the cane growing on lands they used to own. But the industry grew at such a prodigious rate that African slaves were soon being imported in large numbers, displacing the working class English field hands. As well, second sons with no chance at inheritance also found them-selves contemplating a dim future on Barbados.

[6] Roper. Conceiving Carolina: Proprietors, Planters, and Plots, 1662-1729. New York: Palgrave Macmillan, 2004. The Virginia Assembly granted Roger Green land on the Chowan River in 1653. A few years later, in 1662, another

[7] William S. Powell. The Proprietors of Carolina. Raleigh, N.C.: The Carolina Tercente-nary Commission, 1963. Charles Stuart, son of the beheaded King James I, returned from Irish exile to reclaim the throne with the aid of loyal followers like George Monck and Anthony Ashley Cooper. They and six others would play a pivotal role in the develop-ment of Carolina when King Charles II made them the Lords Proprietors of the region, with wide ranging authority to determine the means and locations of settlement in the colony.

[8] J. Leitch Wright Jr. "William Hilton's Voyage to Carolina in 1662." Essex Institute His-torical Collections, April 1969, pp. 96-103.

[9] Daniel Webster Fagg, Jr. "Carolina, 1663-1683: The Founding of a Proprietary." (PhD. Dissertation, Emory University, 1970). Fagg speculates that by the time the New En-glanders reached the Cape Fear, word arrived that the Lords Proprietors had finally established the terms of settlement in Carolina, which contained religious constraints that did not suit them. Rather than waste their efforts under unfavorable terms, they opted to return home or try their luck elsewhere. But the New Englanders left one little sign of their presence other than their cattle – a sign posted at the mouth of the Cape Fear, warn-ing any future explorers that the place was an inhospitable prospect for colonization.

[10] Alfred M. Waddell. "Early Explorers of the Cape Fear." Delivered before the North Carolina Society of Colonial Dames at Brunswick Town site. William R. Reaves Col-lection, New Hanover County Public Library. Vassall, a former New Englander, had emigrated to Barbados from Scituate, after finding dim prospects in the colder climes of the Massachusetts Bay area. He came from distinguished stock, being the grandson of Samuel Vassall, an English shipbuilder who contributed vessels to both the fleet that met the Spanish Armada, and conveyed the first Puritans to Massachusetts.

[11] James Sprunt. Chronicles of the Cape Fear River: 1660-1916. Wilmington, N.C.: Dram Tree Books, 2005 Hereafter cited as Sprunt. Local tradition has it that the Indian chief,

Watcoosa, sweetened the deal by throwing in two of his daughters for Hilton. The English mariner, who already had a wife waiting for him in Massachusetts, managed to debark for Barbados without his native "wives" in tow.

[12] Roper.

[13] Ibid. There were several reasons for this, among them a desire by the Lords Proprietors to provide a buffer between the highly profitable Virginia and Spanish outposts at St. Augustine. They also, in the wake of Spain's weakened global position after the loss of the Armada, wanted to test the Dons' commitment to enforcing claims to lands below the Chesapeake.

[14] Sprunt. This paper consistently uses the modern name for the North Carolina River, Cape Fear, to avoid confusion. The river, the only one in the state with direct access to the Atlantic Ocean, has gone by several names over the centuries, including Rio Jordan and, during the seventeenth century, the Charles River (a tribute to the monarch with whom the colonists were always currying favor).

[15] E. Lawrence Lee. The Lower Cape Fear in Colonial Days. Chapel Hill, N.C.: University of North Carolina Press, 1965. To be fair, the Lords Proprietors were also serving the English government in other capacities. The Great Plague of London (1665), the Great Fire of London (1665), and the Second Anglo-Dutch War took precedence over the fate of 800 settlers an ocean away.

[16] Documenting the American South: Colonial and State Records of North Carolina. Letter from John Vassall to John Colleton, 1667. Vol. 1, pages 159-160. http://docsouth.unc.edu/csr/index.html/document/csr01-0061. Vassal was unaware that the addressee, Lords Proprietor John Colleton, had already died.

[17] Generally accepted as being from 1680-1720.

[18] Angus Konstam. Blackbeard: America's Most Notorious Pirate. New York: John Wiley & Sons, 2007.

[19] 1711-1715.

[20] Sprunt; William S. Powell. North Carolina Through Four Centuries. Chapel Hill, N.C.: Univeristy of North Carolina Press, 1989.

[21] Charles Town would not become known as Charleston until 1783, after the American colonies had all but won their independence from Great Britain.

[22] Claude V. Jackson III; Jack E. Fryar Jr. (ed.). The Big Book of the Cape Fear River. Wilmington: Dram Tree Books, 2008. Hereafter cited as Jackson. Average depth of the Cape Fear River has historically been 9-12 feet outside of the main shipping channel (in modern times, dredged to 38 feet). Making matters worse, a sandy riverbed that constantly shifts in hurricanes and heavy storms makes navigation of the river a treacherous undertaking.

[23] Naval stores is the collective name for tar, pitch, and turpentine from the plentiful long-leaf pine tree of the Carolina coastal plains. They were vital to marine construction, and North Carolina was the biggest producer of them in the British empire.

[24] Louise Pettus and Ron Chepesiuk. The Palmetto State: Stories from the Making of South Carolina. Orangeburg, S.C.: Sandlapper Publishing, 1991. Hereafter cited as Pettus. Eliza Pinckney introduced indigo on her family's plantation on Wappoo Creek, seventeen miles from Charles Town, in the early 1700s. It became a staple of South Carolina's colonial economy. Efforts to replicate her success on the Cape Fear were more moderate.

[25] Several prominent histories of South Carolina credit Dr. Henry Woodward of Charleston with planting the first successful acres of rice in the Low Country around Charles Town in the 1680s. The seeds came from a merchantman out of Madagascar that had to call on the port at Charles Town for repairs.

[26] Sprunt. It has been said that the boundary represented by the Cape Fear River was so distinct that one could tell the difference between rice grown on the west side of the river from that grown on the New Hanover County side by taste alone.

[27] Bradford J. Wood. This Remote Part of the World: Regional Formation in Lower Cape Fear, North Carolina 1725-1775. Columbia: University of South Carolina Press, 2004. Hereafter cited as Wood. While rice was an important part of the Cape Fear's colonial economy, it paled in comparison to naval stores. From 1768-1772, rice only accounted for a little over 1% of total exports from the Cape Fear, while naval stores accounted for roughly 82%. That percentage would increase in later years, after independence.

[28] Roper; James B. Legg and W. Bryan Watson Jr. "The Exploration, Settlement, and Abandonment of the Lower Cape Fear, 1662-67: The Historical Record and the Archaeological Evidence at the Supposed Site of Charles Towne." Unpublished manuscript, May 1979. Author's collection; Richard Waterhouse. "England, the Caribbean, and the Settlement of Carolina." Journal of American Studies, Vol. 9, No. 3 (December 1975), pp. 259-281. For instance, some estimates claim that as much as two thirds of the reported 800 people living within the 32 square miles around the Cape Fear's Charles Town settlement were black slaves.

[29] J.A. Opala. The Gullah: Rice, Slavery, and the Sierra Leone-American Connection. Freetown: United States Information Service, 1987.

[30] Wood. As early as 1734, Cape Fear's John Dalrymple bought 110 slaves from brokers in Charles Town.

[31] Robert M. Dunkerly. Redcoats on the River: Southeastern North Carolina in the Revolutionary War. Wilmington, N.C.: Dram Tree Books, 2008. Hereafter cited as Dunkerly. For instance, Wilmington merchants depended on the British mercantile system for their livelihoods, so they generally tended to support King George III and Parliament. Yet nine of the eleven regiments of the N.C. Continental Line raised during the war were formed at Wilmington.

[32] Ibid. The battle took place on February 27, 1776. Depending on whose account you read, the battle lasted from five to ten minutes. It was a route of the Highlanders, and ended loyalist aspirations in North Carolina for four more years, until Charles Town fell to the British in 1780.

[33] Dunkerly. Aboard one of those ships was Ethan Allen, the famous leader of the Green Mountain Boys and backwoods patriot from Vermont. Allen was a prisoner awaiting repatriation after being captured in the ill-fated 1775 expedition to take Montreal. He would witness British actions both at Cape Fear and Charles Town.

[34] David Lee Russell. Victory on Sullivan's Island: The British Cape Fear/Charles Town Expedition of 1776. Haverford, PA: Infinity Publishing Co., 2002. Hereafter cited as Russell. General Sir Henry Clinton was aboard too, as commander of the ground element of the force. But until such time as the army troops were landed and sufficiently able to conduct independent operations on their own, Parker remained in overall command while the troops were aboard his ships.

[35] Ibid. Redcoat raiders burned the plantation of Robert Howe, a Continental officer of the

Cape Fear who would become the highest-ranking Southern officer in Washington' army. They also destroyed the mill at Orton plantation, and Russelborough, the former residence of two of North Carolina's five royal governors, a quarter mile north of Brunswick. By 1776, the house was owned by ardent rebel William Dry.

[36] Dunkerly; Russell. The expedition's orders instructed them to move on to Charles Town if operations on the Cape Fear River should prove impractical or fruitless.

[37] Russell. The battle occurred on June 28, 1776. Elements of Parker's fleet had been arriving off Charles Town since May, but Parker waited to attack the city until joined by redcoat regulars brought from Ireland under the command of Gen. Charles Lord Cornwallis.

[38] James L. Walker, Jr. Rebel Gibraltar: Fort Fisher and Wilmington, C.S.A. Wilmington, N.C.: Dram Tree Books, 2005. Hereafter cited as Walker. While much of North Carolina was generally Unionist in their attitudes, in southeastern North Carolina, secessionists dominated the discourse. As early as January 3, 1861, a red secessionist flag was hoisted up a flagpole at Front and Market Streets in Wilmington, accompanied by a host of fiery speeches.

[39] Sergeant James Reilly was a unique individual. When the war finally broke out, he resigned from the U.S. Army and enlisted in the Confederate army, where as an artillerist, he participated in seven of the biggest battles of the conflict and rose to the rank of Major. Reilly was also left as the highest-ranking officer at Fort Fisher in January 1865, after Gen. W.H.C. Whiting and Col. William Lamb were wounded in the final battle for the fort. Major James Reilly, the same man who four years earlier had surrendered Fort Johnston to secessionist troops, was left to surrender Fort Fisher to Gen. Alfred Terry. That makes James Reilly the only man who surrendered both a Federal and Confederate fort to the enemy during the Civil War.

[40] Modern Southport, N.C.

[41] Walker. It was customary at the time to leave only caretakers to look out for an installation and keep it ready for occupation by troops should the need arise.

[42] Walker. Scott's plan was derided in the press, who at the time dismissed any notion that the war would last long enough for the blockade strategy to be effective. The label "Anaconda Plan" was one bestowed on it by the media. In the end, Scott proved right, and his detractors proved remarkably shortsighted.

[43] Walker; Chris E. Fonvielle, Jr. The Wilmington Campaign: Last Rays of Departing Hope. Campbell, CA: Savas Publishing Co., 1997. Hereafter cited as Fonvielle. Blockade running would make fortunes for many of the daring captains and crews who risked sinking or capture by the U.S. Navy. Cotton that sold for cents on the pound in the South, sold for dollars on the pound in England, whose industrial age textile mills were starving for all they could get of the fiber. It was said that a captain only had to make one successful run from a port like Wilmington or Charleston, to the transshipment points in British Bermuda and the Bahamas, to pay for his investment. Everything after that was pure profit.

[44] Sevastopol was the virtually impregnable Russian fort in the Ukraine of Crimean War fame.

[45] Fonvielle. Charleston's harbor was successfully closed by elements of John Dahlgren's South Atlantic Blockading Squadron in 1863. Dahlgren is the same man who invented the Dahlgren Gun, a cannon widely used aboard U.S. Navy warships.

[46] Fonvielle. Fraser, Trenholm & Co., Crenshaw & Collie & Co., and even the State of

North Carolina itself operated blockade-running offices in Wilmington. Fraser, Trenholm & Co. and Crenshaw & Collie & Co. both opened offices in the North Carolina town in addition to their main offices in Charleston. When Charleston was closed in 1863, they shifted their operations to the Cape Fear.

[47] Jackson. New Inlet was created by a savage hurricane that hammered the North Carolina coast in 1761.

[48] See the earlier reference to Gov. Sir John Yeamans' flyboat.

[49] Walker; Fonvielle. It was not until late in the war that the Federals finally managed to get enough hulls into the blockade off the Cape Fear to close both entrances with any degree of success. Until then, the Confederates used secure interior lines of communication to signal outgoing blockade-runners which of the two exit points were the least well guarded. If a blockading Federal ship guessed wrong, there was no way they could make it around Frying Pan Shoals in time to capture the fleeing blockade-runner.

[50] Fonvielle. Robert E. Lee readily admitted that if Wilmington fell, he would not be able to keep his Army of Northern Virginia in the field. Rail lines traveling north from Wilmington to Richmond, and south to Charleston, carried offloaded supplies from blockade-runners to chronically undersupplied rebel armies.

[51] Fonvielle. More than a third of the city would die off during the epidemic, somewhere in the neighborhood of seven hundred people (no one knows for sure the correct number). That death toll does not include passings among the slave population, who were not included on official tallies. Slaves were not interred in Oakdale Cemetery.

[52] One of the reasons so few physicians were in Wilmington when the epidemic broke out is that qualified doctors found themselves drafted into the ranks of the Confederate army, and were tending to battlefield wounds far from the port city.

[53] Beverly Tetterton. Wilmington: Lost But Not Forgotten. Wilmington, N.C.: Dram Tree Books, 2005. After the epidemic ended, the nuns returned to Charleston. In 1869, Bishop (later Cardinal) James Gibbons requested that they send a permanent contingent back to Wilmington. They have been in the city ever since.

[54] This refers to sustained war on American soil. Acts of terrorism such as those which occurred on 9/1/2001 do not count in this reference.

Having A Voice: Black Political Activity In
Post-Civil War Wilmington

by
Jack E. Fryar, Jr.

When Union troops crossed Eagles Island in the early spring of 1865 to seal the fate of the last open port of the Confederacy, newly freed slaves took to the streets of Wilmington in droves to celebrate the fact of their emancipation. Under the watchful eyes of federal soldiers and their bayonets, blacks began forging a new identity as participants in the democracy that saw free men choose their own representatives in government. It was a new, heady feeling for a class of people that not too long before had been consigned to lives of servitude in the rice fields of the plantations along the Cape Fear River. In the years to come, before the erosion of civil rights progress ushered in the virtual slavery of Jim Crow, Wilmington blacks managed to achieve a degree of political success that was the envy of other North Carolina and Southern blacks outside the Tar Heel State. But that success was not without its difficulties.

Immediately after the fall of Wilmington, the city became an occupied port under the sway of Gen. Joseph Hawley and the blue-clad soldiers – many of them U.S. Colored Troops – who gave weight to his edicts. Hawley, a North Carolina-born soldier who eventually became governor of Connecticut, pursued a policy that saw secessionist plantations confiscated and divided among the recently freed slaves who used to work them. Hawley understood the caste system that existed in the lower Cape Fear, one that was common among the landed gentry of the former Confederacy across the South. No edict from the Yankee capital would prompt these men to surrender what, to them, was theirs by birth and Divine right. But the political plans of the United States government did not always subscribe to the vision of its dead wartime leader once Andrew Johnson assumed the presidency.

Former Vice President Andrew Johnson was a Southerner, a Tennessean whose initial inclination was to punish the former Confederates harshly. But members of his cabinet prevailed on the new president to follow the example set by his predecessor and show leniency and forgiveness to the rebelling Southern states. Truth be told, many of Johnson's sympathies lay with the vanquished property owners of the South. Under his administration, many of the post-war strictures preventing whites from resuming their dominant positions in society were reversed. In Wilmington, Hawley was replaced with Gen. John Worthington Ames. Under orders from Washington, Ames removed former slaves from their new homes on the sub-divided plantation lands along the Cape Fear River and returned the properties to their former owners. It was perhaps the most significant indication that Abraham Lincoln's promise of freedom might not be as easy to achieve as it was to make.

Almost overnight, control of Wilmington government was returned to those who had occupied city offices before Braxton Bragg's Confederates withdrew in 1865. By 1868, new Black Codes were instituted that replaced the plantation's iron shackles with the bonds of law and municipal code. This return to slavery in all but name did not sit well with the black population of the city. Three riots rocked Wilmington between 1865 and 1868, and despite violent reprisals from Conservatives who sought to put them in their place, blacks in North Carolina's largest city carried out efforts to organize and be politically active.

As 1867 dawned, Wilmington blacks and a small number of white Unionists joined forces to form the Republican Party. This was no small thing, as those who supported the old guard fought at every step to prevent blacks from enjoying any of the freedoms the war supposedly bought them. Under Ames' administration, the military government was often complicit in allowing great latitude to those who would actively work to keep the city's blacks in what they saw as their rightful place. A blind eye was turned to the illegal activities of the Ku Klux Klan, who used intimidation and worse to make their point that blacks in Wilmington forgot their place at their peril. Nevertheless, after enjoying a taste of freedom under Gen. Hawley's oversight, blacks were reluctant to surrender it. Wilmington blacks took steps to preserve what they could of their new-found liberty.

By 1868, Conservative influence in the nation's capital began to wane. In elections that year to the convention to ratify North Carolina's new constitution, Republicans carried all the counties of the southeastern part of the state except Columbus County. When it became apparent that Conservative local governments in the southeastern part of the state had dug in their heels to resist every step towards black enfranchisement, Washington, D.C. put pressure on Raleigh to secure compliance. Governor William W. Holden, the former newspaperman who had opposed secession, used the threat of military intervention to bring local governments along the Cape Fear into line.

While they had been dragged kicking and screaming from their perch at the top of the social, political, and economic hierarchy of the lower Cape Fear by government edict and military managers who, for the most part, had little sympathy for their plight, the old money of the planter class that reigned before and during the Civil War were still potent actors on the political stage during Reconstruction. The size of their pocketbooks, diminished but still sizeable, insured that. But the new kings of the hill in the region were men who moved to the Cape Fear either a short time before the war, or in the vacuum of the post-war era, when the old order was still in disarray with the defeat of the Confederacy. These "carpetbaggers" saw that rice was no longer viable in a slaveless South, and sought to make their fortunes in other areas. These included general business and the naval stores industry, as well as by cotton, shipping, and railroads. Cape Fear blacks found plenty of work in these industries, but in no case did they reach a level of wealth that made them competitive with their white neighbors. Illiteracy, discrimination, disorganization, and a lack of effort on the part of the federal government to insure a level playing field left them in large part limited to menial labor. Black leaders, understanding that they simply could not match the economic power of the white establishment, opted instead for political parity.

Among the newcomers to Wilmington were some blacks who, either with backing from northern whites or of their own design, entered into business. These men, like saloon owner George Moore, catered to a black clientele. Moore's saloon became a gathering place for city blacks, who used his bar as a forum to discuss politics and other issues in an environment that allowed for much freer expression that did black churches. During the late 1860s and through the 1870s, blacks fought with Conservatives (who in 1876 tried to rebrand themselves, adopting the name Democrats) to win the favor of the Cape Fear's business class. It was these men who had the money, and by extension controlled the path to political power.

Republican leaders had varied success wooing the business leaders. In 1868, the party went so far as to put up several candidates more suited to the conservative agenda than what the Republicans ostensibly stood for. It was an effort to capture the support and votes of business leaders in Wilmington, especially among the Germans and Jews. The tactic failed, and Cape Fear business sided almost entirely with the Democrats.

Black business owners in Wilmington were enthusiastic participants in the politics of the era. In part, this was due to the fringe benefits that came of having political connections. James O. Lowrey, for instance, operated a carriage making business for years after the war, but not until he secured a contract with the federal government to repair their carriages in 1878, did R.G. Dun's credit reports show him as earning "$1200 per annum in the U.S. Customs House," where he also had an office. Dun had listed Lowrey as a dubious credit risk up to that point, but their opinion changed after Lowrey secured the government job.

While the two political philosophies - one rooted in the past, the other looking to a future of black equality and inclusion – contested each other at every turn, with economics playing a large part in which party the deep pocketed business leaders supported, blacks did manage to make some gains politically. Of New Hanover County's 6,258 registered voters in the 1868 election, 3,968 were Republicans. Cape Fear blacks took to politics with an enthusiasm, and met with a fair amount of success despite the obstacles in their way.

Abraham Galloway, a Wilmington black who escaped slavery

to become a spy for the Union Army in the war, was one of three local delegates elected to the constitutional convention in 1868. A year later, Solomon Nash and other local blacks led the city's delegation at the Republican convention in Wilmington. During the 1870s and 1880s, Republicans in Wilmington's predominantly black First, Third, and Fourth Wards nominated black candidates for virtually every government office and post that came open. In 1869 election results saw the Republicans garner 68 percent of the vote, but the candidates who assumed office were mostly white businessmen running on the Republican ticket. Still, at least they were Republican, and not openly hostile to black issues.

In Raleigh, it was soon a different story. Democrats took control of the state government in 1877, and control of offices at the local level in Wilmington and New Hanover County soon followed. As the 1880s drew to a close, there was a rift developing in the Republican Party along race lines, and this led to the creation of the Independent Faction of the Republican Party. Wilmington's white Republicans, who were dubbed the "Courthouse Ring" by black dissenters within the party, were businessmen (often "carpetbaggers" from the North) who seemed most concerned with advancing their pro-business agenda, relegating economic, social, and political equality for blacks to something secondary. These men, despite their focus on business, were instrumental in many of the gains that blacks saw in the aftermath of the war.

The Independent Faction called themselves the "true-blue" faction of the party, whose loyalty lay with the state and national party ticket and platform. James O. Lowrey and George W. Price led the breakaways from the Republican mainstream in the local party. When Gov. Daniel Russell wrote the State Executive Committee that North Carolina blacks were unfit to hold office, the rift between the two factions became a chasm. Cape Fear blacks immediately drafted a newspaper article rebuffing the Republican governor for the slight, and soon after held an Independent Republican convention at the county courthouse, in which Lowrey presided over the nomination of an all-black slate of candidates for the next election.

The split in the Republican Party played into the hands of conservative elements in Cape Fear politics. While white Republicans continued to reach office on a consistent basis thanks to black voters who, while perhaps less than enamored with their attitudes, still preferred them to the Democratic alternative, Independent Republicans managed to win some races, but only a few due to the splintered nature of the party. It was not until the party joined with disaffected farmers to form the Populist Party that black candidates began to see real gains in terms of political office holders. This fusion of poor whites and blacks created a voting block that had real power at the polls, something neither group had managed to achieve on their own. Seeing which way the wind was blowing, Republicans quickly joined the Populists, and the resulting party their union created ushered in the era of Fusionist politics in North Carolina.

Black political activism was widespread, found on porches and in pulpits across New Hanover County. In saloons and on street corners, Cape Fear blacks took an active and enthusiastic part in political contests that had real, immediate impact on their lives. Conservative opponents railed against them, and tried to frame the argument so that white fears of black misogyny would dull the threat of poor whites joining Republican ranks. It was one of the strongest weapons in their bag of dirty tricks, as they certainly could not depend on economic arguments to sway common whites to the Democratic cause.

But there was still dissension in the Republican Party, with blacks feeling that their concerns were not being addressed by the mainstream. In response they began forming political clubs to voice their point of view. As black politics became fractious, white conservatives in the Democratic Party saw an opening to oust a race of people they saw as inferior from the political landscape. Their efforts to do just that led to the bloodshed and political coup of 1898 in Wilmington.

A Sampling of Wilmington's Politically Active Blacks, 1865-1898

• Henry Brewington – Republican politician in Reconstruction. Wilmington magistrate (1870s), represented the city's First Ward on the Republican Executive Committee in 1878. Special police deputy, fireman.

• Owen Burney – Wilmington alderman (1870), seven-time candidate for New Hanover County Sheriff, Inspector of the U.S. Custom House (1879-80), New Hanover County treasurer (1882).

• James K. Cutlar – Inspector of Naval Stores (1870), Republican representative of the Fourth Ward on the New Hanover County Executive Committee (1887).

• James Benson Dudley – Register of Deeds, New Hanover County

(1891), delegate to Republican National Convention (1896).

• John S.W. Eagles – former Union soldier, came to Wilmington in after the war. Member of the U.S. House of Representatives (1869).

• Allen Evans – Wilmington city registrar and election judge (1870)

• Abraham Galloway – Delegate tot eh North Carolina Constitutional Convention (1868), senator from New Hanover County in the N.C. Senate (1868-70).

• Eustace E. Green – N.C. House (1883).

• Joseph Corbin Hill – During Reconstruction, served at one time or another as a constable, Register of Deeds, Justice of the Peace, registrar and judge of elections, and city clerk (1871).

• John Holloway – Justice of the Peace (1889), N.C. House (1887 and 1889).

• William J. Kellogg – City alderman (1868), Executive Committee of the Republican Party (1868).

• James Lowrey – Registrar and election judge (1869-1870), magistrate (1871), New Hanover County Commissioner (1872), Wilmington Board of Aldermen (1869, 1879).

• William H. Moore – N.C. House (1874-1875), N.C. Senate (1876-1877).

• Solomon W. Nash, Jr. – Justice of the Peace (1869) and New Hanover County Jailer (1869-1884), Justice of the Peace (1868), candidate for N.C. House (1876).

Endnotes

1. *Dictionary of American Biography*; Putnam, Albert D., ed. *Major General Joseph R. Hawley, Soldier and Editor (1826-1905): Civil War Military Letters*. Hartford: Connecticut Civil War Centennial Commission, 1964. Hawley was born in Laurinburg, N.C. to a Presbyterian minister father from New Haven. The Hawleys returned to Connecticut in 1837.

2. William McKee Evans. *Ballots and Fence Rails: Reconstruction on the lower Cape Fear*. Chapel Hill: University of North Carolina Press, 1967: 249, hereafter cited as Evans.

3. Ibid. Ames was a former officer on Hawley's staff and a conservative reconstructionist who, like his civilian masters in Washington, D.C., upheld every property right except that of slavery.

4. Evans, 250.

5. James A. McDuffie, *"Politics in Wilmington and New Hanover County, North Carolina, 1865-1900: The Genesis of a Race Riot,"* Ph.D. dissertation, Kent State University, 1979: 64. According to McDuffie, Conservatives saw the Republican upstarts as "a dangerous alliance of inferior blacks, incompetent whites, and traitorous Unionists."

6. Evans, 250. Among the steps Wilmington's blacks took included secreting arms and ammunition in places where the Klan and others who sought to oppose their integration into the American landscape on equal terms with whites.

7. Evans, 251.

8. Ibid.

9. Robert C. Kenzer, "The Black Businessman in the Postwar South: North Carolina, 1865-1880." *The Business History Review*, Vol. 63, No. 1, Entrepreneurs in Business History (Spring 1989): 61-87, hereafter cited as Kenzer. Ledgers of the R.G. Dun Credit Rating Service show 126 black businesses in operation in N.C. between 1865 and 1880. New Hanover County, which census records show was 57.9% black, boasted eight firms doing business in 1865-1867. These firms were likely owned by pre-war free blacks, who would have had a head start on business capital with which to found new enterprises over recently freed ex-slaves.

10. Evans, 253-254.

11. Kenzer, 74. Dun's re-evaluation of James Lowrey concluded that was a "Very worthy colored man, said to be a good workman, who has occupied himself with politics and enjoyed an office in the Customs House which is a sinecure." Lowrey later boosted his favorable rating even more in the eyes of the Northern credit evaluators when he became a Wilmington alderman. He was not alone. Of the eight black businesses listed in Dun's ledgers, half of them were owned by men who would hold offices at either the local level or in the state legislature.

12. Karin L. Zipf, "'The Whites Shall Rule the Land or Die': Race and Class in North Carolina Reconstruction Politics." *The Journal of Southern History*, Vol. 65, No. 3 (Aug. 1999): 499-534, hereafter cited as Zipf. A fair number of these were common whites, who to the Conservatives' chagrin, sided with the Republicans against their wealthy white race mates.

13. Bill Reaves. *Strength Through Struggle: The Chronological and Historical Record of the African-American Community in Wilmington, North Carolina, 1865-1950*. Wilmington, N.C.: New Hanover County Public Library, 1998: 239; hereafter cited as Reaves. New Hanover County's population was 58 percent black in 1868.

14. Zipf, 505. Democrat-leaning newspapers explained the loses at the polls by claiming blacks from western North Carolina were relocating to eastern counties and skewing the electorate in favor of Republicans.

15. Zipf. The Democrats in the state legislature enacted a bill in 1877 that removed control of local elections and from New Hanover County politicos – who were overwhelm-

ingly Republican – and placed it in the hands of their conservative brethren in the state house.

16. Reaves, 240. The white Republicans, though not actively hostile to black concerns, were more concerned in many instances with what was good for business. They were also of the opinion that the Cape Fear's largely unschooled black population was unfit to govern themselves, and so should loyally cast their votes for their white party mates without actually participating in the political process.

17. Jack B. Scroggs, "Carpetbagger Constitutional Reform in the South Atlantic States, 1867-1868." *The Journal of Southern History*, Vol. 27, No. 4 (Nov. 1961): 475-493. For instance, "carpetbagger" leadership of ten of the nineteen committees tasked with drawing up the state's new post-war constitution facilitated many elements that were of benefit to blacks and poor whites alike, such as the provision for public education.

18. Reaves, 241. The Independents declared that the party's mainstream – and white – candidates would "sell out the national party to get their way locally."

19. Ibid. Gov. Russell, in what he surely took to be a private missive, had written that "the Negroes of the South are largely savages, and are no more fit to govern than are their brethren in African swamps or so many Mongolians dumped down from pagan Asia."

20. Reaves, 243.

21. Zipf, 510, 514. The Wilmington *Daily Journal* especially targeted black ministers for their political activism, saying in an editorial that they "…carried the Radical platform concealed among the leaves of the Holy Bible." When black delegate Abraham Galloway demanded blacks get equal seating privileges at public lectures, newspapers decried the proposal, claiming it allowed blacks to "…visit places of amusement, frequented by your wives, your mothers, your daughters, and your sisters," permitting them to "occupy seats side by side with those most dear to you in theatres – aye, even in temples of Almighty God!"

22. Reaves, 244. Among the clubs were the Young Men's Republican Club and The Republican Afro League, who promised to fight what they saw as Raleigh's attempts to reduce their civil rights to "mere quasi citizenship." Many other clubs formed, each faction responsible for a further splintering of the once unified Republican vote.

23. Reaves. These short biographies are compiled from the excellent work Bill Reeves did in his one of a kind chronicle of the black experience in the Cape Fear region.

A 30th Infantry Division sniper aims across No Man's Land in Belgium during the First World War.

Fighting The Good Fight in France and at Home: North Carolina Doughboys in World War I

by
Jack E. Fryar, Jr.

When the men of North Carolina answered their country's call to arms in 1918, they left behind their plows and jobs in the banks, railroads, and stores of what passed for cities in the state at the time. By the thousands, they left home to train with strangers from all over the country at depots far from the places they knew so well. The newly minted soldiers of the 30th and 81st Infantry Divisions crossed an ocean after enduring scanty training stateside, and stepped into the furnace of the first global war of the modern age. After the fields of Flanders and the trenches of France, their perceptions of the world they lived in would be forever altered. North Carolina's doughboys would carry that altered sense of self and the world home with them, changing the American landscape as well.

For many of those North Carolina soldiers, World War I would be the first time they were exposed to the wider world beyond their fields and sleepy neighborhoods. For most, it was a terrifying ordeal that brought them face to face with the sad truth of man's inhumanity when acting under the clouds of war. For all of them, it was a life-changing event that would mark them for the rest of their lives. When they returned to the United States, many found resuming their civilian lives to be difficult, with little help to be had from their government.

The Rip Van Winkle State Wakes Up

North Carolina, during the first two decades of the twentieth century, was little different from the defeated Confederate state occupied by Union troops after General Joseph E. Johnston surrendered the last rebel army at Durham's Bennett Place in the spring of 1865. Boasting few cities that were worthy of the name – and none that would compare with the great European metropolis' that Tar Heel doughboys would see in France and England – North Carolina was still primarily rural in nature, and provincial in its outlook on the rest of the world.

Despite innovations like the telephone, electricity, the typewriter and the Wright Brothers' Kitty Hawk experiment that ushered in the age of powered flight, North Carolina for the most part resisted the impact of a changing world and remained predominantly agrarian and rural-centric in character. By 1900, the numbers of the U.S. Census revealed that for the first time in the history of the United States, more people lived in urban areas than rural. But while that may have been true for the nation as a whole, the draw of the big city was not as strong in much of the South. Nevertheless, in the urban centers of the South – including those in North Carolina – the amazing wonders of the age were being embraced, even if those revolutionary inventions had yet to be introduced in the South's rural areas. While new wonders such as the automobile and the electric trolley were proudly touted in Tar Heel cities like Charlotte, Wilmington and Raleigh, in the countryside life was much as it had been for the preceding half century.

In North Carolina, only 318, 474 residents lived in what the U.S. Census Bureau would describe as metropolitan areas, out of a total population of 2,206,287. Yet North Carolina was on the cutting edge of the new technologies sweeping across the nation. In the fifty years from 1870 to 1920, the Tar Heel State would become the most industrialized of the Southern states. Washington Duke was revolutionizing the tobacco industry in Durham, and from his humble homestead would grow a company that would put North Carolina brightleaf in pipes, cigarettes and cigars across the globe. At Wilmington, Alexander Sprunt & Sons would become the largest cotton exporters in the world. North Carolina's Atlantic Coastline Railroad would carry passengers and goods from the northeast states to the tip of Florida, all orchestrated from its Wilmington headquarters overlooking the Cape Fear River.

Yet for all its strides into the new century, North Carolina's people remained, for the most part, firmly rooted in the previous one. The high hopes of better lives for Tar Heels in the wake of the Civil War gradually gave way to something less grand, and became in many cases a quest for simple survival. Emancipation spelled the end of the slave economy that greased the economic engine of the South, but newly freed African-Americans were not suddenly catapulted into socio-economic equality. For most North Carolina blacks - and most poor whites, too – sharecropping and tenant farming became the norm when it came to earning a livelihood. In North Carolina, despite the appearance of wonderful new machines and labor saving devices like tractors, the hoe, plow, and liberal doses of human sweat remained the primary tools of those who worked the state's tobacco, cotton and corn fields.

As most North Carolinians dug in the dirt to earn their sustenance, or worked in the burgeoning textile industry around manufacturing centers like High Point and Greensboro, the men who owned those companies and farms grew progressively wealthier. Durham's James Buchanan Duke (son of tobacco giant Washington Duke), textile magnate Robert Holt, cotton exporter James Sprunt, and railroad impresario J. Pembroke Jones amassed unheard of wealth, while at the other end of the spectrum most working families made due with their own resources. Virtually everyone had a small parcel

James B. Duke

of land set aside as a family garden plot, where food for the dinner table was grown. This was vital to a family's well-being, as there was very little cash income for most families. Between 1860 and 1900, North Carolina's small farms tripled in number from 75,000 to a whopping 225,000, even as the average size of Tar Heel farms shrank from 316 acres to 101. Sharecroppers and tenant farmers would barter with local shops and service providers for the things they needed to get by, using their share of the crop as collateral. By the time the crops actually came in, there was often little in the way of hard cash left. Factory workers were in the same boat, going in debt to company stores established by the factory owners, who extended credit to workers against their expected wages. As many as 200,000 North Carolina workers had migrated from the farm fields to the textile mills as of 1900, working eleven and twelve hour days in less than optimum conditions to put food on the family table. Education in the state, which might have provided a means to escape the grinding poverty and subsistence living conditions most North Carolina workers found themselves living in, was spotty and sporadic at best, especially in the rural countryside.

Given the lives most Tar Heels lived in the early part of the twentieth century, events happening a world away in Europe were of little import to North Carolina's men and women. When war clouds gathered in France and Germany after the assassination of Archduke Ferdinand of Austria and his wife, the consensus among most Americans was to mind our own business. In fact, Woodrow Wilson, the bookish, Ivy League president who had spent much of his youth in Wilmington, N.C. (his father had been the minister of First Presbyterian Church in the city), was elected on a platform of keeping the troubles embroiling all of the European powers at arms length. "He Kept Us Out of War!" exclaimed campaign posters during that election. But when events like the U-boat sinking of the luxury liner *S.S. Lusitania* and its attendant loss of American life, and German machinations against the United States with America's neighbors came to light, the reluctant President Wilson realized the country could no longer ignore the European conflagration. Despite the president's pacifist yearnings, on April 2, 1917 Wilson delivered a message to Congress, asking for a declaration of war against Germany and its allies.

Over There: Tar Heels At War

In 1910, seven years before President Wilson asked for congressional approval to send the nation to war on the side of Britain, France and the rest of the Entente, North Carolina had a male population of 1,098,476. Of these men, 120,248 were between ages fifteen and nineteen; 98,796 were twenty to twenty-four years old; 79,490 were between twenty-five and twenty-nine; and 65,177 were between thirty and thirty-four years old. Despite earlier isolationist sentiment, once the declaration of war was made, large numbers of North Carolina men answered the call to arms with enthusiasm. For the Tar Heels, mobilization may have been a bit easier than for other states, as more than 7000 members of the North Carolina National Guard had already been called to duty in 1916 for service along the U.S.-Mexican border. During that time they served under overall command of the man who would become commander in chief of the American Expeditionary Force (AEF) in France, General John J. "Black Jack" Pershing, as he pursued the Mexican bandit (or revolutionary, depending on whose history you read) Pancho Villa.

Even before the nation officially went to war, numbers of North Carolinians had already joined the fray wearing the uniforms of other powers. Three North Carolinians fought for the British before their own country joined the fight. Five other Tar Heels, including one woman, were already in the field as part of the American Field Service (AFS), driving ambulances in France, when the United States became a belligerent. Men from the Old North State like Kiffin Rockwell (who flew with the famed All-American unit of the French air force, the Lafayette Escadrille), and Wilmington's Arthur Bluethenthal (who flew French bombers), had already followed their consciences and enlisted in the Allied cause. Both would give their lives in the effort. Those early volunteers would soon be followed by wave after wave of American youths wearing the olive-hued wool uniforms of the U.S. Army.

Pilots Arthur Bluethenthal (left), and Kiffin Rockwell (right) were among the first North Carolinians to join the fight against the Germans.

30th Infantry Division unit patch

Some of those young men would be volunteers, others would be draftees. All of them would bring a vigor and youthful optimism to the fight that had been missing for some time, after years of war had sapped the stamina from both sides of the fight in Europe.

With a declaration of war in hand, President Wilson wasted no time bringing the nation to a war footing. In North Carolina, existing National Guard and militia units were called into federal service and reformed as the 30th Infantry Division, nicknamed the "Old Hickory Division" because it was composed primarily of men from the Tar Heel State and Tennessee. The "Old Hickory" label referenced President Andrew Jackson, who had ties to both states. These men were mostly already serving as members of guard units like the 120th Infantry Regiment, or were enlisted volunteers. The bulk of the remainder of North Carolina's men who served in the war were mainly draftees who went to France with the 81st Infantry, known as the "Wildcat" Division. North Carolina's contri-

81st Infantry Division unit patch

bution to the 81st was confined primarily to the 321st Infantry Regt., the 316th Field Artillery, and the 321st Ambulance Regt. The rest of the division was made up of South Carolinians, Georgians, and Floridians. The 81st would arrive later in the summer of 1918, after the 30th Infantry had already been overseas for several months – first, undergoing trench warfare training in Great Britain, then easing into position in the trenches of France. North Carolina's black soldiers served and fought primarily in the segregated 93rd Infantry Division, organized at Camp Stuart, Virginia.

Even with mobilization of regular Army and National Guard units, the United States was woefully unprepared to fight a war on the scale of the one being waged in Europe. It soon became apparent that for the first time, Americans would be compelled to serve in the armed forces via a national draft. The "new" draft of May 1917 covered all males (both black and white) between ages twenty-one and thirty-five. North Carolina, led by enthusiastic wartime Governor Thomas Bickett, actually exceeded the draft quota it was asked to meet. Local county selective service boards registered 337,986 white North Carolina men for the draft, and another 142,505 blacks. The North Carolina draft effort was significant in that it provided no exemptions for college students. Neither did it allow whites to evade service by rigging the draft to put black draftees in their place – a not insignificant fact in a state that is now widely credited with being at the forefront of efforts to usher in the Jim Crow policies that disenfranchised Southern blacks at the turn of the century. As the scope of the conflict became more apparent to General Pershing, he informed his superiors in Washington, D.C. that even with the first draft more men would be needed. Thus, a second round of draft selections were made, this time from a widened pool of candidates up to age forty-five.

Gov. Thomas W. Bickett

Despite Gov. Bickett's best efforts, not everyone in North Carolina came around to his pro-war point of view. Especially in western North Carolina, there were still significant numbers of holdouts who just did not think they had a stake in a war half a world away. The state recorded more than 1500 men who earned the label "slacker" for evading the draft. The U.S. District Court for North Carolina tried 390 evasion cases, and convicted fifty-two draft dodgers. Still, North Carolina's evasion rate was one of the lowest of any state in the nation, at just 2.6 percent of the draft pool. Much of the draft's success was due to Bickett and local draft board officials who took efforts to seek out evaders and convince them to report for duty before the matter could become "official" and require a court martial.

Most North Carolina soldiers carried rifles as infantrymen, or serviced French-provided 75mm guns as artillerymen. The majority of these men in the infantry or artillery (except in the case of mobilized National

Guard units) were draftees. At the war's outset, many volunteers opted to serve as U.S. Marines, or in the navy or air corp. There was a feeling that these services offered options that were somehow more manly, romantic or chivalrous than regular infantry or artillery billets. But whether volunteers or draftees, the Tar Heel State would contribute more than 87,000 of its citizens to the armed forces that made up the American Expeditionary Force. During their six months in combat, from May to November 1918, records show that 629 were killed in the fighting. Another 204 died from wounds sustained in the war, and 1,524 more died from diseases such as dysentery and influenza that were rampant in the ranks of soldiers in the Great War. More than 3,600 came home with debilitating wounds, and scores more with lasting mental scars.

While the mass of American manpower reported for duty at one of thirty-six training camps hastily set up around the country by the U.S. Army, a North Carolina sailor aboard the *U.S.S. Mongolia* claimed the distinction of committing the first hostile act of the war by an American after the nation entered the conflict. Gunners Mate James Goodwin, of Edenton, is credited with damaging a German U-boat while serving on a convoy in the English Channel on April 19, 1917. As well, the first American prisoner captured by German troops after the United States declared war was a North Carolinian.

Gunners Mate James Goodwin

Sergeant Edgar M. Hallyburton, the unfortunate U.S. Army regular who bears that dubious distinction, could at least say he was not the first North Carolinian to be captured. Another Tar Heel, Benjamin Muse, was captured earlier in the war while serving with British forces.

When the 30th Division stepped ashore in France in March 1918, they found an allied force in disarray. The spring of 1917 had been disastrous for the British and French. After French commanders threw wave after futile wave of soldiers against the seemingly unbreakable wall of the German army in an offensive that nearly broke the back of the military's ability to fight, the common soldiers decided they had had enough. Mutinies throughout the ranks threatened to give the Germans the victory over the French that they had not – to date – been able to achieve through

American troops had to rely on Allied vessels to get from the United States to the battlefields of Europe.

outright force of arms. Only a change of command and the adoption of a strictly defensive posture avoided a complete disaster for French commanders. British troops were worn out too, after losing 350,000 men in a 1917 offensive to take some pressure off the beleaguered French. Government leaders at home lost so much confidence in the strategies of their army commanders in the British Expeditionary Force (BEF) that they refused to send any more reinforcements to France, thus forcing the British army to adopt a similar defensive policy. In short order, both French and British commanders looked with covetous eyes at the newly arriving American troops. Pershing was deluged with attempts to co-opt the Americans as replacements for the decimated allied divisions holding tenuous lines of defense in France and Belgium. But Pershing, with the support of his superiors in Washington, D.C., steadfastly refused to allow the American Expeditionary Force to be used piecemeal. The one concession Pershing did make to his desperate allies was to allow whole units to be detached for duty under overall command of French and British commanders. But at no time did Pershing contemplate allowing individual soldiers to be used as a replacement pool for the kind of attrition tactics the allies had adopted on the trench-scarred French battlefields.

Pershing's hope was that he could postpone deployment of his fresh American forces until 1919, when he would have a completely trained and provisioned force to put in the field. He disdained the static tactics that trench warfare had devolved into as being wasteful of life and resources, and unsuited to the American style of combat, which was characterized by open field, small unit fire and maneuver, rather than massed advances into the teeth of enemy machine guns, artillery and gas shells.

But plans made in cozy staff quarters seldom survive in the real world, and Pershing's were no different. First, there was the problem of supplying the new American army. From the moment war had been declared until the first American went "over the top" to face combat for the first time, getting men and materials to the army had been a problem. American industry was slow to ramp up for the war effort, and actually getting troops to France was complicated by the fact that America did not have enough ships to move large numbers of men and their equipment across the Atlantic Ocean in short order. That lack of hulls meant Pershing had to rely on ships provided by the British, at the time the world's premiere maritime power. Disagreement over which troops should be sent complicated the process even further. Pershing wanted logistical support troops to have equal priority of movement. British and French allies wanted combat troops – infantry, artillery and engineers – to be sent first (hoping, of course, to use them to replenish their own depleted ranks). On top of everything else, not even the mighty merchant fleet of Great Britain was big enough on its own to conduct such a mass movement. The British had to lease and buy ships from all over the globe to meet the demands of moving the American army and all of its equipment.

Gen. Erich von Ludendorf

As a result, American forces were slow to reach France. Still, by December 1917 General Pershing had 176,000 troops at his disposal in the AEF. He would soon need them. As the Russian war effort came apart under the stresses of the Bolshevik revolution, the Russians signed a separate peace that took them out of the war in March 1918. General Erich Ludendorf and the German high command immediately began transferring their freed up divisions from Russia to the western front. Ludendorf hoped to launch an offensive against the flagging British and French that would win the war before Pershing's fresh troops could arrive in enough numbers to make a difference. By late March, the Germans had amassed over a million men to face the combined strength of 1,476,000 allied forces in France and Belgium. By this point, American strength had risen to 287,500. When Ludendorf launched his great offensive in the Somme, those Americans would be very much in demand.

Seeing the Elephant

Ludendorf's plan was ready to launch by March 21, 1918. The Germans had managed to gather seventy-five divisions, organized into three armies, along a seventy kilometer front facing British General Sir Douglas Haig's three battered armies. When Operation St. Michael was launched, it fell on the hapless British like a hammer. Haig's forces were sent reeling, as on the opening day of the offensive alone, British forces suffered 17,000 casualties and lost 21,000 men as prisoners. The British fought heroically despite losing as much as eighteen percent of their combat effectiveness, and managed to inflict 39,000 casualties on the attacking Germans. But Ludendorf's armies were several times as large as the British force they faced, and consequently could absorb the losses over the short term. By March 26, the British were forced to withdraw in the face of a superior enemy. Ludendorf squandered a chance to knock the British out of the war, however, by failing to press the issue. The British, with French assistance, manage to consolidate their defenses with their backs to the English Channel. Now Ludendorf would turn his attention to the French. It was here that North Carolina troops would receive their baptism of fire.

The Tar Heels were called into action as soldiers and Marines of the Second Corp, against the third major German offensive launched between May and June 1918. They would also see extensive action during the ensuing allied counteroffensive from August to November. When German forces participating in Operation Blucher threatened to make a breakout in the area of Cantigny, Chateau-Thierry, and Belleau Wood, along the Marne, French commanders implored General Pershing for help. Americans, serving under their own officers, went into the line as the battered French were in full retreat. The Marine brigade, especially, earned lasting acclaim while stemming the oncoming German tide at Belleau Wood, then actually pushing them back. Astounded by the Marines' ferocity in the attack across machinegun-swept fields, German soldiers labeled the Amer-

U.S. Marines of the 6th Marine Regiment scramble into the woodline after crossing the wheat field at Belleau Wood.

icans "teufel-hunden," or devil dogs, a nickname that Marines are proud to claim today. All glory aside, the victory around Chateau Thierry and vicinity came at a high price. Pershing lost 8,000 American lives to win what became known as the Second Battle of the Marne, but the Germans were stopped thirty miles from Paris. Represented among those killed and wounded were men from North Carolina.

Meanwhile, in July, the 30th Division was sent to Belgium as part of the British forces defending the front around Ypres. In August 1918 they took over the section of the line known as the Canal Sector, running from Ypres to Voormezeele. After a month of training alongside the 27th Division (made up primarily of New Yorkers), both divisions were sent to the British Second Army. The Old Hickory Division found itself a part of the army's Second Corp. With the New Yorkers on their left flank, the Tar Heels of the 30th Division entered the trenches at Ypres on July 2, 1918. The young men of the division would find themselves faced with the reality of war in short order.

Assigned to a relatively quiet section of the line initially, the North Carolina men found themselves relegated to menial labor rebuilding collapsed trenches when they moved on July 16 to support two British divisions south of Ypres. The Tar Heels, who had so enthusiastically answered the call to arms when their nation went to war, resented the work. They came to France and Belgium to fight, not dig. They would get their chance before another month passed by.

Sensing a fatigue among their German foes, allied commanders began planning for a new counteroffensive even as doughboys and Marines were still earning their reputations in the Second Battle of the Marne. That offensive stepped off on August 8, 1918 when British, French and American troops began a push that would end in what Ludendorf would label "the black day of the German army." Allied success was such that German troops seemed completely demoralized. Encouraged by their successes, hoping to capitalize on the German collapse around Amiens, British high command gave the go ahead to launch a new offensive around Ypres. It was a fight in which the Tar Heels would lead the charge.

Called by military planners the Ypres-Lys Offensive, the men of the 30th Infantry Division would play a dominant role for the first time in offensive operations. Beginning on August 19, 1918, the North Carolina men would lead the way in the attack. This was especially true of the Sixteenth Infantry Brigade, to which North Carolina's 119th and 120th Infantry Regiments were attached. These men took their places in front line trenches and stayed there until the attack ended on September 4. The high ground of the line was dominated by Mount Kemmel, part of the Bailleul heights. The mount gave German defenders a wide view of the Flanders plain to the south, east and north. To be successful, Mount Kimmel had to fall.

As night fell on August 30, British commanders believed enemy forces were falling back from trench lines opposite the Old Hickory Division. Scouts, sent to confirm that information the next day, found something entirely different. Each company of the 119th Infantry sent single platoons out into No Man's Land early the next morning to conduct a reconnaissance towards the village of Voormezeele. In less than 200 meters they began encountering stiff resistance from machineguns and mortars. At least at this point on the line, Ludendorf's men seemed determined to make a stand.

Division commanders discussed after action reports from the day's fighting later that evening. The consensus seemed to be that no clear picture of the enemy's determination to hold the sector could be discerned from the results of action on August 30. Units expecting light resistance suddenly found themselves in disarray and out of touch with command.

Accordingly, 30th Division commanders decided to press forward again the next day. Orders went out to units already engaged in No Man's Land to continue their slow advance toward German lines. At first light, a general advance by both the 119th and 120th Infantry Regiments would follow.

Some of the Tar Heels assumed that they would occupy the recently vacated heights of Mount Kimmel when the attack commenced on September 1, 1918. Instead, the two battalions of the 120th ordered over the top at 7:30am that morning were aimed at the trenches directly opposite, where German troops were still offering a spirited defense near the Lankhof farm. Despite stiff fighting, by nightfall the Americans held a new line that included the Lankhof farm trenches taken by the 120th, and the town of Voormezeele, secured by elements of the 119th Infantry. The next day, a German counterattack failed to dislodge the Old Hickorys. The Tar Heels stuck.

Having proven their ability at Ypres, army commanders replaced the 30th Infantry Division with British troops over the next few days, shifting the North Carolinians to other areas in preparation for the coming Somme offensive and the assault on the Hindenburg Line. From July to September, the 30th Infantry Division as a whole lost 777 men. The 119th and 120th Infantry Regiments suffered the vast majority of those casualties, with 296 and 269 respectively, between July 11 and September 6, 1918.

Breaking the Line: St. Mihiel and the Hindenburg Line

To this point American units had fought well as units attached to British and French armies. Now General Pershing was about to get his wish. The AEF would launch an offensive of its own. The French had lost the area around St. Mihiel to the Germans in 1914, and the enemy had managed to repulse a French effort to take it back again in 1915. Strategically, the salient around St. Mihiel threatened the stability of the entire allied front. It also was important because of the railroad junction within the salient that was critical to German logistics. French commander Marshal Ferdinand Foch assigned the task of retaking the salient and capturing the rail junction to the Americans.

For whatever reason, Pershing abandoned his preferred doctrine of small unit fire and maneuver at St. Mihiel. American soldiers assaulted the trenches of the enemy in the classic wave formation that had proven so costly to that point during World War I. The attack came in three stages. First, sappers and engineers were sent out into No Man's Land at night to cut lanes through the wire for follow-on troops in the assault to come. Second, a huge artillery barrage was laid on to soften up the enemy's defenses and provide a curtain of steel to mask the advance of the infantry. The third phase of the plan was sending the infantry against German trenches.

Three thousand artillery pieces opened the bombardment one hour after midnight on September 12, and kept it up for four straight hours, pummeling German lines before the infantry assault. While the 119th and 120th regiments of the 30th Division were still engaged at Ypres, around St. Mihiel the 113th Infantry and 105th Engineers were meeting stiff resistance from the Germans. But the stiff resistance was just a rearguard action. German troops, expecting an attack by the end of the month, had already begun withdrawing from the salient. Five hours after the artillery began raining down, allied forces had occupied most all of the area around St. Mihiel. A day later allied elements of the three-pronged attack linked up at Vignuelles, and the salient was no more.

St. Mihiel was a tough fight to endure, as the rain of artillery was incessant. As a result, North Carolina doughboys reported nineteen cases of "shell shock." Also known as neurasthenia and war neurosis, symptoms included anxiety, nightmares, exaggerated startle response, tremors, nightmares, hallucinations, delusions, withdrawal and catatonia. Today it is more familiarly known as post-traumatic stress disorder.

For the next few weeks, both sides were content to rest and regroup. Artillery kept up a steady bombardment to dissuade any plans to alter the status quo, but by October the allies were ready to shift operations to the Meuse-Argonne front. Just a week after the fighting at St. Mihiel ended and the Americans were replaced in the trenches there, the Tar Heels who had been fighting under British command at Ypres rejoined their countrymen and started training for the upcoming offensive.

On September 23, 1918 the 30th and 27th Divisions were sent to General Sir Henry Rawlinsons' British Fourth Army. The Old Hickory troops relieved Australians in the line before Bellicourt and Nauroy, towns occupied by Germans anchoring the toughest part of the famed Hindenburg Line. The sector lay between the larger French cities of Cambrai and St. Quentin. Three days later, the attack began.

The Hindenburg Line was a massive, heavily fortified defensive line that stretched across the French countryside. The Germans began its construction early in the war, and had spent the ensuing four years making it stronger and more impregnable with each passing week. The section the

27th and 30th Divisions in Somme Offensive
September 24-30, 1918

Tar Heels of the 30th Infantry Division was to attack was widely believed to be the strongest section of the line. Centered around the town of Belli-court, along the St. Quentin Canal northeast of Paris, it would be a tough obstacle for the Americans. First, there were three rows of heavy barbed wire, each row thickly woven to a depth of thirty to forty feet. Artillery did little to remove it from the path of the advancing infantry. Next came three rows of the Hindenburg Line trenches, a bristling collection of machine-gun nests with interlocking fields of fire. Finally, there was Bellicourt and the St. Quentin Canal tunnel, also fortified with machinegun emplace-ments to guard the massive German army barracks, command, control and communications centers, and hospital complex located there.

By the night of September 27, the 119th and 120th Infantry Reg-iments had moved into position for the main assault scheduled for Sep-tember 29, 1918, when the men would step off at 5:50am. The 117th and 118th Regiments of the 30th Division were ready as reserves if needed. The attack would be supported by artillery and thirty-four British Mark V tanks. When the time came, a creeping barrage of artillery led the men of the 119th and 120th into No Man's Land, advancing at a rate of one hundred yards every four minutes. The artillery fire was not just outgoing, either. German guns began dropping shells among the Tar Heel soldiers massing for the attack. Rainy weather, fog, and gun smoke created a thick curtain that masked the advancing Americans from each other, reducing the war to just what each man could see in his immediate vicinity. Lost in No Man's Land, the North Carolinians advanced, often separated from their own of-ficers, small bands of men walking into the most heavily fortified German defenses in France.

Despite the confusion and carnage, the men of the 120th Infantry pressed on. Company A was the first to break through into the concrete reinforced bunkers of the Hindenburg line around 7:30 that morning. Men from the company captured their section of the supposedly impregnable line and used compasses to advance beyond the first row of bunkers. With little command guidance, noncommissioned officers acted on mission objectives given before the attack started to press home the gains they had made. On their left, the 119th Regiment was having a tougher go of things. They too had reached the Hindenburg Line as scheduled, but heavy machinegun fire caused their assault to falter. As well, the slow advance of the New Yorkers of the 27th Regiment lagged behind that of the North Carolinians, leaving the Tar Heels' left flank exposed to enfilading German machinegun fire. The exposed flank, a half-mile deep, resulted in whole-sale slaughter of the North Carolinians. It was not until reinforcements of the 117th and 118th Infantry Regiments arrived late in the afternoon that the exposed flank was secured, and the 119th was able to gather its dead and wounded and secure their section of the line.

Taking the Hindenburg Line was an impressive win for Pershing and the Allies. With North Carolina men leading the way, American forces captured forty-seven German officers, plus 1,432 enlisted men during the three-day assault. Large stores of ammunition and weapons were also captured. Yet for all the losses suffered, it still only amounted to just 3000 yards of territory. To get it, North Carolinians of the 30th Infantry Division suffered 2494 officers and men killed or wounded. The 119th Infantry Regiment lost 874 men, while the 120th lost 994. During the two weeks ending October 20, 1918, the British Third Army, to which the 30th Infantry Division was attached, suffered 121,000 casualties in total.

The Meuse-Argonne, 1918

After being beaten to a pulp taking the Hindenburg Line, the bulk of the 30th Infantry Division was too worn out to participate in General Pershing's move against the German line in the Meuse-Argonne region of southwest France. The campaign, launched in September 1918, would last until the armistice was announced in November. Even though most of the 30th was too fatigued to participate, Pershing did have the services of the division's 113th Field Artillery, plus the as yet untested 81st "Wildcat" Division. The green nature of the 81st was not unique in the force Pershing assembled. Five of his nine divisions for the offensive had never been in

American troops service a belt-fed machine gun in the Meuse-Argonne in 1918. North Carolina troops played a major role in the fighting .

combat.

The Meuse-Argonne was a region the Kaiser's troops had held since 1914, after their first assault on Verdun. In the years since, they had invested a lot of time and effort into strengthening their defenses there. The Meuse-Argonne campaign was part of a larger offensive devised by France's Marshal Foch, designed to cut German rail lines at Mezieres, Sedan, and Aulnoye, hopefully forcing Ludendorf's troops to retire within German territory before the onset of winter.

The doughboys' part in the plan was to advance against the German line west of Verdun, with a jump off date for the attack of September 26, 1918. The Americans would be supported by 190 French light tanks and 800 aircraft, plus the usual artillery. It would be a formidable task. Thick forest and a landscape studded with natural and German-made obstacles, dominated by three lines of defense in depth featuring trenches, barbed wire, deep dugouts, and concrete reinforced fighting posts faced the attacking Americans in the area. A fourth such line was even then under construction. The Meuse River formed the right boundary of the American sector for the attack, while the thickly wooded ground of the Argonne Forest, riddled with deep ravines, machinegun nests, and barbed wire entanglements, bounded the left side. A high, hogback ridge commanded the center of the line between forest and river, bristling with stonewalled villages and fortified spurs. The dominant feature of the ridge was the heavily fortified town of Montfaucon. To take this piece of real estate, General Pershing massed three corps, giving him an eight to one edge in manpower for the attack. Pershing hoped to advance at least ten miles in the opening, unyielding push. The general would be disappointed.

Even after a three-hour artillery bombardment to prep the battlefield, the attack ran into trouble early on. While the American III Corps did manage to gobble up five miles in their drive, their sister units in the center and on the left had less success. The V Corps was able to make little headway against the German defenses along the ridge in the center, while I Corps on the left advanced barely a mile into the thick tangle of woods that was the Argonne Forest. This left V Corps overextended. Over the next few days, after wave upon wave of Americans advanced in murderous frontal assaults, V Corps managed to penetrate into the Germans' second line of trenches near the Meuse. But the lack of progress by the other two corps allowed the Germans on the central ridge and in the forest to hit them with flanking fire. By the end of September, the attack had bogged

Tar Heel soldiers of the 30th, 81st, and African-Americans of the 92nd Divisions played pivotal roles in the Meuse-Argonne campaign that resulted in 24,000 allied casualties.
down.

While the main thrust of the offensive was grinding to a halt along the banks of the Meuse, the Wildcats of the 81st Division, as well as African-American soldiers of the 92nd Division, were assigned to what until then had been a fairly quiet sector near the Vosges Mountains. When Pershing's offensive kicked off, their mission was to do what they could to draw off German troops that might otherwise be used against the Americans closer to the Meuse-Argonne. After some heated exchanges with the enemy, the two divisions were moved closer to the main thrust in the Meuse-Argonne. By the end of September, the offensive had ground to a halt.

Pershing, recognizing that much of the problem lay in the inexperience of his green divisions, had to regroup. The American general had a lot to overcome. Logistical support was far outstripped by the demands of the war, and so trucks, mules, and all the other things an army needs to continue the fight was slow in coming from home. Battlefield losses were outstripping the rate of replacement from training camps in America, so newly arrived troops were thrown into line divisions unprepared for what they were about to face. Thirty of the French tanks seconded to his command for the attack were destroyed in one two-mile advance, and the rest seemed plagued with the usual miscellaneous mechanical troubles. The battlefield itself was daunting. Pocked with shell holes already, many doughboys must have felt even God was against them, as a hard rain fell for forty of the forty-seven day offensive.

The Americans regrouped, with veteran units that included the Second Division being brought to the fight, and resumed the attack in early October. Stiff resistance persisted from the Germans, but slowly, inch by muddy, shell-torn inch, the doughboys cleared the Argonne Forest, and eventually forced the Germans to fall back to Sedan. North Carolina men played a significant role in the fight, from start to finish. The last German trench line was breached by the Americans on November 1, but the success came at a steep price. In a month of fighting, Pershing's forces had suffered 24,000 casualties.

Under pressure from internal strife and Allied successes, Ludendorf resigned on October 27, 1918. The inexorable pressure being brought to bear on the exhausted Germans by the Americans and their British and French allies finally caused the Kaiser's ministers to sue for peace. On November 11, 1918, the guns fell silent. The armistice went into effect, and the soldiers could go home – in time.

American soldiers, including those from North Carolina, would be in Europe up to a year longer before boarding transports that would take them back to the homes they had left behind more so many months before. Both the 30th Infantry Division and the 81st Infantry Division stayed in France during the winter of 1918-1919, until boarding American ships for the voyage back across the Atlantic. The North Carolinians touched American soil again at east coast ports like Charleston, Newport News, and Boston. From there, they rode by train back to the same camps they had left behind on the way to France, where they were given sixty dollars travel pay and mustered out of their country's service. The Tar Heels were home.

After Johnny Came Marching Home: Re-assimilation

The men who came home from Europe's battlefields were not the same men who had marched off to war singing patriotic songs in 1917 and 1918. From lives centered around family, friends, crop planting schedules, and daily clock punching at jobs in North Carolina factories and offices, the men of the AEF re-entered civilian life changed by their wartime experiences. They returned from France and Belgium missing limbs, with seared lungs from exposure to mustard gas, and a less naive (if not outright jaded) view of the world and their place in it. While most were glad to be home, many also harbored a resentment that they were not allowed to finish the job.

It is difficult to find data specific to North Carolina when it comes to determining how well Tar Heel doughboys managed to fit in with the lives they left behind after coming home. Given the resources available, the best we can do might be to look at World War I veterans as a whole, in that the issues facing North Carolina veterans must have been similar to those facing their brothers from other parts of the country.

North Carolina veterans, like those from other states, carried baggage home with them that they did not have when they embarked for France in 1917 and 1918. Even among those that may not have been clinically diagnosed as suffering from Post Traumatic Stress Syndrome (or shell shock, as it was known then), there was still an abundance of nightmares and memories they often spent the rest of their lives trying to bury deep inside themselves.

The mental residue of the veterans' time in combat often became an insurmountable obstacle for loved ones hoping to get their friends, lovers, husbands, brothers and fathers back again at the war's conclusion. They either could not understand what their men had been through, or did not want to. Then too, the veterans themselves bore their share of the blame. Said one ex-doughboy, "It was a long hard job for Walt (his brother) and me to adjust to civilian life. We were both partially deaf from exploding shells. My throat was damaged by gas, and Walt had a breaking out on his face from cootie bites. We had traveled so much that we had the wanderlust. Every time we heard a train whistle, we wanted to get on it and go somewhere. Every horizon beckoned. No matter where we were, we wished we were somewhere else.

"However, our worst handicap was a callous indifference to everything and everybody."

While troubles reintegrating into civilian life was widespread among veterans, within the ranks of America's African-American doughboys, including those North Carolina men of the 93rd Division, it was compounded by racism at home. World War I was the largest transatlantic movement of African Americans since the days of the slave trade, with more than 200,000 black American soldiers serving in France until the Armistice. Those men were exposed to a society in which men of their color were not the social outcasts they were at home. In France, there was no segregation (at least among French civilians). The racial, social and sexual equality they found among French men and women sowed the seeds of social activism in the black soldiers who would shortly return to Jim Crow-era America. The men had thought their sacrifices in Europe would pave the way for changes in civil rights in America. They were wrong.

The war changed the men and women who lived through it, and in turn those men and women changed the world they lived in. Skirts got shorter. The teetotaler movement was bolstered in their efforts to usher in prohibition by a wartime ban on the sale of alcohol as a scarce resource, which in turn spurred the rise of criminal elements represented by men like Chicago gangster Al Capone. Jazz, deemed immoral by government authorities, spread across the country after the ghettos it was born in were made off-limits to U.S. servicemen during the war. Free or almost free cigarettes provided to the military hooked a generation of soldiers, sailors and Marines on tobacco products. American soldiers who had been part of the occupation forces in France and Germany brought home foreign-born wives, whose cultural influences were felt in the communities they lived in. Maybe more to the point, any lingering fascination with European sophistication among American veterans went by the wayside. By the 1920s, as more and more families began to suffer economic decline, many veterans began to feel like the nation had been hoodwinked into a costly war for a bunch of people who did not deserve it. The experience of life among the British, Belgians, Germans, and especially the French (who most doughboys grew to detest as ungrateful for the sacrifices they had made), left most veterans of the opinion that it should be a good long time before American blood and treasure was spent on helping out with troubles across the Atlantic Ocean again.

The American public had a hard time understanding their returning heroes, in part because the soldiers who had seen combat saw it in varying degrees. While all may have served in France, the experiences – and therefore the psychological impact of the war – of each man was different. An ambulance driver saw the end results of combat, but his experience never approached the blood chilling terror felt by an infantryman scrambling for a gas mask as a fog of lung-searing death floated inexorably closer along his trench line. An artilleryman's experience of the war would be different from that of a scout trapped in a shell hole while German machineguns chewed up the air above him.

The U.S. government tried to help its returning soldiers, but in too many cases the effort was ineffectual. Part of this might be attributable to corruption on the part of the men tasked with administering the newly created Veterans Bureau. Yet even if the Veterans Bureau had been a model of efficiency, the task it faced was daunting. While historians generally date

the Great Depression as beginning in 1929, the seeds of that global disaster were sowed in 1919, when four million hastily discharged American
soldiers were unceremoniously dumped into a job market that had no jobs
to fill. The G.I. Bill of World War II did not exist for the soldiers of the
Great War (though the experience of those World War I vets was a cau-
tionary tale that influenced the creation of the bill in 1945). There was no
money for re-educating returning soldiers, no job training on the national
level, although attempts were made to find employment with some new
government programs for returning veterans. After World War I, veterans
were basically expected to fend for themselves, no matter the financial loss
their service might have burdened them with. Making things worse for the
veterans were the blinders that many civilians wore when it came to their
returning soldiers. In too many cases, they seemed intent on returning the
men to a simpler, more docile past that just could not exist anymore in a
time when the idealism of the Wilson administration was often seen as a
laudable but naïve failure. The nation was ready to put the ugliness of the
war behind them, and the painful reminder of the conflict represented by
maimed or destitute veterans was something most people of America just
refused to see.

Some thought had been given to the problem of returning soldiers,
however fleeting or poorly executed it might have been. In the past, soldiers had been given homesteads as thanks for their service, but Congress
ended that program after the Civil War. Veterans from all ensuing conflicts
were forced to settle with something less than what their grandfathers had
been given via the "bounty" system that existed in their time. By the time
the veterans of World War I came home cities were growing, and the slums
and other problems that came from urban living were, too. The cities just
did not have the infrastructure to offer returning soldiers a home and a job.
Couple that with the fact that as the economic situation in the nation wors-
ened, so too did the city's ability to support those who were unable to fend
for themselves through charitable organizations. Therefore, many people
began to advocate "back to the land" schemes for returning Great War soldiers. The idea was to return some of the urban population to communes in
the countryside, where the occupants would be able to achieve self-suffi-
ciency (or some degree of it) by growing and raising the things they needed to survive. Wilmington, N.C.'s Hugh MacRae was one such advocate of
communal living for the returning vets and their families. As early as the
turn of the century, literature put out by advocates of such policies painted

a romanticized picture of life on bucolic patches of land, where formerly harried city dwellers got back in touch with their agrarian roots and fashioned livelihoods from God's country bounty. Planners of the soldier resettlement for the most part operated under no such illusions, realizing that agrarian living was often "unprofitable, uncomfortable, and dull." They hoped that a cooperative effort between private sector developers and the national government could sidestep many of the pitfalls of the plan. Secretary of the Interior Franklin Lane was an advocate of veteran colonization.

He proposed a "communal plan" in which one hundred families or more would be grouped together to work allocated land. According to Lane's thinking, the reason for the decline of rural communities was "dissatisfaction with social conditions," and that the new communal system would have the advantage of neighborliness. Lane anticipated that returning soldiers would precipitate a deep bout of unemployment, and hoped that such a planned commune would lessen its impact. The plan was that states would furnish the land, while the federal government provided the financing for development. A much broader plan, that included agricultural, forest, and mineral lands, and

Franklin Lane

the establishment of a "United States Construction Service" as a buffer against unemployment, was put forth by the Labor Department. Even the American Legion endorsed such plans, and adopted soldier resettlement as one of their four points for dealing with returning veterans. Plans for soldier resettlement were never adopted at the national level, due in large part to opposition from large farming interests. Thirty-seven states did, however, pass legislation creating such colonizing plans. The agricultural depression of the 1920s and the dependence on funding from the federal government to see the projects through doomed them all to extinction by 1930.

Such plans would likely have found fertile soil among veterans

Penderlea, in Pender County, N.C., was a planned community established by Hugh MacRae under the New Deal to provide work and homes to people during the Great Depression.

in North Carolina, where by 1920 half the total population still lived on working farms. But increasing mechanization and a glut of agricultural product made farming a tenuous occupation even among people who had made their living tilling the soil for generations. This was a situation that would be compounded when the Great Depression gripped the country beginning in 1929. Franklin D. Roosevelt's election to the presidency saw the unveiling of new programs under his "New Deal," including subsidies for *not* growing crops (to decrease the surplus and stabilize the markets), and in 1933 the new Resettlement Administration. This organ of the federal government, created by Congress in 1935, moved select families to federally planned resettlement farms. One such communal farm in North Carolina is the community known in 2010 as Penderlea. The Civilian Conservation Corp, organized by the federal government in 1933, also offered some help to veterans caught in the throes of the depression. Through it, men worked on civilian infrastructure projects nationwide for thirty dollars a month in pay, plus room and board.

Other programs, both governmental and privately administered and supported, tried to offer the wounded and maimed rehabilitation, retraining, and support. But in a perverse sense, sometimes veterans found the medicine worse than the cure. For men used to making their own way in the world, finding themselves relying on government subsidies and the charitable efforts of strangers – no matter how well intentioned – often had the effect of making them feel less than a man. For a veteran who might already be suffering from self-esteem issues stemming from a missing a limb, blindness, or shell shock, even an unintended blow like that could be a serious setback. Even when a veteran did swallow his pride and apply for retraining under one of the federal programs, red tape and delays often saw the men drop out in disgust.

It was this disgust and desperation that led to one of the most horrific scenes in the aftermath of the war, when unemployed veterans at the height of the Great Depression joined their brothers in a mass march on Washington, D.C. to demand the bonus promised them by Congress. The bill to compensate World War I veterans for the difference between their service pay and what a civilian was being paid at the time over the length of their wartime service was passed in 1924. Called the Adjusted Compensation Act, it compelled the U.S government to pay World War I vets a dollar for every day they served, while those who saw overseas duty would be paid $1.25 per day, plus interest at a rate of four percent. The checks were to be issued in 1945, delaying the hit to the treasury during the height of the country's economic woes. Some veterans stood to be paid as much as $1600, money that desperate veterans and their families could surely use in the days after the stock market crash of 1929. When the market bottomed out, cash strapped doughboys began calling for their "bonus" to be paid immediately, and they did so with the support of new but powerful veterans advocacy organizations such as the Veterans of Foreign Wars and the American Legion. The need was certainly evident. Veterans Administration studies show that in 1930 and 1931, veterans suffered almost fifty percent higher unemployment than their civilian contemporaries, and that their plight on average lasted longer. Over one nine-day period in the first month of 1930, 170,000 World War I veterans applied for first-time loans against the monies promised them by their bonus certificates. But the demands from veterans for immediate relief from the government by paying them their bonuses butted up against efforts by the Hoover administration to cut spending to reign in Depression-fueled deficits. Hoover was adamantly against paying the bonuses early. Faced with no other options for relief, many veterans across the country decided they would go to the seat of government and ask for their money in person.

The Bonus March of 1932

The nation's capitol was sweltering in the summer of 1932, and the heat came from more than just the weather. For weeks, caravans of former soldiers of the Great War had been arriving in Washington, D.C. to put

Veterans of the Great War set out for Washington, D.C. to demand Congress pay the "bonus" they had been promised immediately instead of in 1945.

their demand for payment of back pay, what was popularly termed a "bonus," to the President and Congress in person. As many as 20,000 combat veterans – some with their families in tow – gathered on the outskirts of the city in makeshift tents and derelict buildings. The men were led by a thirty-four-year-old former sergeant from Portland, Oregon named Walter Waters. Collectively, the men came to call themselves the Bonus Expeditionary Force, an undisguised reminder of the last time they had gathered together en mass, as their country's American Expeditionary Force being sent off to fight a war.

The House passed a bill that would have paid the vets their bonus money, but the Senate blocked it with an overwhelming vote against the measure (18 for, 62 against), and Congress adjourned for the summer. Realizing there would be no satisfaction until the legislators returned in the fall, about a fourth of the veterans availed themselves of a government offer of free transportation home. The rest settled in to wait in their shantytowns in parks on the flood plain of the Anacostia River, and in a row of condemned buildings along Pennsylvania Avenue. From there, they staged peaceful demonstrations in front of the White House, depending on charitable contributions to feed themselves and their families.

The real trouble came when members of the American Communist

Party sent John Pace to stir the pot and incite a riot. While it is uncertain if he had any success, his mere presence set off alarm bells in the seats of power. Hoover and others in the halls of Washington were only too aware of the bloody chaos that had ensued when Communists in Russia had set the people there to overthrowing the Czar's government. They also were aware of worker unrest in the war-ravaged countries of Europe. Hoover did not want any such scenarios happening in the United States, especially among wounded, unemployed and starving veterans – and certainly not with the White House as a backdrop to whatever pictures of the unrest that might appear in the newspapers. To evict the veterans, Secretary of War Patrick Hurley turned to the army.

Hurley ordered Washington, D.C. police superintendant Pelham Glassford, who had been a friend to the veterans and their cause, to re-move the men from the capitol. When police officers tried to move the squatters out of their camps, they came under attack with thrown stones and bricks. One officer suffered a fractured skull. Police opened fire on the veterans, killing one and mortally wounding another. Glassford sought the counsel of the city's Board of Commissioners, who passed the buck up to the federal government. Hoover used it as an excuse to call out troops from Fort Myer to restore order.

Secretary Hurley issued marching orders to Major General Doug-las MacArthur, who on July 28, 1932, led five Renault tanks and a brigade of rifle and bayonet-toting soldiers to the squatters' village. After ordering

Gen. Douglas MacArthur sent troops and tanks in to the Bonus Army camps to evict the veterans at the point of bayonets.

Fire rips through the condemned buildings where veterans and their famiies had taken up shelter after the army moved in to evict them.

them to disperse, the soldiers began a steady march through the shanties, driving the veterans ahead of them like cattle. Angry pockets of resisters threw glass bottles and bricks, but to little effect. In short order MacArthur had driven the ex-soldiers out of the downtown area of the capitol. Then his men proceeded across the 11th Street bridge and into the camp where the soldiers and their families were camped. No one really knows how it happened, but suddenly the highly combustible shacks the veterans were living in were aflame. Before the day was over, fifty-four veterans would be dead, and another 135 would be arrested – and the nation would be stunned.

The backlash was almost immediate. In the presidential election soon after, the public expressed their displeasure with Herbert Hoover, the man they held responsible for what happened to the "Bonus Army" in Washington, D.C., by voting in Franklin D. Roosevelt. The Congress eventually did vote give the men their bonus ahead of time, but not until 1936.

Henry L. Stevens, Jr., a North Carolina veteran of the Wildcats of the 81st Infantry Division, was the national president of the American Legion. At the group's 1931 national convention in Detroit, the membership of the legion was on the verge of passing a resolution demanding the payment of the promised bonus money. Before the measure could come to a full vote, President Herbert Hoover arrived and made a plea to the American Legion leadership not to push for the bonuses. The measure was defeated, and Stevens spent most of the rest of his tenure defending the decision to his rank and file.

In North Carolina, Tarboro veteran Henry C. Bourne, the president of the state chapter of the American Legion, was adamantly opposed to the position taken by Stevens and nation leadership. A vote by all Legion posts in the state sent a resounding message in favor of asking congress to pay the bonus immediately, and that became the position that Bourne adopted. Meanwhile, Walter Waters' band of veterans was gaining new followers on their way to the nation's capitol. Men from all states began to journey to Washington, D.C. to press the bonus issue with the president and the members of congress.

North Carolina's volunteers in the Bonus Army came mostly from the central piedmont and western parts of the state. While the Great Depression brought hardship to virtually everyone across North Carolina, people living along the Coastal Plain were less severely impacted. Nevertheless, 276 Tar Heel doughboys joined the march and took their complaints to the capitol. These men, living mostly in a derelict building along Pennsylvania Avenue, suffered along with all the rest of the veterans from hunger, dysentery, sore mouth, venereal diseases, and other minor injuries. None of them had beds, the sides of the building were open to the air, and there was no plumbing to offer a sanitary means

American Legion commander Henry L. Stevens

of dealing with bodily wastes. It would have been a miserable way to live in the heat of a Washington, D.C. summer.

The Doughboys' Legacy

World War I tore the globe apart, ripping asunder ways of life that existed before what historian Barbara Tuchman dubbed the "Guns of August" roared. That was as true for North Carolina as it was for everywhere else. The profound impact of the war on the men who left homes

Men of the 81st Infantry Division, largely made up of North Carolinians, muster into formation in France.

and loved ones to serve in the muddy, blood-soaked trenches of France could not help but change the Tar Heel State, too. Until the declaration of war came, most North Carolinians were isolationist in their tendencies. But when the war came to America, North Carolinians of all races and backgrounds answered their nation's call. They served admirably on the fields of France and Belgium, achieving notable victories against their German enemies. They helped keep order in a war-torn, post-armistice Europe – despite being surrounded by allies who seemed less than grateful for the blood the Americans had shed. They came home missing limbs, psychologically scarred, often unemployed and finding themselves playing catch-up in a world that had somehow passed them by. Doughboys from North Carolina joined their brethren from other states in a desperate plea to their government, not for special perks, but for what was simply their due for a job well done. They came home optimistic that their sacrifices had some greater meaning and had changed the world for the better. Then they felt that sense of accomplishment fade, as two short decades later, they watched their own sons march off to bleed on European battlefields against the same enemy they had faced. And then they faded into obscurity, trying to put the things they had seen and done on behalf of their flag behind them. The North Carolina veterans of World War I are all gone now, but there was a time when they did all that their country asked of them, when they were all "soldiers once, and young." Through the lens of a century later, their sacrifices may seem somehow less significant than those made by their sons who fought World War II. But there was nothing easy about fighting a war in the trenches, the wounds they sustained did not bleed any less. Their sacrifice is no less noble because politicos gave them something less than the victory they all thought they were fighting for. In France and at home, the Tar Heel doughboys did their jobs.

Captain William F. Lynch began his career in the United States Navy, but ended it in the Confederate States Navy. Lynch commanded naval forces on the Cape Fear River.

"Per Mare, Per Terra:"[1]
The Confederate Marines and Navy on the Cape Fear

by
Jack E. Fryar, Jr.

Despite its proximity to the Atlantic Ocean and its importance to the war effort of the Confederacy, the presence of the Confederate navy and Marines in the lower Cape Fear was never very large. Leaders in Richmond assigned them to the area almost as an afterthought, and neglected to man and supply the Cape Fear Naval Squadron once they did establish it. Nevertheless, Southern sailors and Marines performed their duties well and with valor, in spite of making up only a fraction of the total military strength stationed in and around the port of Wilmington.

Gen. Winfield Scott, Chief of Staff of the United States Army on the eve of the War of Rebellion, recognized the chief weakness of the South as its lack of an industrial infrastructure to provide the logistics that keep an army fighting in the field. His plan to blockade Southern ports and cut off the Confederacy from its overseas suppliers, derisively dubbed the "Anaconda Plan" by newspapers and critics of the day, would eventually make Wilmington, North Carolina perhaps the most important place in the Confederacy.[2]

Wilmington's importance stemmed from its location and geography. In the southeastern corner of North Carolina, the city was the largest in the state. Situated twenty-eight miles north of Old Inlet at the mouth of the Cape Fear River, the city's role as a destination for blockade-runners would play a key part in Southern military plans during the war. The Cape Fear River is the only one in North Carolina with direct access to the Atlantic Ocean, with a length of 147 miles that bisects the state to the northwest. It was navigable all the way from Wilmington to Fayetteville in the nineteenth century. Railroads running north to Petersburg, and south to Charleston, allowed freight and troops shipped from Wilmington to be dispatched to the fronts where Union and Confederate armies clashed. Robert E. Lee famously said in the latter stages of the war that if Wilmington fell, he could not keep his army in the field.

To protect the port and its railways, Confederate war planners designed a series of eleven major forts and batteries at strategic points between Old Inlet and the city itself. The chief of these was Fort Fisher, a massive sand-walled fort at Confederate Point in southern New Hanover County that mounted forty-seven main guns behind defensive works shaped like an inverted "7". The land face of the fort ran for more than 600 yards from the river to the Atlantic Ocean on the east. The sea face of the fort extended south for more than a mile to New Inlet. At the junction of the river and the inlet, a huge four-gun battery dubbed Battery Buchanan anchored Confederate defenses. Fort Fisher was the key to any effort to reduce Wilmington, since it commanded access to the Cape Fear River and offered protection for blockade-runners trying to outrun elements of the Union navy's North Atlantic Blockading Squadron. The fort was manned by Confederate army troops under the command of Col. William Lamb, a former Virginia newspaper man turned military engineer. Overall command of Cape Fear defenses rested with Gen. William Henry Chase Whiting until late in the war. Despite the relatively few Confederate sailors and Marines attached to the Cape Fear Military District, they performed admirably in the struggle to defend Wilmington. That internal strife between army and navy commanders complicated those defensive efforts only makes their performance more laudable.

The South's New Navy and Marines

As it became clear that the Union would soon be ripped asunder over the issues of states' rights and slavery, officers in the United States military services began choosing sides. Many of those serving officers, Southerners who fought side by side with Northern compatriots in the Mexican-American War of the 1840s and elsewhere, opted to surrender their commissions rather than take up arms against their home states and the institutions they believed in. As a result, the South's lack of an industrial base was somewhat offset by a core of talented military leaders who were, at least early in the war, more than capable of challenging the U.S. on the battlefield.

Officers of the United States Navy and U.S. Marine Corps faced the same choices as their army counterparts. Many, like William F. Lynch, who would come to command the Cape Fear Naval Squadron, were veteran tars who had served with distinction before the great rift between the North and South forced them to declare their loyalties. Most Confederate naval standouts – men like John Newland Maffitt, John Taylor Wood, William T. Muse, and Raphael Semmes – all could list service in the United States Navy on their resumes.

When the Confederacy split the nation in half, its navy was for all intents non-existent. No resigning naval officer left the U.S. Navy and brought his ship with him when he went south. Within the boundaries of the Confederacy there were no shipyards capable of real heavy ship construction, or ancillary factories to manufacture cordage and the myriad other things needed to provision a warship.[3] The only saving grace the South could point to was the fact that the United States Navy was not in much better shape.[4] When Federals recaptured the naval facilities at Nor-

CSS Virginia (formerly the Merrimac) duels with Union ironclad USS Monitor (right) at Hampton Roads in 1861.

folk, not long after they fell to Confederate forces at the beginning of the war, the only real navy yard available to the South was denied them. The Confederacy turned to ironclads to rectify the imbalance between their navy and that of the enemy. Ironclads, as proven at the great Hampton Roads showdown between the *Monitor* and the *Virginia*, offered a way for a cash, technology, and infrastructure-strapped South to equal the odds to some degree.

The Confederate States Marine Corps, like the other branches of the South's military, found its initial leadership within the ranks of existing Union forces, in this case the United States Marine Corps. When the war broke out, a high percentage of trained, experienced, and capable company-grade officers resigned from the USMC to accept positions in the CSMC.[5] Evidence supports the position that Confederate Marines were in high demand, although the ranks of the CSMC never rose above 600 men.[6] Commands throughout the Confederacy that had a naval presence, or bordered waterways that could support naval operations, all clamored for the gray-clad sea soldiers to flesh out the often pitifully small ranks of Confederate Navy personnel on hand. That the Marines were capable of duty aboard ship or on land, and had proven capabilities as artillerymen, put their services at a premium.[7]

The Confederate States Marine Corps organized differently from its northern brothers, into three company-sized elements that saw service in part or in whole in virtually every theater of the war, including at Wilmington, N.C.

The Cape Fear Naval Squadron

The Confederate navy presence on the Cape Fear River around Wilmington was, of necessity, relegated to a subordinate position behind the army that manned the eleven forts and batteries defending the port city. The army had the most men and materiel there, and ultimately any defense would hinge on the ability of land-based troops to deflect the efforts of Union war planners to reduce the port by land or sea. Add in the fact that Confederate naval authorities were slow to establish a C.S. Navy presence in the region, and it is not surprising that the army dominated military planning and efforts in southeastern North Carolina.[8]

Originally, the Confederate navy planned a much more robust presence around Wilmington, but for a naval service bereft of much in the way of warships, those plans depended on the ability of local shipyards to construct vessels to implement those plans. At Wilmington, the Beery brothers and James Cassidey operated shipyards on the banks of the Cape Fear River capable of building small craft and repairing others. The Confederate States Navy made contracts with both concerns to build small patrol boats, convert captured tugs and other vessels to military purposes, and to build three ironclads to safeguard access to the Cape Fear River at New and Old Inlets. Supervising all of this activity was the commander of the newly formed Cape Fear Naval Squadron, William T. Muse.[9] Chronically undermanned, the sailors and Marines who made up the Cape Fear Naval Squadron did their best to carry out their duties under trying circumstances.

Cape Fear shipbuilder Benjamin Beery

Those duties, early on, seem to have consisted of doing odd jobs for the army. Until the Confederate navy undertook a program of gunboat construction in late 1861, the navy apparently believed that Forts Caswell and Johnston, at Old Inlet below Smithville, were sufficient to dissuade any Federal incursions to the Cape Fear. For months, the only Confederate States Navy vessel mounting any significant firepower was the old converted tug, the *Uncle Ben*.[10] After the fall of the Albemarle region and Outer Banks to a resurgent Union, the only North Carolina port left in Confederate control was at Wilmington. Protecting it became a paramount concern for Southern war leaders.

To that end, in March 1862, Confederate Secretary of the Navy Stephen Mallory instructed Capt. William T. Muse to begin building two ironclad rams at Wilmington.[11] The C.S.S. *North Carolina* and the C.S.S. *Raleigh* were plagued by problems from the outset. The Beery and Cassidey shipyards, owned by brothers William and Benjamin Beery and James Cassidey,[12] lacked the material to build them, and getting those materials was a chore that tested the patience and resourcefulness of both Muse and

The ironclad CSS Raleigh was one of two such vessels constructed at Wilmington shipyards.

his successor, Capt. William F. Lynch. The South only had two iron mills capable of rolling the huge sheets of metal needed to armor the ships, the Tredegar Iron Works in Richmond, Virginia, and another in Atlanta.[13] The Tredegar Works was always besieged by army, navy, and railroad interests who all needed scarce iron and steel, and needed it yesterday. To make matters worse, the yellow fever epidemic of 1862 cut a swath through Wilmington that left more than 700 people dead. Those marine carpenters and shipwrights who did not die from the scourge fled Wilmington for safer environs, effectively halting the work on the ironclads.[14]

Orders from Secretary Mallory sent William F. Lynch to Wilmington in October 1862. The commodore, with four decades of naval experience under his belt, arrived in November 1862 during the last days of the epidemic at the port city. Nevertheless, he immediately took charge of Confederate naval activities in the Cape Fear and began an energetic program to whip the existing infrastructure into shape, complete construction of the two ironclads, and generally enhance the navy's standing and role in the defenses of the strategic port.[15] Still, the navy would be woefully undermanned for the remainder of the war, and Lynch's prickly personality would cause a host of troubles that ultimately cost the navy's efforts.[16]

The Confederate Marines at Wilmington

Into this mix of ego and insufficiency, the Confederate States

Marines tried to make themselves useful in whatever ways they might. As trained artillerists, Col. William Lamb welcomed them as supplements to his undermanned garrison at Fort Fisher. The construction of Battery Buchanan at the southern tip of Confederate Point, close by New Inlet, allowed the Confederate sailors and Marines to make an active contribution to the defenses of the Cape Fear River.

Captain Alfred Van Benthuysen, CSMC, assumed command of the Marine Guard at Wilmington in June 1862. Van Benthuysen led a colorful life prior to his Confederate service. He is thought to have fought in China during the Tai-ping Rebellion, served in Guiseppe Garibaldi's Italian campaign on the staff of General Avezzano, and fought in the Battle of Caesaria. Van Benthuysen was present and played a major role in the bombardment of the Federal installation at Pensacola, Florida. His CSMC service took him to Mobile, New Orleans, and Drewry's Bluff before taking him to southeastern North Carolina.[17] Van Benthuysen commanded Company B of the CSMC, that was serving as an independent company both afloat and ashore, but it was another two years before he had much to command. Company B's Marines served primarily as infantry or artillerists, and as a rapid reaction force in both defensive and offensive operations.[18] The core of the new Company B was made up

Lt. Henry Doak, CSMC

of former Company C Marines led by 1st Lieutenant Richard Henderson, whose thirty men reported to Wilmington early in 1864 for duty aboard the two ironclads being built there. Lt. Henry Doak joined the new company on March 1, 1864 from Savannah and assumed command of the Marines aboard the C.S.S. *Raleigh.* As the naval and Marine strength at Wilmington was beefed up, Commodore Lynch and his officers could finally begin planning offensive operations against Federal forces.[19] Those operations were highlighted by a spectacular nighttime naval engagement that, if not big on results, was great entertainment for Fort Fisher's bored defenders.

Keeping Busy and Making Enemies

Commodore Lynch did not always play well with others. In virtually every place he served, his sense of honor and naval pride caused him to alienate others who were crucial to the success of his mission. At Wilmington the enmity between Lynch and the commander of the Cape Fear Military District, Gen. William Henry Chase Whiting, grew so bad that eventually Secretary Mallory replaced Whiting with Braxton Bragg. While relations between the army and navy on the Cape Fear were not the primary reason behind Whiting's replacement, it was certainly a contributing factor. That Lynch had managed to get on North Carolina Governor Zebulon Vance's bad side, too, did not bode well for the future of Confederate navy operations around Wilmington.[20]

Gen. W.H.C. Whiting, CSA

The ill will between Capt. William Lynch and the other military and civilian leaders of the Cape Fear defenses stemmed in large part from Lynch's quick temper. The naval officer had already had a run-in with Gen. Henry Wise over operations in the Albemarle and at Roanoke. The hard feelings between the two likely contributed to the success of the Federal fleet that wrested control of the Outer Banks from Confederates in 1862.[21]

When Lynch initially arrived in the Cape Fear, he formed a good working relationship with Gen. W.H.C. Whiting. That working relationship soured after Lynch felt Whiting was mismanaging the Indian Wells battery north of the city. The guns of the fort would bear on any attacker attempting to destroy the two shipyards at Wilmington and across the river on Eagles Island, where Lynch's ironclads were under construction. Lynch asked for army troops to man the guns of the battery, as the lack of navy personnel under his command left him too shorthanded to send sailors to the fort. Whiting replied that he was having staffing problems of his own, and could not spare any men to garrison Indian Wells. Lynch took it as a slight to the navy, and protested to Sec. Mallory. The relationship between the two officers went downhill from there. The climax came when Lynch refused to let the blockade-runner *Hansa*, carrying army cargo, depart from the Cape Fear, despite having an authorization to do so from Whiting. Lynch put Marines aboard to make sure the ship did not depart without his permission while the matter was sorted out. Whiting dispatched army troops to oust the Marines, and a nasty stalemate ensued. Finally, officials in Richmond had to settle matters. After that, Whiting simply ignored Lynch's messages.

Scarce manpower and materials also plagued the defenders of Wilmington. Both the army and the navy needed warm bodies and iron to enact their defensive plans, neither of which could be readily had around Wilmington. Both branches of the service found themselves in competition with railroads for the rare supplies of used rail iron that became available, and in bidding wars to secure some of it for military purposes. Even when the army and navy had requisition authority from the Confederate government, it was difficult to get the materials they needed. Despite the shortcomings, by the time Federal warships assembled off Confederate Point, both the army and the navy rallied to fend off the impending attacks. In some cases, enterprising officers made plans to execute daring operations despite their manpower deficiencies.

Raids and Raiders

Confederate Marines from the Wilmington station participated in at least two operations before the final reckoning at Fort Fisher in 1865. Under the command of Capt. John Taylor Wood, Wilmington Marines joined a force of 220 sailors from stations in North Carolina, South Carolina, and Virginia to attack and capture the U.S.S. *Underwriter* at New Bern.[22] Later, more Marines traveled to Wilmington from Drewry's Bluff to board two blockade-runners for an aborted attack on the prisoner of war camp at Point Lookout, Maryland.

Wood, a veteran of the ironclad duel in Hampton Roads between the Monitor and the Virginia, led his force to the Neuse River early in February 1864. The Federals had been in control of the strategic coastal town of New Bern for more than a year, and Confederate forces were determined to take it back. Eliminating the threat posed by the 186-foot long warship was part of the overall plan to eject Union forces from the town at

Confederate Marines from the Cape Fear River were among the 200 others who launched a daring raid to capture the USS Underwriter at New Bern.

the confluence of the Trent and Neuse Rivers.

Wood split his command into two elements that rejoined at Kinston before heading downriver to where the *Underwriter* lay anchored on the New Bern waterfront close by the guns of Fort Stephenson. At 2:30 a.m., two boats commanded by Wood and Lt. Benjamin Loyall made for the side wheel of the ship and engaged in a hot fire with defenders once spotted from the *Underwriter*'s deck. While Marines in the boats picked off any head that showed above the gunnels, more sailors and Marines swarmed aboard to take the ship by force from the skeleton crew. The original plan had been to get the ship underway and steal her from the Federals. Unfortunately, the ship's boilers were cold, and engineers determined it would take more than an hour to fire them up and get under way. Wood was forced to fire the *Underwriter* and escape to their waiting boats, as the sleepy gunners in Fort Stephenson finally began lobbing shells at the Confederates. Wood and his men stroked back up river to Kinston. If they failed in their mission to capture the *Underwriter*, they could at least take satisfaction in her destruction, announced by the explosion behind them once the flames found the cruiser's powder magazine.[23]

Later, in early July, Capt. George Holmes and his men of Company A, CSMC, departed Drewry's Bluff for Wilmington. The Marines were part of a battalion-sized operation, again under the command of John

Taylor Wood, to free and arm captured Confederates penned up at Point Lookout, Maryland. Holmes' ninety men joined other sea soldiers gathered from throughout the Carolinas for the expedition. By July 6 Holmes and his men were briefed and provisioned, then loaded aboard the *Florie*, one of two ships acting as transport for the proposed amphibious landing. The ships moved down to anchor off Fort Fisher, awaiting favorable tides and conditions to dart through New Inlet to thread through the Federal blockade offshore. As they waited, Wood received word that the mission had been compromised. With the element of surprise gone, the mission was scrapped. Holmes and the men of Company A returned to duty in the Richmond area, while the others returned to their duty station at Cape Fear and further south.[24]

The Joust of the C.S.S. *Raleigh*

Commodore Lynch was a man who worked mightily to make something of the Cape Fear squadron, despite tribulations that rivaled those of Job. Finding men to man his ships became almost an academic exercise, because finding the material to finish building them was an equally exasperating task. If the ships could not be completed, what was the point in finding men to man them? Fires destroyed irreplaceable shipyards and materials. A lack of properly seasoned timbers left ship's carpenters to use green wood for the timbers of the naval vessels under construction at the Beery and Cassidey yards (something that would come back to haunt Lynch later). Nevertheless, by April 20, 1864, both the ironclads, the *Raleigh* and the *North Carolina*, were anchored in the river off Fort Fisher. Lynch was ready to take the offensive.[25]

The *Raleigh* and *North Carolina* were slightly different ships. The *Raleigh* mounted one IX-inch gun, one VII-inch Brooke rifle, and two 6.4-inch Brooke rifles. It is likely that one of the VII-inch Brooke guns was mounted in the bow because its rifling would have enabled the Confederates to engage targets at longer distances. Since the *North Carolina* was too heavy to negotiate New Inlet, Lynch decided it would be the *Raleigh* that would lead the attack against the Federal blockaders.[26]

Lynch stripped the crippled *North Carolina* of men to crew the *Raleigh* in the attack. Thirty-five of those men were veterans of the expedition against the *Underwriter* lead by John Taylor Wood, but most of the sailors and Marines were untrained and unblooded in naval combat. Lynch and Lt. J. Pembroke Jones began a training regimen to prepare the crew.[27]

The night of May 6, 1864 was balmy, the ocean calm with a partial moon obscuring much of the view to Union blockaders cruising silently past the sand behemoth guarding the entrance to New Inlet. Unknown to Federal blockaders, the newly readied C.S.S. *Raleigh* and two escorts, the gunboats *Yadkin* and *Equator*, were on their way to introduce themselves to the Union fleet. Confederate naval lieutenant J. Pembroke Jones commanded the 150 foot-long ironclad, its sloping casemate giving it the appearance of, as one observer described it, a "low-slung house" with one stack protruding above it.[28] The *Raleigh*, steaming at seven knots, mounted one gun in both the bow and stern. Three others were mounted amidships, able to fire to either port or starboard through three gun ports down both sides of the ship. Marines manned some of those guns, as the *Raleigh* steamed out of New Inlet to challenge the Federals offshore.[29] Aboard the U.S.S. *Britannia*, Volunteer Lieutenant Sam Huse noted the appearance of a hulking shape emerging from the inlet off Fort Fisher, and immediately fired off two rockets to alert the blockading fleet. The *Britannia,* believing the ship to be a blockade-runner, took the ironclad under fire with her 30-pound Parrot gun to no effect. Huse then opened with a 24-pound Howitzer that also failed to turn the Confederate ship. As the Federals turned to run for open sea, flame belched from the forward gun on the *Raleigh*, its shot demolishing the binnacle light aboard the *Britannia*. A second round flew past the Union vessel's starboard paddle box before Huse was able to distance himself from the seemingly indestructible Confederate.

Lt. J. Pembroke Jones, CSN

For the rest of the night, the *Raleigh* challenged other Union warships to combat. The U.S.S. *Howquah, Nansemond, Mount Vernon, Fahkee, Niphon*, and *Kansas* all traded shots with Jones' ironclad, but none could land a telling blow. The *Raleigh*'s shot failed to seriously damage the Federal ships, but many landed uncomfortably close. The gunnery of the Confederates, including that of a starboard gun manned by Marine Lt. Henry Doak and his men, made the Federals nervously aware of the damage that might be done. Rather than risk it, the Federal tactic turned into one of avoidance, the blockading ships outrunning the *Raleigh* for the open sea.

It was all great fun for the watching soldiers at Fort Fisher, despite Doak's accidentally firing on the fort.[30] As sunlight lightened the horizon offshore, the *Raleigh* came about and steamed back into New Inlet, retiring from the engagement without having caused real damage or accomplishing much else, other than putting on a good show and depriving the hapless blockaders of a night's rest. Along the traverses of Fort Fisher, Col. Lamb and his men raised a lusty cheer as the ironclad steamed through the channel, and fired off nine guns in salute to the navy's efforts. Whether the salute from the fort distracted *Raleigh*'s helmsman, or whether it was sheer incompetence, disaster struck as the ship nosed back into the Cape Fear River. A sand shoal extended from Zeke's Island opposite the fort and into the river. As the cheers of the soldiers rang in their ears, the *Raleigh* ran aground on it and broke her back as the tide receded underneath her. The accident ended on a sour note what would have otherwise been a notable accomplishment. The ship was lost, taking on water from the stern and eventually breaking in half over the course of two days.[31]

The loss of the *Raleigh* was disastrous for the Cape Fear Naval Squadron. The other ironclad, the C.S.S. *North Carolina*, was barely able to stay afloat due to unseasoned wood used in its construction. Its heavy weight also left it unsuitable for navigating the shallow depths of the Cape Fear River. After the loss of the *Raleigh*, Commodore Lynch was left with just a small collection of gunboats to patrol the waterways between Wilmington and the Federal menace offshore.[32]

Is It Still A Navy If They Have No Ships?

The mood of Confederates at Fort Fisher was as gray as the late autumn skies that frequently cast a pall over the peninsula, where Col. Lamb kept watch over the Federal fleet steaming back and forth in the Atlantic. Commodore Lynch had played out his string at the Cape Fear, and was replaced by Secretary Mallory in early September. Lynch's constant conflict with army commanders in the Cape Fear lead Mallory to the conclusion it was time for a replacement, though that was never explicitly said. By the fall of 1864, Wilmington was the last open port of the Confederacy. It was vital that the defenders of the Cape Fear work well together. With that in mind, Mallory made the change. Assuming command of the Wilmington station was Capt. Robert F. Pinkney.[33]

As Federals began to focus their attention on the Cape Fear, Pinkney found himself with little to command. The *North Carolina* sank at Battery Island off Smithville in July. The *Raleigh* was a broken hulk marking the obstacle to navigation that claimed her. The third ironclad, the *Wilmington*, was still on her ways, a victim of the animosity between Commodore Lynch and Gen. W.H.C. Whiting, the army commander refusing to do anything to help n the construction of the ship. The only Wilmington-built naval vessel still afloat was the gunboat *Yadkin*.[34]

Because there were no ships to man, the navy became useless in its current configuration, its sailors and Marines being wasted on guard duty and make-work details that failed to use them to their full potential. Gen. Whiting ordered the construction of a new battery at the tip of Confederate Point that would command the entrances to New Inlet. Manned by naval personnel and armed with navy guns, Battery Buchanan was where most sailors and Marines of the Wilmington station would see the elephant. The fortification was complete by October 1864, and Pinckney ordered officers, men, and Marines to garrison it by November 6. After some jockeying between Gen. Whiting and Richmond as to the ordnance to be mounted in the battery, two VII-inch Brooke rifles and two VII-inch smoothbore cannon were chosen as naval contingent's main weapons at Battery Buchanan.[35]

The construction and arming of Battery Buchanan was among the last acts of William Henry Chase Whiting as commander of the Cape Fear Military District. Confederate President Jefferson Davis replaced Whiting

Battery Buchanan, the southernmost installation of Fort Fisher, guarded New Inlet. It was manned mostly by Confederate Marines and sailors.

with an old friend, Gen. Braxton Bragg, soon after. Bragg was probably the most vilified Confederate general of the war, one who the public held responsible for the disasters that befell the Confederacy in the western theater of the war. The move to Wilmington prompted the *Richmond Enquirer* newspaper to announce the change of command with a bold headline that read in part, "Goodbye Wilmington!" The local newspaper, the *Wilmington Journal*, came to Bragg's defense as a native North Carolinian who would do all in his power to safeguard the port. The editorial smacks of wishful thinking as much as sincere endorsement. Bragg's mettle was soon to be tested, as was that of the other Confederate defenders of the vital port city. Col. William Lamb noted in his diary in late October that word had reached him of a great Union fleet assembling to attack Wilmington.[36]

Gen. Braxton Bragg, CSA

Defending the Fort

Lamb's diary entry would prove prophetic. As day dawned on December 20, 1864, lookouts at Mound Battery spotted row after row of Federal warships, monitors, and transports taking station off the Cape Fear coast. It was a fearsome flotilla.

Union Secretary of the Navy Gideon Welles had been lobbying for an attack to reduce the port at Wilmington for most of the war, but Federal war planners had other objectives. That changed in 1864, when the Union navy's closure of Confederate ports and victories by the Union army made conditions right to look to Wilmington. Command of the land element of the expedition fell to Benjamin Butler, the political general from Massachusetts who had seen action at Forts Hatteras and Clark in North Carolina, and in New Orleans. Admiral David Dixon Porter commanded the naval elements of the fleet that gathered at Hampton Roads before loading men and material and steaming south to the Cape Fear.

The U.S. Navy and U.S. Army operated under separate command structures during the Civil War, with separate responsibilities and spheres of authority, even on the same operation. Both services guarded their prerogatives jealously. David Porter disliked the droop-jowled and balding Butler from the beginning, and especially disliked Butler's plan to load a ship with gunpowder and detonate it against Fort Fisher to force a breach. Maybe that explains why he lit the fuse on the U.S.S. *Louisiana* on the morning of December 23, after it was beached at Confederate Point, while Butler was still enroute to the operation. The result was something less than impressive. The explosion did little more than cause a few Confederate defenders to roll over in their sleep.[37]

The powder ship a failure, Porter's fleet commenced a massive bombardment beginning at dawn on Christmas Eve and lasting until 5:30 p.m. Union ships fired nearly 10,000 shells at the fort while Confederate defenders, including Battery Buchanan's sailors and Marines, hunkered down in their bomb proofs to wait out the rain of iron. Lt. Francis Roby lead a crew of Marines manning two VII-inch Brooke guns salvaged from the C.S.S. *Raleigh* and mounted by Col. Lamb between Mound Battery and the sea face. All through the bombardment of December 24, Roby's men worked their guns until the tubes finally exploded, wounding several men but not killing anyone.[38] As the bombardment tapered off in the late afternoon, Federals assumed the lack of return fire meant that Fort Fisher's guns had been silenced. The next morning, Christmas Day, Butler's infantry began embarking in boats to land on the beach north of the fort.[39]

At 3:30 on December 25, Federal ships began probing New Inlet to do a reconnaissance prior to bigger ships forcing their way into the river. The Marines at Battery Buchanan let the Federals know Fort Fisher was not ready to give up the ghost just yet, when they opened fire and sank one of the Union barges and drove the others off. The action secured the fort's southern flank for the rest of the attack. To the north, Butler's infantry began massing to attack the land face of the fort. Col. Lamb, with only an undermanned garrison of army troops to repel it, sent word to Capt. Van Benthuysen, asking for Marines to help in the effort. Van Benthuysen immediately sent two thirds of his command to help Lamb and the army, double-timing across the sandy fort interior for roughly a mile to reach the land face defenses. The Marines arrived in the nick of time. The fire they delivered on the advancing bluecoats was so fierce it sent the Federal troops reeling back, leaving their dead and dying on the field. Soon after, the Union troops re-embarked on their boats to withdraw. The first attack on Fort Fisher was a failure, in no small part because of the tenacity

Federal troops assault Fort Fisher's river side during the second attempt to reduce the fort. Confederate sailors nd Marines joined in the defense with Col. Lamb's troops.

and skill of Capt. Alfred Van Benthuysen's Marines of Company B.[40] But among the Confederate casualties of that first battle, nineteen of the twenty-nine men in Roby's detachment lay dead or wounded.[41]

As the Federals steamed away from New Inlet on December 28, 1864, the fort band played "Dixie" to send them off. Col. Lamb and Gen. Whiting both were effusive in their praise of the naval contingent who had performed so well when the air became thick with shot and shell.

"I could mention numberless cases of daring equally deserving commendation," Lamb wrote, "...I would make special mention, however, of the detachment of officers, sailors, and Marines from the Navy...who came as volunteers from Battery Buchanan." Whiting's praise was even more heartening to sailors and Marines who had received precious little accolades to date. "No commendation of mine can be too much for the coolness, discipline, and skill displayed by officers and men."[42]

Braxton Bragg chose to celebrate the victory by withdrawing the men of Gen. Robert Hoke's division from the Sugar Loaf line of defenses that stretched from the huge sand dune on the river side of the peninsula to the Atlantic on the east. The men were moved to Wilmington where, among other things, they took part in a parade to entertain the townspeople of Wilmington. Two weeks later, when the Union fleet returned, Hoke's

U.S. Navy ships assembled off Fort Fisher in January 1865 to deliver the largest naval bombardment in history until World War II.

men were still in Wilmington.[43]

If losing Hoke's men was the blow that ultimately doomed Lamb's efforts to defend Fort Fisher, Bragg's failure to resupply the embattled fort with the men and materials needed to prepare for another attack was certainly a contributing factor in what came next. Lamb and the less than 1,500 men and boys he had to face the enemy with were essentially left to fend for themselves. Van Benthuysen's Marines made up a significant part of that force, but the effort left Pinkney's sailors and Marines seriously depleted of manpower. To rectify the losses of the first battle, Marines and sailors from Savannah were ordered to Wilmington. As the New Year dawned on January 1, 1865, fifty-one men, including nine free blacks, reported for duty to Battery Buchanan.[44]

The second weekend of January 1865 saw the return of Porter's warships. This time the ground element of the Union attack would be shepherded by the capable Gen. Alfred Terry, a professional soldier far superior to the disliked Benjamin Butler. Terry and Porter established a good working relationship, and the bombardment and landing proceeded with much better coordination this time around. The affable Terry made sure to consult Porter on his intentions, and included him in planning the attack. That made a world of difference.[45]

Porter's fleet began a methodical bombardment of the guns still mounted along the sea and land faces of Fort Fisher. The land face that bisected the peninsula came in for particular attention from the gunners aboard Porter's ships and monitors. It was the land face guns that posed the greatest threat to Terry's assaulting columns. From January 15-17, 1865, Federal guns pounded the fort until virtually all of its guns were disabled. The Confederate commerce raider C.S.S. *Chickamauga* steamed downriver to send shells into the assembling ranks of Terry's troops on the beach at the request of Gen. Whiting.[46]

Offshore, Admiral Porter did not want to see the U.S. Navy be relegated to spectators of the battle for Fort Fisher. Porter was determined that the navy receive its fair share of the credit, not just for the bombardment, but for actually taking the fort by force of arms. To that end, Porter gathered sailors and Marines from the ships of his flotilla and landed them under the command of naval Capt. Kidder Breese. Breese and his 2000 men – including 600 Marines - were supposed to attack the northeast bastion of the fort at the same time that Terry's army column attacked on the river side of the land face. But Breese jumped the gun, sending his sailors and Marines across hundreds of yards of open sand to attack the one place at Fort Fisher where guns from the land face and sea face both could engage any assaulting force.

Inside the fort, Col. Lamb and his men emerged from their bomb proofs to deliver a withering fire against the Federals, most of who were armed only with cutlasses and pistols. Again Confederate Marines from Battery Buchanan double-timed to the fort to assist in the defense.[47] The attack was a dismal failure that resulted in the only time in the history of the U.S. Marine Corps that it has been refused a beach. The one good thing that came of the assault was that it provided a distraction from Terry's assault on the fort through the gate that lead to the road for Wilmington. By the time Lamb and Gen. Whiting realized the error, Federals were inside the fort, fighting hand to hand with Confederate defenders to take the land face gun emplacements one by bloody one. Whiting, while trying to rally his men against the Yankees sweeping into the fort by way of "Bloody Gate," was mortally wounded in the hand-to-hand combat along the traverses. Fighting like men possessed, the Confederate Marines managed to recover the fallen officer before being driven back.[48]

Making matters worse, Confederate navy lieutenant Robert Chapman, in command of the guns back at Battery Buchanan, was alarmed to see Union flags flying from the traverses a mile to the north. Without thinking, he turned the battery's guns on the melee along the land face, shelling friend and foe alike. Col. Lamb quickly sent a runner to order a

ceasefire. What followed was a slow, inexorable retreat to the south, the
defenders of the fort, now under the command of Major James Reilly
as the highest ranking officer left fighting, made their way to what they
thought was a redoubt at Battery Buchanan. When they arrived, they found
the remaining guns spiked and the men of the navy and Marines who
manned them nowhere to be found. With nowhere to go and nothing left to
fight with, Reilly surrendered Fort Fisher.[49]

With Honor, With Valor

The Confederate sailors and Marines assigned to the Cape Fear
during the Civil War did not lack for courage or enterprise. The successful
raid on the U.S.S. *Underwriter* and the blood spilled by them in defense of
Fort Fisher in not one but two overwhelming Federal assaults is testimony
to their mettle. The ill-fated adventure of the C.S.S. *Raleigh* in sallying
forth to do battle with a numerically superior foe off New Inlet speaks to
the eagerness of the navy and Marines of the Confederacy to do their part
to engage and defeat the Union forces arrayed against them. That they
performed as well as they did, given their chronic shortages of manpower,
machinery, and raw materials to fashion the tools of war speaks volumes
about the resiliency of the CS Navy and CSMC and their determination
to fulfill their missions. Despite split command structures and clashing
personalities that had detrimental impacts on their ability to achieve those
objectives, when the chips were down the sailors and Marines of the Cape
Fear stood to and met the enemy in the best traditions of their respective
services. Had the South won the war, their example would likely have
formed the basis of lore that set the standard for future generations of Marines and sailors who wore the gray.

Endnotes

[1] "By Sea, By Land" – the motto of the Confederate States Marine Corp.
[2] Robert M. Browning, *From Cape Charles to Cape Fear: The North Atlantic Blockading Squadron during the Civil War* (Tuscaloosa: University of Alabama Press, 1993) 1. Much of the criticism stemmed from elements in the North who sought a more aggressive land based effort to reduce Richmond. Eventually, a compromise was reached on a strategy that incorporated both Scott's blockade and a land campaign.
[3] John Thomas Scharf, *History of the Confederate States Navy: From Its Organization to the Surrender of Its Last Vessel* (J. McDonough, 1894) 17. Hereafter cited as Scharf.
[4] Scharf, 27. At the time the war broke out, the U.S. Navy only had a total of ninety ships, and twenty-one of those were unfit for duty. A great many of the remainder were dis-persed on show-the-flag missions around the globe.

[5] Michael E. Krivdo, "Marines in Gray: The Birth, Life, and Death of the Confederate Marine Corps" (master's thesis, Texas A&M University, 2006), 6. Hereafter cited as Krivdo, "Marines in Gray." Of fifty-four Confederate Marine officers at the start of the war, seventeen had served in the USMC. Most of the Marines lost to the Confederacy had substantial expeditionary experience. That not only gave them operational know-how, but a dexterity that allowed them to improvise and adapt to situations on the ground much more readily than the U.S. Marine Corps proved able to do.

[6] Krivdo, "Marines in Gray," 13. Those 600 marines represented roughly twenty percent of the total manpower of the Confederate States Navy. By comparison, the USMC counted 4,000 men on its rolls, making up only about ten percent of the 50,000 men of the U.S. Navy.

[7] Krivdo, "Marines in Gray," 7.

[8] Edwin L. Coombs "On Duty at Wilmington: The Confederate Navy on the Cape Fear River" (master's thesis, East Carolina University, 1996), Forward. Hereafter cited as Coombs.

[9] Kelly Agan, "Muse, William T.," *NCpedia*, 2014, accessed 4/16/2014. http://ncpedia.org/muse-william-t.; Coombs, 9. Born in 1800, Muse was a capable officer and well liked by his men, though by the time he was sent to Wilmington (October 1861) he was already in his sixties. Nevertheless, Muse proved a capable administrator, slowly bringing together the structure of a Confederate naval presence despite having far too few resources at his disposal to accomplish the task.

[10] Coombs, 11.

[11] Coombs, 13-14.

[12] Claude V. Jackson, III; Jack E. Fryar, Jr. (ed.), *The Big Book of the Cape Fear River* (Wilmington: Dram Tree Books, 2008), 202-203. The Cassidey yard was located on the Wilmington bank of the river, across from the Beery yard (also known as the Navy yard) on Eagles Island. The Beery yard was the larger of the two.

[13] Coombs, 73. After Federal attacks on Charleston stepped up, armor sheets from the Atlanta mill were redirected to Wilmington to complete the construction of the ironclads there.

[14] Coombs, 20. Work was effectively at a standstill by October. Though the epidemic had passed by November, workers refused to return to Wilmington and resume construction until January 1863.

[15] Coombs, 37-42. Upon Lynch's arrival, the naval roster counted only thirty men. Lynch immediately began recruiting, and requested that the army detach some soldiers for temporary duty with the navy. Gen. W.H.C. Whiting granted the request, lending Lynch almost two-dozen men.

[16] Coombs, 38. Lynch's feud with the commander of he Cape Fear Military District, Gen. William Henry Chase Whiting, reached such heights that both dispatched troops on one occasion to thwart the efforts of the other regarding the status of the blockade-runner *Hansa*.

[17] Ernest Kniffen, unpublished research files on the Confederate States Marine Corps in and around the Cape Fear, provided by Kniffen to the author. Hereafter cited as Kniffen. Van Benthuysen also had his run-ins with authority. A conflict with a navy doctor at Drewery's Bluff resulted in the Marine's first court martial. Another happened as a result of alcohol and attitude, when he refused to acknowledge the authority of another Marine

captain while still under arrest from the first charge. Both incidents were nullified by higher ranking officers who saw in Van Benthuysen a fighting man whose skills were much in need. That Van Benthuysen was related by marriage to Jefferson Davis may have played a role, too.

[18] Krivdo, "Marines in Gray," 181, 189. Realizing the importance of Wilmington, Marines from other areas close by the port city were transferred into a newly formed Company B assigned to the Cape Fear Naval Squadron, under Van Benthuysen.

[19] Krivdo, "Marines in Gray," 190.

[20] Coombs, 57. Lynch and Vance clashed over the defenses of the Albemarle and New Bern before he came to Wilmington.

[21] Coombs, 34-37.

[22] "USS Underwriter Expedition," *Biographies: Teaching Through Our Historic Sites*, N.C. Historic Sites, published 8/31/2011, accessed 4/19/2014. http://civilwarexperience. ncdcr.gov/biographies/underwriter.htm. Hereafter cited as *Underwriter.*

[23] *Underwriter,* http://civilwarexperience.ncdcr.gov/biographies/underwriter.htm.

[24] Krivdo, "Marines in Gray," 178.

[25] Coombs, 102-103. Lynch's original plan was to use his new torpedo boats to engage the blockading fleet offshore, but those were destroyed by a fire that swept through the Beery yard on April 26. The fire originated at the government cotton yard on Eagles Island, and spread to the terminus of the Wilmington & Manchester Railroad. It also destroyed a sawmill at the Beery yard. Over all, the damage to the shipyard was relatively light. Unfortunately for the Confederate navy at Wilmington, among the materials consumed by flame were the torpedo boats being built there.

[26] Coombs, 104-105.

[27] Coombs, 105.

[28] James L. Walker, *Rebel Gibraltar: Fort Fisher and Wilmington, C.S.A.* (Wilmington: Dram Tree Books, 2005) 211-214. Hereafter cited as Walker.

[29] Walker, 211.

[30] Walker, 213. Doak had been ordered to fire on the next visible light, under the assumption that it had to be a Federal warship. In the confusion, Doak's gunners sent a round careening at the fort, where the light at Mound Battery signaled the mouth of New Inlet to incoming blockade-runners. Commodore Lynch was not pleased, and placed Doak on report, until Lt. Jones persuaded Lynch that the fault was his for issuing a vague order to fire on the "next light he saw."

[31] Walker, 211-214; Krivdo, "Marines in Gray," 188-191. Guns and other materials from the *Raleigh* were salvaged and put to other uses in defense of the Cape Fear. Marine Lt. Doak was reassigned to the C.S.S. *Arctic*, the receiving ship at Wilmington.

[32] Chris E. Fonvielle, Jr., *The Wilmington Campaign: Last Rays of Departing Hope* (Mechanicsburg, PA: Stackpole Books, 2001) 81. Hereafter cited as Fonvielle. The unwieldy ironclad had been tied up at Smithville for use as a floating battery, its pumps running nonstop to try and stay ahead of the water she constantly took on. Eventually, the teredo worms eating through her hull won out, and the ship was towed to Battery Island, across from the town, to be swallowed by the waters of the Cape Fear River.

[33] Coombs, 120-121. Pinckney entered the U.S. Navy in 1827, and during the Civil War served aboard the ironclad C.S.S. *Savannah*, but other wise had scant time in combat.

[34] Coombs, 128.

[35] Coombs, 129-130.

[36] Walker, 243-246.

[37] Fonvielle, 119-125.

[38] Coombs, 132. One observer described what happened: "The gun burst into a thousand pieces, knocking everybody down, but fortunately killing none…The other 7-inch Brooke was then fired, and burst worse than the other. How many men escaped God knows."

[39] Krivdo, "Marines in Gray," 193.

[40] Krivdo, "Marines in Gray," 196.

[41] Coombs, 132.

[42] Coombs, 133.

[43] Fonvielle, 182-183. Bragg seems to have been the only Confederate leader in the Cape Fear who thought the Federals were through with Wilmington. Col. Lamb, Gen. Whiting, and Hoke himself all suggested the Yankees would be back. Bragg, though, insisted both Hoke and Kirkland's brigades be withdrawn from Sugar Loaf and bivouacked at Camp Whiting outside the city.

[44] Fonvelle, 182; Coombs, 134. Needing ordnance and other supplies, Lamb wrote that "…it was impossible to get what was needed."

[45] Fonvielle, 201.

[46] Coombs, 135.

[47] Walker, 317. Seaman Robert Watson, formerly of the C.S.S. *Chickamauga* and drafted to help man the guns at Battery Buchanan, was among the men who rallied to the land face attack. In his diary, he remembered that the men ran with "…the shell bursting around us in large numbers…We manned three guns and commenced firing at 1 p.m. The Yankees had been firing on the fort all day with 3 monitors and the *Ironsides*."

[48] Fonvielle, 249-297; Coombs, 135; Walker, 306-335.

[49] Coombs, 135; Walker, 348-354; Fonvielle, 245. Reilly, who before the war was Sgt. James Reilly, U.S. Army, may have the distinction of surrendering both a Union and Confederate fort to the enemy in the war. While the caretaker of Fort Johnston before North Carolina seceded from the Union, secessionists from Wilmington marched on the fort and its sister, Fort Caswell on Oak Island, and demanded the keys to both. Reilly found himself again surrendering a fort he was in charge of at Battery Buchanan in 1865.

New York playwright Edna Ferber, who used the James Adams Floating Theater as inspiration for her most famous work, "Showboat."

Showboat:
The James Adams Floating Theater
by Jack E. Fryar, Jr.

dna Ferber looked doubtfully at the miracle of improvisation that was the ancient Ford truck, its door held open for her by a smiling African-American boy. His worn clothes said that he did not come from money – then again, no one in this remote part of coastal North Carolina did, at least by New York standards. But the inviting smile on his face spoke volumes about his hospitality. The truck was a patchwork example of mechanical ingenuity, held together with baling wire and rust. Its roof was a piece of canvas, and not much protection from the unforgiving Carolina sun. Swallowing her doubts, she climbed in and watched as the boy secured the door with a piece of cotton string.

While some of her friends might have looked upon a ride in the battered old Ford as an unacceptable risk, Edna Ferber did not. The up and coming playwright and novelist was on a mission to research an idea for her next book. She had heard that there were places in America where relics from theater's past still brought the footlights to remote communities far removed from Broadway. Ferber had managed to track down one such

The James Adams Floating Theater made the rounds of ports along the Chesapeake and North Carolina coast in the early years of the twentieth century.

dinosaur from the stage's romantic past along the coast of North Carolina. She was on the way to see it for herself, and if finding the James Adams Floating Theater required a ride in a truck that would be illegal on most roads in America, then so be it.

Ferber glanced back and saw the quiet coastal town of Washington fade away in the distance. Thirty miles later, the truck pulled to a stop at a rickety old wharf. Out on the water, a small tug guided what to all appearances was a floating barn across the water. Ferber just stared, overcome with delight at the sight of an actual floating theater.

The James Adams Floating Theater was really a 128-foot long scow, thirty-four feet wide and drawing a scant fourteen inches of water. Built in Washington, N.C. in 1914, it had no power of its own, so it had to be towed from place to place. It was unusual in that most floating theaters were confined to rivers, but the James Adams Floating Theater ventured out into the sounds along the North Carolina coast and the Chesapeake Bay. Each season the theater traveled from Elizabeth City, north to the Chesapeake, then south again all the way to Wilmington, before returning to Elizabeth City for the winter.

"Hello the boat!" Ferber yelled through cupped hands, hailing the rangy man coiling lines on the floating theater's deck. "I'm Edna Ferber, from New York. I'm writing a story about floating theaters, and I was hoping I might be able to talk you."

The man, Charles Hunter, may not have recognized the woman, but he recognized her name. Hunter and his wife were fans of the New York author's earlier work. He quickly summoned his wife, Beulah, known as "the Mary Pickford of the rivers," and who also happened to be the sister of the theater's owner. The Hunters were the lead actors in the

James Adams Theater's company. Both Hunters were fans of Ferbers.

As it happened, Ferber was late in undertaking her journey to find the James Adams Floating Theater. When she met the Hunters outside of Washington, N.C., the cast and crew (often the same people) were leaving for Elizabeth City, where they would tie up for the winter. But Ferber did not leave empty handed. Before she headed back for New York, the members of the theater extended her an invitation to return for the next season. She vowed to meet them when the first show opened at Bath the following April.

James Adams

When spring arrived, Ferber went south again, and found the Bath that existed in 1925 to be charming in its decay.

"Elms and live oaks arched over the deserted streets," she wrote. "Ancient houses, built by men who knew dignity of architectural design and purity of line, were now moldering into the dust from which they had come."

The New York writer found Bath's one hotel, a "fine old brick mansion," and checked in to one of its spacious rooms. That hotel was the Palmer-Marsh House, part of the modern Bath State Historic Site, then run as a boarding house by Henry Ormond. Once she had checked in, Edna Ferber asked after the floating theater. A note for her from the Hunters explained that they had been delayed, but would arrive within a day or two. Ferber went to her room, to find that while the house may have been a grand place in the past, it was something less in 1925. The air was thick, and smelled of mold and

Gertrude Adams

unchanged linen. Edna asked for, and grudgingly received, fresh sheets, but the night she spent in Ormond's house was not a very comfortable

This diorama model of the James Adams Floating Theater is on display at the Museum of the Albemarle in Elizabeth City, N.C.

one. It would be two more days before the James Adams Floating Theater arrived at Bath.

Once the theater arrived, the discomfort of Ferber's previous nights vanished, and she quickly became reacquainted with the Hunters and the rest of the of the crew and company. The boat itself loomed above the rickety dock on the Pamlico, two stories tall, painted white with dark trim. Four the next four days, Edna Ferber would soak up everything should could learn about the James Adams Floating Theater and the people who acted and operated aboard her. Those lessons would provide the fodder for Ferber's most famous work, and the play based on it that has been produced countless times all across the globe, *Show Boat*.

The Hunters played delighted hosts to the New York author, explaining that the troupe's schedule was best described as flexible. They might stay just a day or so at any given location, or they might stay a week, depending on how the receipts were. There were ten actors in the ship's company when Ferber was with the floating theater, and her new friends Charles Hunter and Beulah Adams were the stars of the shows.

As anyone who has spent time aboard a ship knows, space is at a premium, so what room there is often does double or even triple duty. In the case of the James Adams Floating Theater, that was doubly true. Not only did they have to have public spaces for the audience and the performances, but the cast and crew needed space to live in, too. The dining hall, or mess, was located directly beneath the stage. Ferber found the food to be a vastly better than the fare served at Mr. Ormond's house. Dressing rooms also doubled as sleeping quarters for the members of the cast and ship's company. The floating theater even had a balcony in the auditorium reserved for use by African-Americans. The actors rehearsed and slept during the day, and performed at night.

That schedule made it difficult for Ferber to corner Charles Hunter, who proved to be one of her best sources of information about how the theater operated. Hunter was a theatrical Jack-Of-All-Trades, not just headlining, but directing and writing the productions, too. But by the end of her four-day stay, Ferber had what she needed to pen her most famous novel.

By the time Edna Ferber saw the James Adams Floating Theater, it was quite possibly the last such enterprise remaining in America. Originally owned by James and Gertrude Adams, the theater was known to federal marine officials as the *Play House*. James and Gertrude had been circus aerialists, and had transitioned to the floating theater after running vaudeville-style tent shows until they became unprofitable.

Adams designed his theater himself, and hired Washington builders like Sam Green Spencer to construct it. When it was finally finished, James Adams could boast a floating playhouse that was solidly built with 4.5 feet from deck to keel, beams that ran the length of the boat without scarfs, heavy thirty-two-foot planks across the bottom, a skin four

When the James Adams Floating Theater was arriving, it was often front page news, like in this story in the Baltimore Sun.

FICTION   THE   SUN   AUTOS

Salt-Water Showmen Roam The Chesapeake

COMING SOON
JAS. ADAMS
FLOATING THEATRE

Floating Theater Makes Week Stands, Playing Popular Bills At Towns Along The Shores Of Bay

inches thick, that were drift bolted every two feet with 27-inch bolts. The original floating theater was described in loving detail in an article in the Washington, N.C. *Daily News*:

> *"To the rear of the stage are situated eight comfortable and convenient living quarters for the performers; underneath the stage is located a spacious and sunny dining room, also the cook room which is sanitary and airy. In this section of the boat is to be found the electric plant for the entire boat. Mr. Adams has on board his own water plant.*
>
> *"At the front of the 'Playhouse' is seen two offices, one being a ticket office and the other the private office of the owner. Between the two rooms is the main entrance to the theater proper which is eight feet wide. Above the main entrance Mr. and Mrs. Adams have their living quarters, which are convenient and attractive, being Bungalow in style and finish. There are three large rooms, besides closets, a bathroom, etc. These quarters are finished in Beaver board. The boat is provided with a telephone system running all over the boat.*
>
> *"The main attraction to the visitor, of course, is the main auditorium. This room is 30 by 80 feet, with a balcony running all the*

The auditorium could seat as many as five hundred people on the deck, and another 350 African-Americans in the wrap-around balcony.

way around the room. The first floor is provided with steel folding self-righting opera chairs and has a seating capacity of 500 people. To the left and right of the stage is installed two boxes, having accommodations for five persons each. The balcony is reserved exclusively for colored people and will seat 350 persons. Two boxes are also on this floor. The main auditorium is attractively finished with steel ceiling and the color scheme is surely one of good taste, being white trimmed in blue and gold. In the center of the auditorium has been placed an electric chandelier and also on the walls chandeliers of a similar design. When all these lights are turned on a person will be enabled to pick up a pin on the floor.

"The stage has an opening of 19 feet and is equipped with scenery manufactured by John Herfurth & Co. of Cincinatti. An orchestra pit is located just in front of the stage...Mr. Adams has provided a ten-piece concert band and a six piece orchestra."

Actors pulled double duty aboard the James Adams Floating Theater, serving as ushers and ticket takers, while boat crewmen often filled out casts by playing small parts or helping out with special effects and lighting. At stops from Beaufort to Belhaven, Edenton, Hertford, Williamston, and Wilmington, the Adams company thrilled their customers with productions like *The Little Lost Sister* and *Smilin' Through*. One particular production, of *Ten Nights In a Barroom*, roused the ire of clergy along the North Carolina coast, until James Adams defended the play by claiming it had been instrumental in "reforming many a drunkard."

Regardless of what the local preachers might have thought, the people who lived in the isolated hamlets called on by the floating theater awaited its arrival eagerly. In a time when money was hard to come by, you could see a show for a quarter (only a dime for children). Better seats cost more, at thirty-five cents. Later, prices reached a high of fifty cents. Visitors to the "op'ry boat" who were willing to pony up another ten or fifteen cents could remain after the theatrical show to be serenaded with a concert by the orchestra. The floating theater offered shows six nights a week, Monday through Saturday, although if receipts were slow, James Adams would cancel the remainder of an engagement and ship out for the next port, where hopefully the grass would be greener. The plays inevitably had happy endings, and the bad guys always got what was coming to them by the closing curtain. In between acts, vaudeville performers entertained the audiences while set changes went on.

The 1936 movie starring Irene Dunne was based on the Ferber play of the same name, which was based on the author's experiences aboard the James Adams Floating Theater.

The James Adams Floating Theater was a bit of a pig to maneuver, and rough seas were both uncomfortable and dangerous for the cast and crew. In fact, the floating theater sank four times during the years it plied the waters along the east coast. The first time came in the summer of 1920, when a storm appeared as the theater was crossing the Chesapeake Bay. When the crew and cast reached shore, half of them decided there were safer ways to make a living – meaning, on dry land. The next sinking happened after the boat hit a submerged object not far from Norfolk, Virginia on November 24, 1927. A submerged stump in the Great Dismal Swamp Canal claimed the floating theater in November of 1929, but the damage was repaired in time for the beginning of the 1930 performance season. The last sinking took place nearly nine years to the day after the November 16, 1929 mishap. On November 6, 1938, the boat hit a snag in the Roanoke River and went down again. And again, she was refitted and put back in service.

Edna Ferber's novel, *Show Boat*, arrived in bookstores in 1926. When it did, the James Adams Floating Theater enjoyed the acclaim it received as being the inspiration for the book. But the boat's time in the spotlight was coming to an end. Radio and silent movies were replacing repertoire theater as the diversion of choice for people across America, and ticket sales began to drop even among the isolated audiences along the Chesapeake and the North Carolina coast. The ship was sold in 1930 to Nina Howard, of St. Michael's, Maryland, but by then its glory days were behind it. By 1939, even the new owners had given up hope of making a go of it as a floating theater.

The James Adams Floating Theater had its last curtain call in Thunderbolt, Georgia in January 1941. Not long after, the boat and its tugs were sold at auction to E.A. Braswell, of Savannah. Braswell intended to convert the floating theater to a cargo barge, but it was lost in a fire while being towed to the Georgia port for refitting.

The floating theater may have been lost, but its memory lives on even today, whenever Edna Ferber's book or the shows it spawned are read or performed.

Flora MacDonald, the Scottish heroine credited with saving the life of Prince Charles Stuart in the aftermath of the battle of Culloden, was perhaps the most famous loyalist to settle in North Carolina.

They Had Their Reasons:
Loyalism In Revolutionary North Carolina
by Jack E. Fryar, Jr.

It has been estimated that during the Revolutionary War the population of Great Britain's North American colonies was split roughly into thirds on the question of independence from the Mother Country across the Atlantic. One third sought a complete break, another third favored staying a part of the British Empire (though certainly with some serious discussions about the degree of autonomy they would be allowed within that construct), and yet another third that only wanted to be left alone to pursue their own interests, without being sucked into the quagmire of politics and violence that seemed to be consuming their neighbors. In North Carolina, whether or not a person became a Loyalist or a revolutionary – Tories or Rebels, to use the pejorative terms of the times – in many cases depended on a number of factors, but more often than not Loyalist allegiance was determined more by personal interest and the course one's neighbors took than the policies of Great Britain. For Highland Scot immigrants, all of this was true.

Much has been written of the Highland and Lowland Scots who poured into the country after the loss at the Battle of Culloden that ended the Jacobite Rebellion and the pretensions to the English throne of Charles

Stuart in 1748. In the ensuing hard times that followed, a mass exodus of those seeking new lives in a new place led to a massive infusion of Celtic blood settling largely in the piedmont region of North Carolina and in upstate New York. Most early scholarship paints the Scots who sided with King George III as enemies of the freedom sought by right-minded American patriots. Later work explores more deeply the clan system that was transplanted to the New World when the Highlanders came to America, and builds a fuller picture of the Scots as a distinct people. Still later work tries to tease out the reasons why a people who had been poorly used and defeated by an English king would ever take up arms in defense of a Hanoverian monarch.

British policy regarding Loyalists in America was never a cohesive one. In most cases, efforts to make use of pro-British elements of the colonial American population were strictly ad-hoc, with no cogent strategy that was applied to the colonies as a whole.[1] At no time, but especially in the early years of the conflict, did British leaders think that the revolution in the American colonies was anything more than troubles incited by a small, disaffected, rabble rousing minority.

That belief led to a weak, confusing policy of firmly disciplining the rebelling colonies, while at the same time offering forgiveness and at least implied consideration of Whig[2] complaints. Parliament feared the British army on hand in the Northern colonies was inadequate to the task of stamping out the rebellion, but held high hopes that in other parts of the colonies it was a different story. Reports by governors like North Carolina's Josiah Martin and Virginia's John Murray, Lord Dunsmore, reinforced the idea that large numbers of Loyalist sympathizers could be found in the Southern interiors. All it would take was a show of British force to unite them in a common cause to defeat rebellious agitators there.[3]

Though there were warning signs that perhaps things were not as sunny as the governors led them to believe, other factors influenced British war planners to stay the course regarding the notion of Loyalist willingness to rally to the British cause in the South. Strong economic ties in the South, where the colonies were dependent on imported commodities, persuaded British leaders that many below New England would be reluctant to severe their ties with the Mother Country. Slaves, Regulators, and Scots Highlanders were also populations in the South that London felt certain they could co-opt for the king.[4]

A New Start in a New Land

North Carolina in the late eighteenth century was a colony where what passed as civilization was clustered primarily along the coast. Wealthy planters there cultivated rice and indigo, and harvested the bounty of plentiful long leaf pine trees to feed the voracious appetite of the naval stores industry. In the piedmont and mountainous parts of the colony, known somewhat nebulously as the "backcountry," the social niceties and deference to authority found among the coastal merchants and planter elites was far less common.

Backcountry settlers in North Carolina were largely minority groups. Quakers, Moravians, and Highland Scots, among others, immigrated into the colony seeking a place where they could build their own lives free of the persecutions (real or imagined) that came with living in more settled places where England and its Anglican church held sway. In settlements like Salem and Bethabara, Quaker Friends and Moravians built communities that thrived under their own creeds. Large numbers of Highland and Lowland Scot immigrants flocked to North Carolina in the wake of the Stuart defeat at Culloden in 1748,[5] planting the seeds of Presbyterianism and seeking a new place for a fresh start. The one thing they all seem to have had in common was feeling weak and threatened by the English-American majority clustered in older, wealthier, and more developed cities and towns closer to the sea.[6]

Loyalism in the American colonies came with different levels of conviction. Some who would be labeled Tories by their independence minded neighbors may have differed from Whig views only by a matter of

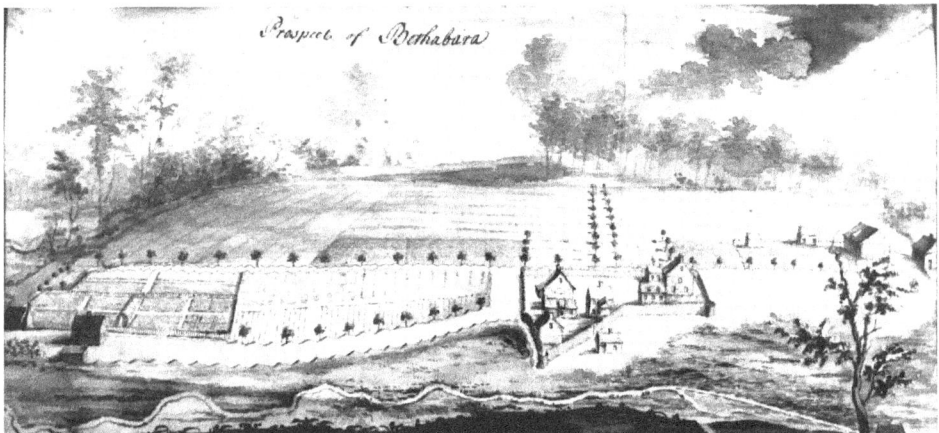

The Moravian settlement of Bethabara in central North Carolina as it looked at the time of the Revolutionary War.

Gov. William Tryon led coastal militia against Regulators at the Battle of Alamance in what many deem to be the first battle of the American Revolution.

degree. Some hid their Loyalist feelings from their fellow citizens in hopes of avoiding the ostracism that they knew would follow if their true colors were known. Some were opportunists, people who were enthusiastic when the redcoats were successful, but who faded into the woodwork when things were not so rosy. Others ended up siding with the British because of their religious or tribal ties.[7]

The reality is that, at least in North Carolina, a streak of fierce independence was a common trait of many who later chose to support the British when war came. These were people who often refused to recognize the power of either side to claim their allegiance.[8] This untamable independence was at the root of several missteps by the Whig powers of the time that tended to force these North Carolinians – especially the Highlanders - into the waiting arms of the British. Many of the seeds of this discontent were sowed in the years before the conflict with Great Britain began, in episodes like the Regulator Rebellion (1770-1771) and the strategy of non-importation pacts that hurt the mercantile trade.[9]

Once hostilities broke out, Whig policies and legislation earned the cause of independence enemies among Highlanders and other Loyalists, who found themselves forced to make choices they did not want to make. Nine months after Loyalist Highlanders were dealt a crushing defeat at Moores Creek by Whig militia under Richard Caswell and Alexander Lillington, legislation was passed to require oaths of allegiance from those who had taken up arms against the revolutionary cause, or else be treated as enemies by a rebel government on the rise.[10]

Reluctant they may have been, but once committed to the fight, Loyalists in the Carolinas – both North and South – undertook a guerrilla war that was savage, unrelenting, and fraught with consequences for both sides in the conflict. The Revolutionary War was a civil war in the truest sense of the term. Nowhere was that more true than in North Carolina.[11]

While several demographics filled the ranks of the Loyalists who championed King George III's cause in the Carolinas, the ones most closely associated with the British side in the war are those immigrants from Scotland who populated the central part of North Carolina during a wave of trans-Atlantic immigration that began in 1732, but which became a flood after the Jacobite Rebellion.[12]

Early Birds of a Feather

In the early days of discontent between Great Britain and its American colonies, many of those who would later choose to stand with the British rather than their friends and neighbors were of similar minds with those who they would later oppose. British steps to rearrange its colonial empire and increase the colonists' share of the burden for their protection and government in the wake of the French & Indian War were greeted unfavorably by King George III's subjects in North America. While Americans of all stripes generally concurred that the British government's policies were objectionable, few colonials (outside perhaps a small number of New England malcontents like Samuel Adams) foresaw a time when the colonies would take up arms to break from the king's dominions.[13]

The split between Loyalists and Whigs evolved gradually. Many in North Carolina who would eventually take a stand under the king's banner initially joined their more nationalistic neighbors in organizations seeking redress of colonial grievances with the crown. In provincial congresses, and later in the Continental Congress, Loyalists added their voices to the American chorus pleading for relief from what they saw as heavy handed and unfair treatment from the British government. As relations deteriorated, Loyalists found themselves at odds with their neighbors. Early on, Loyalists objected to the steps taken by the Continental Congress to oppose British edicts. As hostilities commenced, others were unwilling to reject their allegiance to Great Britain and serve in Whig militias. By the time muskets balls were flying in earnest, still others found themselves taking up arms against revolutionary neighbors to defend British-American unity.[14]

According to one historian, American Loyalists were largely "native officeholders" or politicians with close ties to the British administration. Their endorsement of the colonial status quo stemmed from deference to the "legal, historical, and constitutional ideas that held the empire together." Colonial freedom could not be allowed if that system was to remain intact.[15]

Wilmington merchant and planter John Burgwin held Loyalist sympathies.

In North Carolina those who stood by the crown did so for a number of reasons. Loyalism in the colony emerged early and in considerable numbers. Highland Scots, merchants, African-American slaves, and ministers and their flocks all had significant numbers who actively took steps to counter revolutionary efforts in the colony. Among the most prominent among them were the tartan-clad kinsmen who homesteaded in the North Carolina piedmont.[16]

The 1745 Jacobite rebellion that saw Charles Stuart make a claim to the English throne with the support of Scotland's Highland clans was a bloody affair that ended only with a brutal defeat at the hands of King George II's champion, the Duke of Cumberland, in 1748. In the wake of the defeat, Scots were forbidden to wear their distinctive tartan colors, Gaelic was outlawed as a language within the country, and those who supported the insurrection bore the wrath of the victors by enduring land confiscations and a host of other humiliating and debilitating measures.[17]

By the time Highlanders were immigrating in large numbers to the American colonies, British leaders (William Pitt among them) initiated a reconciliation with the Scots. When war with France threatened, the British realized that their Highland subjects would be valuable assets on the battlefield. This was especially true in North America in the early 1750s, where French troops in Canada and in the western territories bordered by the Mississippi River threatened Britain's colonies. For their part, the Highlanders were glad to answer the call to arms during what was, in America, known as the French & Indian War. The Scots' martial prowess during the Stuart rebellion and during the French & Indian War earned them a reputation for battlefield ferocity that Great Britain coveted by the time hostilities broke out in America.[18]

In the meantime, Scottish opinions of Great Britain were greatly rehabilitated. Thanks to domestic improvements at home in Scotland such as the construction of roads and schools, and the liberal land grant policies of colonial governors like North Carolina's Gabriel Johnston,[19] who actively encouraged Scottish immigration, the general opinion of most Highlanders of Great Britain was favorable. The relatives of Highlanders in North Carolina communicated these improvements to the old homeland in letters and stories passed along by recent immigrants. By the 1770s, that rapprochement between Britain and the Scots was such that one of George Washington's general officers complained that the Highlanders looked upon the revolutionaries in much the same unfavorable light that they did other undesirable elements.[20] In the years that followed, British officers were instructed to carefully cultivate good ties with those who might be sympathetic to the Loyalist position.[21]

Scottish regiments gave good service during the French & Indian War, bolstering their reputations as fierce fighters.

Highland Scot immigration to North Carolina began in earnest in the 1730s, and peaked in the 1750s and 1760s. The British were not particularly forgiving conquerors immediately after Culloden, and rising rents and other factors forced many Highlanders to seek better opportunities elsewhere. When restrictions on Scottish martial activities forced the clans' tacksmen to abandon their traditional role as organizers of the clan chiefs' militaries, they instead began managing their clan chief's land leasing. This role became increasingly obsolete as Scotland shifted from agriculture (or to less labor intensive agricultural techniques) to large-scale sheep management instead. Lease prices for land rose as well, and soon the position of tacksmen no longer made economic sense. For these people especially, the invitation to relocate to North America was very attractive.[22]

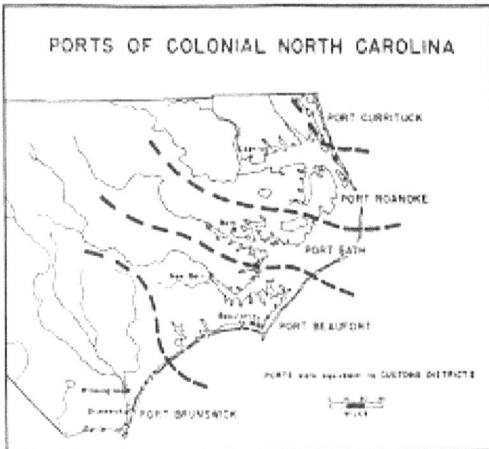

PORTS OF COLONIAL NORTH CAROLINA

Those circumstances dovetailed nicely with efforts by North Carolina governors George Burrington and Gabriel Johnston, who energetically encouraged their fellow Scots to cross the Atlantic and help populate the vast Carolina backcountry. They did, by the shipload. By the time of the Revolution, more than 20,000 Scots had settled in the American colonies, with the lion's share in New York's Mohawk Valley, around Darien, Georgia, and along the Cape Fear Valley in North Carolina.[23]

Most of those immigrants, including Flora MacDonald and her husband, Allan, passed through the Cape Fear ports at Brunswick and Wilmington before journeying to their new homesteads in the interior. One of the stipulations before the royal governors would hand over grants to those new lands was that the newcomers swear a loyalty oath to the British crown. That promise of fealty would come into play later, when redcoats called for friends of the king to rally under the British standard.[24] A central premise of Robert O. DeMond's study of Highlander Loyalism in North Carolina during the Revolutionary war is that faith and fealty were both foundations of the Scots' rationale for siding with the British. Highlanders who came to North Carolina after 1748 were extremely religious and felt bound by their loyalty oaths. In their view, the second chance at new lives they were being afforded in America was a direct result of King George III's generosity. Being "accustomed to a government by a king," he writes, "they could conceive of no other."[25]

Scottish immigration to the Carolinas came from two basic directions. The trans-Atlantic route took them from ports in Scotland and England, to the West Indies, and then to ports at Charleston, Brunswick, and Wilmington. Others came overland along the Great Wagon Road, from Pennsylvania and New York. The two main waves of immigration are separated by as much as thirty years, and did not end until the outbreak of hostilities in 1776. Highlander populations settled generally in the piedmont, while Lowland Scots tended to cluster closer to the coast. While the common perception is that all Scots were Loyalists, that conclusion would be incorrect. Studies have shown that in North Carolina, Scots chose both sides in the conflict, though which side they chose – Loyalist or Whig – usually depended on several social factors. Highlanders who arrived between 1730 and 1750, direct from Scotland, gathered in family based communities that prospered. Their land holdings were large, their wealth substantial by their standards (though nowhere near that of wealthy planter elites along the coast), and their social, commercial, and familial ties with kinsmen in Scotland were strong. All of which contributed to a class of Highlander who differed greatly from those who came after.[26]

Crippling poverty among the Highlanders was a prime reason for coming to America.

Immigrant Scots of the 1760s and 1770s came to America out of desperation, when their lives in Scotland left them no choice but to seek new starts elsewhere. In 1792, a survey of Highlanders settled in North Carolina asked them their reasons for immigration. They gave three: (1) poverty; (2) the oppression of landlords; and (3) encouraging letters from friends and relatives singing the praises of the new lives they had found in America.[27] These people farmed land that was sizeable by Scottish standards, but still significantly smaller than the property holdings of their earlier arriving Highland brethren.[28] They were poorer, and their desperation made them skittish about siding with any entity that opposed Britain. Their Presbyterian faith and the loyalty oaths exacted from them in order to get the land they so desperately sought in the colonies also pointed them in the direction of the Crown when choosing sides became unavoidable.[29]

For many Highlanders of that later wave of immigrants, Great Britain represented a stable system that offered peace and security, ingredients necessary for economic growth. The Scots generally saw Great Britain as the political system best able to provide them with what they needed to grow and prosper in the American colonies – economic opportunity, military protection, and benevolent government, to name a few. The highly industrious Scots made up a significant portion of the mercantile class in North Carolina, especially in coastal centers like Wilmington. Within a short time after arriving in the colonies, Scots had achieved a dominant position in the cattle business. Great Britain also provided an outlet for young Scots seeking fame and adventure in martial pursuits via its army. Sentiment was, therefore, largely with the British in the Revolution even without considering any loyalty oaths the Highlanders may have taken. When representatives of the Revolutionary government began demanding the Scots swear an oath to their cause and serve in the militia, it forced the hand of the immigrants and caused them to gravitate to the British side of the argument. [30]

That Highlanders made up a disproportionate percentage of Loyalists in North Carolina is something of an aberration when considering the colonies as a whole. In most places, those who lived in the rural countryside tended to be either neutral, or to side with the Whigs. Reasons for this included an aversion to the mercantile system that made Loyalism so attractive to those rich, urban and urbane colonists close to the coast. Such social stratification was incompatible with the equality afforded farmers and others who shared the hardships of living on the frontiers. The British

This map of the lower Cape Fear was used by British forces in 1781.

military occupation of the colonies was generally found close to the coast in the towns and ports like Wilmington and New Bern, leaving the rural colonist untouched by the restrictions and impositions of military rule. As well, those living in the inland territories were much closer to Native American forces like the Cherokee and Catawba, who allied themselves with the British.[31]

Despite being routed at the short, sharp battle at Widow Moores Creek in February 1776, Highland zeal for the British cause continued. While many returned to their farms and kept a low profile in the four years that followed until the British took Charleston, S.C. in 1780, many others joined up with British regiments to form a potent force in the field against Revolutionary armies. These Scots would continue their service for the remainder of the war. When Major James Henry Craig landed redcoats at Wilmington in January 1781 with the mission of sending supplies to Cross Creek in support of Cornwallis' Carolinas campaign, his force was made up mainly of the 82nd Regiment of Foot, a Highlander regiment with a large number of former Carolina Scots who had fled to British lines in the wake of the defeat at Moores Creek in 1776.[32]

Yet the allegiances of most Highlanders, like that of other Loyalist leaning groups, changed with the conditions on the ground. At Ramseur's Mill in North Carolina, Whig militia crushed nearly 1300 Loyalists - including many Highlanders among them - on June 20, 1780. The Loyalists were embodied at the order of Gen. Charles Lord Cornwallis, who intended to use them to retain local control of lands his British regulars marched through and liberated from Whig control. Therein lay a key weakness of Cornwallis' strategy. During the Carolinas Campaign of 1780-1781, Cornwallis counted on the support of Loyalist levies to supplement the ranks of his redcoat regulars. The object of the exercise was to march into Whig controlled areas of North and South Carolina and wrest the territory back from revolutionary governments and militias. When the army marched on to another area, local Loyalists were to assume control and governance of the recently liberated territories. After the defeat at Ramseur's Mill, North Carolina Loyalists were much more reluctant to show their true colors in the face of Whig reprisals. Making things worse, Cornwallis' declared use of the Loyalists as administrators of liberated territory went by the wayside when he began drafting them to fill the depleted ranks of his redcoat army. Loyalists who showed themselves would too often find themselves marching off with the British army, leaving wives and loved ones undefended and subject to the retribution of vengeful Whigs. As a result, Cornwallis found Loyalist support in the Carolinas far less substantive than the British imagined.[33] Yet North Carolina Whigs still managed to lose the opportunity to quell Loyalist activity by insisting that they join the revolutionary cause.[34]

Highlanders found themselves in a difficult position, with no good choices at hand. Both sides in the conflict seemed intent on co-opting them to one side or the other, and both sides threatened reprisals if the Scots did not comply. Along Fishing Creek on the North Carolina-South Carolina border, Whig militia burned the Presbyterian Meeting House and the home of its pastor, Highlander John Simpson. It is just one example of the atrocities that pushed neutral colonists into one camp or the other. After Ramsour's Mill, it became increasingly difficult for neutrals to remain that way. Many began taking up arms for the British. How many of them did so out of enmity for the American cause is a difficult question to answer.[35]

James Henry Craig in later life. Craig occupied Wilmington in 1781 as part of Cornwallis' Southern Campaign.

For Highlanders who made their living in the mercantile trades, a break from Great Britain represented potential ruin. British laws and infrastructure provided a stable, profitable system for the conduct of commerce between the colonies and the rest of the world. That laws such as the Navigation Acts gave Britain a monopoly on trade did not negate the fact that it also gave colonial merchants and their suppliers in England a smoothly running business model where product was easy to come by, bills were generally paid, and credit was readily available between suppliers and merchants. If the colonies were sheared from Great Britain, then that model was in danger.

The peril posed by the revolutionaries to colonial commerce was doubly threatening, because colonial American merchants stood to lose a great deal if the Whigs were successful.

North Carolina merchants, conservative by nature, generally disapproved of the revolutionaries, seeing them as troublemakers and opportunists, creating a rift between America and the Mother Country for their own benefit.[36] Expressing those opinions was a quick road to persecution by those who sided with the Whigs, often in ways that involved unpleasant encounters with tar, feathers, and trips out of town on a rail (or worse). During the course of the war the revolutionaries plundered freely from Loyalist belongings, and confiscated merchandise and supplies from Loyalist merchants at will. It is small wonder that many merchants sided with the crown.[37]

In Wilmington for example, Robert Schaw, a North Carolina merchant of Scottish extraction, took the king's side during the war. A partner in the general merchandise firm of Duncan, Ancrum, & Schaw, he was generally held in high regard by his neighbors. His name is found on many documents as a trustee, witness of wills, or executor of estates, and he even served as a justice of the peace and a colonel of artillery in Gov. William Tryon's expedition to put down the Regulator Rebellion in 1771. But Schaw's support for the Revolution was lukewarm at best, and he refused to take the oath of allegiance to the Whig government. Forced to leave the colonies because of his intransigence and Loyalist sympathies, Schaw lost his lands and most property to sequester at the end of the war.

Robert Hogg came to Wilmington in the years immediately following the French & Indian War, another Scottish newcomer who quickly opened a store that soon made him one of the most affluent of the port town's citizens. Hogg was a moderate who failed to see the need for bloodshed or independence from British rule. To that end, he chose to sail for England when the political climate in North Carolina made life for men of political moderation a risky proposition.

Samuel Campbell, another Scot and a merchant partner of Hogg's, actually took the oath of allegiance to the revolutionary cause, and became a captain of the local militia in Wilmington. Nevertheless, when ordered to proceed to the mouth of the Cape Fear River and assist in the dismantling of Fort Johnston in 1776, he refused. Though threatened with court martial, Campbell retired to the countryside and paid for a substitute to take his place among the Whig troops. When Major James Henry Craig and the 82nd Regiment of Foot occupied the town in January 1781, Campbell was again posted as a captain of militia – this time for the British. When Craig led expeditions into the countryside to harass revolutionary forces and sympathizers, Campbell was left in charge of the city the redcoats left behind.[38]

In Halifax, Scottish immigrant John Hamilton and his two brothers established a mercantile firm after arriving in North Carolina sometime prior to 1760. The Hamiltons did brisk business lending money to High-landers and others establishing farms in the piedmont of the colony. When war broke out, Hamilton sided with the British out of the belief that Great Britain had the right of things. When his Loyalist sympathies drew the ire of North Carolina Whigs, he left the colony for New York. British Gen. William Howe quickly commissioned him as a recruiting officer for the Southern theater of the war, a job in which his ties to Highlanders in the piedmont bore fruit. Hamilton commanded the Royal North Carolina Reg-iment in several major campaigns, before leaving for London when the war ended.[39]

Hogg, Campbell, and Schaw were exceptions to the rule in Wilm-ington, where most merchants sided with the rebellion. In the Albemarle, at Cross Creek (modern Fayetteville), and elsewhere, those in the mer-cantile trades were by far a Loyalist majority.[40] Whether Highland and mercantile allegiance to the crown stemmed from principle, as a reaction to Whig coercion and harassments, or economic concerns, the fact is that if they had been embodied in large numbers with the support of British army regulars to back them up, they may have played a decisive role in the outcome of the war.

Strategic Missteps

The national unity we celebrate each Fourth of July is an inac-curate reflection of the condition of the American public over the course of the war years that severed our ties with Great Britain. Especially in Southern colonies like North Carolina, the British were correct in their as-sumption that there were large numbers of sympathizers who disapproved of Whig efforts towards independence. The failure to capitalize on that sentiment was a strategic error that likely cost Great Britain the war.

That most Highlander Loyalists from North Carolina were recent immigrants who had yet to form an American identity cannot be stressed enough. These Scots never had time to find common cause with their

Whig neighbors and it showed in the enrollment lists of Loyalists who took up arms for the crown. For instance, of the forty officers of the loyal North Carolina Volunteers regiment, thirty listed their residence as Scotland. Only nine claimed America as home.[41]

In the Carolinas, the proximity of British troops accounted for a rise in Loyalist sentiments. This is especially true after the British occupation of Charleston in 1780, lasting until the British withdrew from the field in 1782. Places like Ninety-Six and Camden in South Carolina, for example, were inland headquarters for the redcoat army under Cornwallis. The same was true at Wilmington and Cross Creek in North Carolina. With British bayonets so close, prudent self-interest drove many colonists to cheer for the king's men. As well, records sustain the claim that most who took up arms in the Loyalist cause were recent immigrants who had yet to become "Americanized." These people felt a greater loyalty to the British because it represented a system that they were familiar with. Too, the lands they settled in North Carolina in most cases were theirs due to the largesse of Great Britain and the royal governors who gave them land grants. To take up the Whig cause posed the serious risk that if they bet wrong they could be dispossessed. In North Carolina, the Highlanders had few strong Whig examples to follow. That being the case, most took the side that other family members and friends did.[42]

In testimony before Parliament after the war, one British general estimated that two thirds of the people in North Carolina harbored Loyalist sympathies, but never acted on them. There could be some truth to that, as the consequences of declaring for the king were serious. Loyalists who came out for the crown in North Carolina were subject to lose their lands and other property to confiscation laws enacted and enforced by the Whigs. Yet on the other side of the coin, those who declared for the Whig cause and joined the war effort had their homes and property protected and vouchsafed.[43]

As with most people, self-interest was often the determining factor in deciding North Carolina allegiances during the Revolutionary War. Whether those interests were religious, economic, in support of a system that provided them with employment and power, or born out of a taste for revenge, the Loyalist presence in the colony was large enough to present rebel leaders with a formidable foe who remained in the field even after the British themselves had abandoned it.

For the Highlanders who sided with the British, a key element in their choice of allegiance was their relatively new arrival in North Carolina. Had they been in America long enough to develop a stake in its future, or to be swayed to the notion of democratic government, the level of British sympathies among the Scots may have been different. Had the Whigs made greater efforts to win over the Highlanders, to make them feel welcome within the bosom of the revolutionary movement, things may have been different. Instead, they too often chose to antagonize the Highlanders with oppressive legislation and punishments for those who sat the fence over which side had the right of things in the conflict. If revolutionary zeal had not resulted in actions that turned those colonists against the independence movement, it may be that British designs in America may have ended well before their surrender at Yorktown. Conversely, if the British had not bungled their utilization of Loyalists in America by drafting them into an army that left their families unprotected, perhaps our history books might tell a radically different story.

Endnotes

[1] Paul H. Smith. *Loyalists and Redcoats: A Study in British Revolutionary Policy*. Chapel Hill, N.C.: University of North Carolina Press, 1964:ix (hereafter cited as Smith).
[2] "Whig" is the proper name of the American colonists who agitated against Great Britain in the Revolutionary War. I dislike using the term "patriots," because in their own minds, each side in the struggle was behaving patriotically.
[3] Smith, 18-19. As politicians are wont to do, Dartmouth's administration failed to adjust their expectations when later communications with royal governors in the South sang a different tune. In April 1775, Virginia's Dunmore reported, "I have not at present the least expectation of assistance from the Country. The enemies of government are so numerous, and so vigilant over the conduct of every man, that such as have manifested till now very different sentiments have been so intimidated that they have entirely shrunk away." In North Carolina, the situation was much the same.
[4] Smith, 21.
[5] Walter H. Conser. *A Coat of Many Colors: Religion and Society along the Cape Fear River of North Carolina*. Lexington: University of Kentucky Press, 2006, 58, hereafter cited as Conser. The earliest Highlander land grant in North Carolina is dated 1732, for land in the area of Rockfish Creek outside Cross Creek (modern Fayetteville). The grant was made to James Innes, from Caithness, Scotland. The Highlanders tended to take lands in the interior of the colony, while Lowland Scots tended to cluster closer to the coast and its mercantile centers like Wilmington.
[6] Carole Watterson Troxler. *The Loyalist Experience in North Carolina*. Raleigh: N.C. Department of Archives & History, 1976, viii, hereafter cited as Troxler. Troxler quotes William Nelson, who said of North Carolina's Loyalists that, "…Almost all Loyalists were, in one way or another, more afraid of America than they were Britain."
[7] Catherine S. Crary. *The Price of Loyalty: Tory Writings from the Revolutionary Era*.

New York: McGraw-Hill, 1973: 4, 64 (hereafter cited as Crary). Two such North Carolina Loyalists were Farquard Campbell and Thomas Rutherford, of Cumberland County, who managed to conceal their British sympathies so well that they were elected to serve in the North Carolina Provincial Congress.

[8] Crary, 281. Twice the British called on North Carolina Loyalists to rally around the king's banner in large numbers to fight the rebels, and twice they were disappointed. Moores Creek (1776) and King's Mountain (1781) were defeats that caused Lord Cornwallis to suspect that estimates of Loyalist zeal may have missed the mark.

[9] Paul D. Escott, and Jeffrey J. Crow. "The social order and violent disorder: an analysis of North Carolina in the Revolution and the Civil War." *The Journal of Southern History* 52.3 (1986): 373-402. The authors point to political strife in the case of the Regulator rebellion that carried over to the Revolution, when Whig forces called on the citizenry to make "relentless sacrifices" and enacted laws for expropriating the property of those who would not join their movement, or for confiscating the belongings of those who openly sided with the British.

[10] Robert M. Dunkerley. *Redcoats on the River: Southeastern North Carolina in the Revolutionary War*. Wilmington, N.C.: Dram Tree Books, 2008: 34, hereafter cited as Dunkerley. The act requiring an oath of allegiance was passed by the North Carolina legislature on November 22, 1776, and was followed in April 1777 with a concrete definition of what constituted treason. Two years after that, in 1779, legislation was passed that allowed for the confiscation of Loyalist property for noncompliance with Whig edicts and taking arms against the revolutionary cause.

[11] Calhoon *Loyalists*, 493. Depredations by factions on both sides became so heinous that British commanders were forced to urge Loyalist partisans to "gentle" their methods when dealing with suspected rebels. Their guidance was seldom heeded.

[12] Duane Meyer. *The Highland Scots of North Carolina, 1732-1776*. Chapel Hill: University of North Carolina Press, 1957 (hereafter cited as Meyer).

[13] Robert M. Calhoon. *The Loyalists in Revolutionary America 1760-1781*. New York: Harcourt Brace Jovanovich, Inc., 1973: 17 (hereafter cited as Calhoon *Loyalists*). In Britain's view, colonies existed to enrich the power and wealth of the Mother Country.

[14] Troxler, 1.

[15] Calhoon *Loyalists*, 41.

[16] Calhoon, 439. As early as 1775, royal governor Josiah Martin issued a proclamation condemning plans for a second North Carolina Provincial Congress. He was gratified to receive as many as 500 signatures on petitions sent by sympathizers declaring their loyalty to the crown.

[17] Meyer, 21-26 *passim*.

[18] Ibid, 149.

[19] Conser, 58-59. Royal governor Gabriel Johnston was himself a Lowland Scot, who championed Scottish immigration to North Carolina. A graduate of Scotland's St. Andrews University, Johnston saw in the Scots the industrious immigrants he sought to help populate the vast empty spaces of his colony. Johnston initiated a policy that was continued by his successors, in which Scottish immigrants were granted money and tax exemptions to come to North Carolina. In 1739, for instance, 350 Scots from County Argyll landed at Brunswick Town and were granted a subsidy by Johnston of £1000 to be split among them. The governor also granted them a ten-year exemption from any taxes owed.

[20] Meyer, 150. Continental Army General Philip John Schuyler made the complaint in New York. "These people have been taught to consider us in politics in the same light that *Papists* consider *Protestants*," he said.

[21] Smith, 22. This was so true that Lord Dartmouth's instructions for General Howe, commanding British troops in America, advised him to pay particular attention to Loyalists in the South: "...In truth, the whole success of the measure His Majesty has adopted so much upon a considerable number of the inhabitants taking up arms in support of government, that nothing that can have a tendency promote it ought to be omitted..."

[22] Conser, 59. Tacksmen were "moderately well off individuals" who made up the gentry – or middle class - of Scotland. The political and economic changes that came to in the wake of the Stuart revolt led to a breakdown of their roles in relation to their clan chiefs. As a result, the "special bond" between the tacksmen and their clan chiefs was effectively broken. This left the gentry no real choice but to seek better opportunities elsewhere.

[23] Matthew P. Dziennik. "Through An Imperial Prism: Land, Liberty, and Highland Loyalism in the War of American Independence." *The Journal of British Studies*, Vol. 50 (2011): 332-358, hereafter cited as Dziennik. In North Carolina, Highland Scot settlement was heaviest in the modern piedmont counties of Anson, Hoke, Scotland, Bladen, Cumberland, Duplin, and Rockingham.

[24] Dziennik, 337; Robert O. DeMond. *The Loyalist Experience in North Carolina During The Revolution*. Hamden, CT: Archon Books (1964): 51, hereafter cited as DeMond. Flora MacDonald, a heroine to Highlanders for her efforts to protect Charles Stuart in the wake of the Culloden disaster, was feted with balls and receptions at both Brunswick and Wilmington as residents basked in their proximity to celebrity

[25] DeMond, *passim*.

[26] Peter N. Moore. "The Local Origins of Allegiance in Revolutionary South Carolina: The Waxhaws as a Case Study," *The South Carolina Historical Magazine*, Vol. 107 (Jan. 2006), 35, hereafter cited as Moore. One table in Moore's article shows that around Waxhaws, Highlanders who immigrated to North Carolina by or before 1765 constituted 42 percent of enlistments in the Whig militias, as opposed to 28 percent from among post-1765 immigrants. By 1781, those who came to the colony after 1765 constituted 72 percent of enlistments in the British cause – a 162 percent increase. On the Whig side of the ledger, the increase over the same time period was only to 38 percent.

[27] James D. MacKenzie. "The Highlanders of the Cape Fear." *International Review of Scottish Studies*, Vol. 1 (2008), pp. 18-23.

[28] Moore, 37. According to Moore, Loyalists on average owned 336 acres of land in 1780, as opposed to the 717 owned by the earlier Scottish immigrants who arrived prior to 1765 (and who sided with the Americans more often than with the British).

[29] Ibid, pp. 26 41. Though Moore's essay centers around the Waxhaws community in upcountry South Carolina, it can serve as a legitimate example for North Carolina, as well. In fact, at the time of the Revolutionary War, exactly which Carolina Waxhaws was located in was a matter of some dispute (see the competing claims to Waxhaws' most famous resident, Andrew Jackson, for example).

[30] Dziennik, 340.

[31] Wallace Brown. "The American Farmer in the Revolution: Rebel or Loyalist?" *Agricultural History*, Vol. 42 (October 1968), pp. 327-338, hereafter cited as Brown. Of the North Carolina Loyalists who made claims against the British government in the years

after the war, almost half (46.5%) listed their occupations as farmer.

[32] Dunkerley, 115. Craig occupied Wilmington from January to November 1781. His primary mission was to send supplies via the Cape Fear River to Cross Creek, so that Gen. Charles Lord Cornwallis could resupply while on the march as he chased Greene's Continentals towards the Virginia border. He failed because there were no boats of sufficiently shallow draft available at Wilmington to ferry the supplies upriver, and because local Whig militia under Alexander Lillington created an insurmountable chokepoint on the river above Wilmington at Heron's Bridge. Craig's mission changed after the surrender at Yorktown to one of guerrilla warfare. This involved utilizing Loyalist raiders like David Fanning to scour the countryside, while holding Wilmington as a safe haven for the Loyalists when things became too hot to stay in the field.

[33] Smith, 146. "We receive the strongest professions of Friendship from North Carolina; our Friends, however, do not seem inclined to rise until they see our Army in motion," Cornwallis confided to British officials in New York on August 29, 1780.

[34] Ibid, 142-144. Some 800 Loyalists from the Yadkin River area led by an officer named Bryan fled North Carolina to enlist with the British in South Carolina after Whig officials left them little choice. "The say," wrote Colonel Francis Lord Rawdon from Charleston, "that they had been drafted to serve in the [revolutionary] militia, and, refusing to march, had no alternative but joining us or going to prison."

[35] Moore, 33. Cornwallis, fearing that unattached Loyalists would be cowed into nonparticipation or worse, that they would be coerced into joining the Whig ranks – took draconian steps of his own in regards to Carolina Loyalists. After the American victory at Ramsour's Mill, it became British policy to demand that neutrals either take up arms for the crown, surrender their horses and arms, or face execution.

[36] W. S. MacNutt. "The Loyalists: A Sympathetic View." *Acadiensis* (1976): 3-20. MacNutt characterizes the Loyalist view of the revolution as "the antithesis of modernity and freedom, a conspiracy of reckless and designing men to raise themselves from adversity to affluence, from public disfavor to high prominence."

[37] DeMond, 53. Of sixty-eight people designated by name in the North Carolina Confiscation Act of 1779, more than half – forty-five – were merchants.

[38] Janet Schaw. *Journal of a Lady of Quality: Being the Narrative of a Journey from Scotland to the West Indies, North Carolina, and Portugal, in the Years 1774 to 1776.* U of Nebraska Press, 1934. Information on Robert Schaw, Campbell, and Hogg all comes from appendices of Janet Schaw's book. An online edition can be found at: http:www. ncpublications.com/colonial/Bookshelf/Schaw/loyalist.htm.

[39] DeMond, 53; Troxler, 27. According to DeMond, Hamilton was well thought of by his enemies. This in large part was due to his aversion to the often savage tactics employed by fellow Loyalists like David Fanning. Hamilton's kind treatment of the Whigs who became his prisoners of war, says DeMond, "won for him their lasting gratitude." Though he lost by some estimates in the neighborhood of £200,000 when the war closed down his business, Hamilton was well thought of enough on both sides of the Atlantic that he was sent to Norfolk, Virginia to serve as British consul in 1790.

[40] DeMond, 54. Among the other Wilmington merchants who sided with the British were John Cruden, George Hooper, James Glass, and Samuel Cornell. DeMond makes the observation that the loyalty of merchants in the Albemarle region may or may not have been heartfelt. He points out that the British had a much firmer grip on the Albemarle region

than they did on other parts of North Carolina due to its proximity to the Chesapeake and British forces there under Lord Dunsmore. That being the case, they may not have been able to support the rebellion in any meaningful way.

[41] DeMond, 59.

[42] Brown, 336-337. North Carolina Highlanders, especially, feared becoming (in Brown's words) "three time losers" if they sided with the wrong faction in the conflict. Without strong leaders, these recent immigrants tended to follow the example of their clan leaders. In North Carolina, those clan chiefs were overwhelmingly Tory.

[43] DeMond, 60-61.

The Great Fire of London in 1666 was just one factor that led to the failure of the Charles Towne settlement on the Cape Fear River.

The Lords Proprietors, Charles Town, and Neglect: A Matter of Priorities
By Jack E. Fryar, Jr.

ohn Vassall,[1] and the few hundred settlers scattered along the banks of the Cape Fear River near Town Creek in 1664, counted on the Lords Proprietors in London to insure the nascent settlement would have what it needed to carve a home from a wilderness of long leaf pines in the colony called Carolina. But the colonists from Barbados and Massachusetts had no inkling that events in England and on the world stage would make the fate of a handful of settlers an ocean away among the least important problems the eight Lords would have to deal with.

In recounting the story of the Barbadian settlement that was the first along the Cape Fear River, historians have generally attributed neglect by the Lords Proprietors as a leading reason for the failure of the Vassall-led effort to plant an English settlement in the southern part of what is now North Carolina. Yet a closer look at the history of England and the world between the years 1664 and 1667 reveals that, while neglect did occur, there were mitigating circumstances that might tend to exonerate the Lords – or at least persuade an objective person that the neglect was unintended.

When the Stuart line of the English monarchy was restored to the throne in 1660,[2] after years of Oliver Cromwell's Interregnum, the King recognized that he owed a debt to a number of loyal nobles who had been instrumental in his return from exile in Scotland and Ireland. To reward these men, King Charles II declared them Lords Proprietors of the American colony of Carolina. For their loyalty, Edward Hyde, 1st Earl of Clarendon; George Monck, 1st Duke of Albemarle; William Craven, 1st Earl of Craven; John Berkeley, 1st Baron Berkeley of Stratton; Anthony Ashley Cooper, 1st Earl of Shaftesbury; Sir George Carteret; Sir William Berkeley (brother of John); and Sir John Colleton, found themselves exercising almost absolute power over every aspect of settlement in the virtually undeveloped colony a half world away.[3]

While the Lords preferred that settlement take place at Port Royal, south of the Cape Fear River in what would later become South Carolina, they made Vassall the Deputy Governor of the Carolina colony behind Governor Sir John Yeamans, the Barbadian who spearheaded efforts to place a colony on the Ashley River.[4] With Sir John Colleton and Sir William Berkeley living practically on-site in the Americas, they trusted their intentions would be carried out.[5] The Lords' assumption proved incorrect. Aside from troubles with the local Indians, and being second to the Yeamans' colony to the south, events in England conspired to derail the promised support from the Lords Proprietors for the Barbadians and Puritans trying to carve a home from a wilderness along the Cape Fear.

The Second Anglo-Dutch War

At the time that John Yeamans was securing the permissions of the Lords Proprietors to establish a settlement in Carolina that would eclipse the Vassall settlement in 1665, simmering tensions between Great Britain and Holland were once again heating to a boil. Both nations were major players in the burgeoning Atlantic Trade between Europe and the New World colonies, both possessed mighty navies capable of projecting their power at the global level, and both were jockeying for supremacy on the European continent and in North America. The trigger for the Second Anglo-Dutch War was the English seizure of the Dutch colony of New Amsterdam in the Americas in 1664.[6] By March 1665, a state of war existed again between the two great maritime empires. The conflict would stretch into the summer of 1667.

General George Monck,[7] a Carolina Proprietor and distinguished English soldier, was called into service to command King Charles II's fleet in a joint command with Prince Rupert. The two took that fleet into battle against the Dutch off the Flemish coast in the summer of 1666.[8] Monck distinguished himself in the Four Days Battle, and remained on active duty with the navy through the St. James Day Battle a month later.[9]

Another of the Lords Proprietors, Edward Hyde, Earl of Craven, was also occupied with the war as King Charles II's Lord Chancellor and most trusted advisor. Yet Craven's favor with the monarch began to wane over the course of the conflict, and military setbacks[10] suffered by the English ultimately saw him flee to French exile. Anthony Ashley Cooper, 1st Earl of Shaftesbury, also played a role in the conflict as Chancellor of the Exchequer to the Crown. Sir George Carteret served as Treasurer of the Navy. Even those Proprietors without a military role in the war against the Dutch, as prominent men of the realm, would have been at least peripherally involved with the war. It would be a safe assumption that wartime obligations to the government, against a foe capable of bringing the fight right to the heart of England, might relegate colonial matters to a back burner.

The Great Plague of London

London was no stranger to epidemics, and as plague episodes went, the one that cut a swath through Britain's largest city and capital beginning in 1665 was not even the worst such outbreak its citizens had endured. That said, the epidemic of bubonic plague that tore through London and the surrounding countryside between the summer of 1664 and 1665 was certainly bad enough by any objective standard. The 1665 outbreak was the last major bout of the disease that had been a recurring problem since 1499. The difference this time was that London had been experiencing something of a population boom, swelling the city to some 499,000 residents at the time of the outbreak. Before it was finally stamped out with the help of the Great Fire of London, the plague would claim roughly one fourth of that population.[11] As government ministers, the Lords Proprietors had duties that demanded their attention and which, given the immediacy and scope of the public health emergency, took precedence over colonial matters half a world away.

Edward Hyde, Lord Clarendon, was vilified in some circles as the minister most responsible for London's unpreparedness for the epidemic.[12] George Monck, on the other hand, was lauded for taking charge of desolate, disease-ridden London in the absence of not just the King, but also everyone else with the wherewithal to abandon the capital. Given the scope of the disaster, Monck's efforts to restore public health and the disposal of plague victims' remains would have demanded a great deal of his attention. William Craven established a hospital for plague victims in Marshall Street. Pest House Close, as it was called, was a place where people dying of the disease could be attended by physicians and provided what comforts were available, instead of expiring alone in the exile of their own boarded up homes. Meanwhile George Carteret, after having been captured aboard ship in transit from America to England by the Dutch in the summer of 1665, finally managed to make his way to London in time to witness the epidemic in full swing. Few of the Lords Proprietors were untouched by the multiple disasters that struck the capital between 1664 and 1667.

The Great Fire of London

"I saw a fire as one entire arch of fire above a mile long: it made me weep to see it," wrote Samuel Pepys of the great firestorm consuming his city in the fall of 1666. "The churches, houses are all on fire and flaming at once, and a horrid noise the flames made and the cracking of the houses."[13] Between fifteen and twenty thousand buildings along the north bank of the Thames River perished in the conflagration triggered when a maid of King Charles' baker forgot to douse fires in the bakery's ovens at the end of the day. The ovens overheated, igniting adjacent straw and kindling, killing the neglectful maid[14] before sweeping beyond the walls of the bakery to engulf the capital.

If the people of the Vassall colony on the Cape Fear had reason to wring their hands at their situation, seemingly abandoned in a strange wilderness that was growing more hostile by the day, then the residents of London must have wept at the calamities of biblical proportions visited upon them between 1664 and 1666. George Monck was not in London when the fire broke out, but he made it to the capital in time to see the flames rage between Cheapside and the Thames. After it was over, Monck would join George Carteret in offering plans to rebuild King Charles II's capital city.[15] Monck and Carteret, like all of the other Lords Proprietors except William Berkeley and John Colleton, lived, worked, or owned homes in London. In addition to the general and the vice chancellor, many of them held important posts in King Charles' government. There was plenty for all of them to do.

War, pestilence, and flames – the people of England must have wondered what they had done to bring such Godlike wrath down upon them. Certainly the men who were in many cases among the King's most trusted advisors had their hands full just trying to keep the nation from descending into anarchy from which it might not recover. Notable among those ministers were the eight men whose obligation to support the English Barbadians camped along the muddy banks of the Cape Fear went by the wayside. The failure of the Vassall colony at Town Creek was not entirely due to the failure of the Lords Proprietors to send along the material support the settlers needed, but it was most assuredly a factor. Nevertheless, events in England that coincided with the Barbadian attempt at settlement might offer at least some modicum of excuse for the Proprietors' failure.

Endnotes

[1] William S. Powell. Dictionary of North Carolina Biography, Vol. 6. Chapel Hill, N.C.: University of North Carolina Press, 1996. John Vassall was the Barbadian planter, originally from Massachusetts, who headed a group of colonists called The Company of Barbadian Adventurers, that established a colony at the mouth of modern Town Creek in 1664.

[2] Antonia Fraser. King Charles II. London: Weidenfeld and Nicolson, 1979.The Stuart line of the English monarchy was restored with the return from exile of Charles II to England in 1660.

[3] Powell, William S. The Proprietors of Carolina. Raleigh, N.C.: The Carolina Tercentenary Commission, 1963. Hereafter cited as Powell.

[4] Wesley Frank Craven. The Southern Colonies in the Seventeenth Century: 1607-1689. Baton Rouge: Louisiana State University Press, 1949. Yeamans founded the second Charles Town settlement at Port Royal on the Ashley River.

[5] Powell. Berkeley was the colonial governor of Virginia, and Colleton was a planter living in Barbados.

[6] J.F.C. Fuller. A Military History of the Western World: From the Defeat of the Spanish Armada to the Battle of Waterloo. New York: Da Capo Press, 1955. Hereafer cited as Fuller. The British assault on New Amsterdam happened on August 27, 1664.

[7] Powell. At this period in history, British general officers also sometimes doubles as naval commanders. George Monck was one such soldier/sailor hybrid. Monck earned his command after serving at sea under Admiral Robert Blake during Cromwell's reign.

[8] Fuller. June 1-4, 1666. The Four Days Battle is still one of the lengthiest naval engagements in history.

[9] Fuller. July 25, 1666. It would be Monck's last sea battle.

[10] Fuller. For instance, in the summer of 1667, Dutch warships under De Ruyter sailed up the Thames and destroyed much of the English fleet anchored at the Medway.

[11] Lloyd A. Moote and Dorothy C. Moote, 2004. The Great Plague: The Story of London's Most Deadly Year. Baltimore: Johns Hopkins University Press, 2004.

[12] Ibid. The epidemic happened at a time when Clarendon's influence was on the decline.

He was also blamed for the Medway Raid, and the Great Fire of London.

[13] "The Diary of Samuel Pepys." http://www.pepysdiary.com/archive (accessed 09/14/09) Entry for September 2, 1666.

[14] Neil Hanson, 2002. The Great Fire of London: In That Apocalyptic Year, 1666. Hoboken, New Jersey: John Wiley and Sons. Amazingly, the maid was one of the only fatalities of the Great Fire. Official records put the death toll at just five (although that count may be skewed, as it is not unreasonable to assume some lives were lost in the flames and never discovered). Part of the reason for the low death toll may lay in the fact that much of the city had been evacuated or killed in the previous summer's plague epidemic.

[15] Adrian Tinniswood. By Permission of Heaven: The True Story of the Great Fire of London. New York: Riverhead Books, 2003.

The King's Americans:
The Colonial Regiment at Cartagena During the War of Jenkins' Ear

By Jack E. Fryar. Jr.

hen James Innes and 99 other men from North Carolina sailed past the mouth of the Cape Fear River on 15 November 1740, enroute to join Admiral Edward Vernon's fleet at Jamaica before the assault on the Spanish bastion at Cartagena, most of them believed the expedition to be a bit of a lark. For some it was a break from the everyday routines of colonial life, while for others it was a ticket out of the gaol. After all, men of English stock had a generally poor opinion of Spanish martial prowess. The expedition was significant because it was the first time American colonials had been enlisted to fight under the British flag outside the North American continent. Two years later, only one in four of them set foot on Carolina soil again after a campaign marked by disaster, disease, and command dysfunction.

Since 1650, British policy towards Spain was based on Spain's weakness. While England lacked the military power to challenge Spanish dominion over New World lands in the Caribbean basin directly, it was able to pursue a policy of what was - plainly speaking - piracy, to carve off a piece of the treasure making its way from Havana to Madrid. What made this possible were tensions between France and Spain. While Spain's rulers were forced to keep an eye on their neighbor to the north, they did not have the military resources to end the predations of England's sea rovers. The Treaty of Utrecht, in 1713, ended the War of Spanish Succession and the French threat to the Spanish crown. In the process, it freed Spain to turn her attentions to annoyances coming from the British.

Admiral Edward Vernon

By the early years of the eighteenth century, Great Britain's burgeoning mercantile fleet was chafing at their exclusion from potentially lucrative markets in the West Indies, Central, and South America. Spain, the colonial power that staked the earliest claim to the wealth of the New World, was jealous of its holdings and vigilant in its efforts to insure no rival power had unfettered access to its territories. The decades-long friction between Spain and England needed only a spark to turn into full fledged war, as the great powers of Europe each vied with their rivals to secure a piece of the profitable western lands for themselves. That spark came in the spring of 1731.

In April of that year, after leaving Jamaica, the Glasgow brig *Rebecca* was tacking north for home when the *San Antonio,* of the Cuban *guardacosta* out of Havana, intercepted the ship. During an inspection, Cuban captain Juan de Leon Fandino and his crew ransacked the *Rebecca*, and in a final fit of pique, sliced off Capt. Robert Jenkins' ear. According to Jenkins' testimony before parliament, the Cuban captain told him to "carry it to his majesty King George." Jenkins did, and relations between Spain and Great Britain deteriorated from there.

By 1738, King George II issued a proclamation allowing any British subject with a claim against the Spanish coast guard to engage in privateering. A year later, British merchants with assets in the Caribbean were advised to remove them. By 1739, the privateers were joined by a massive fleet led by Admiral Edward Vernon, who intended to take a strategic port in the West Indies to protect British aspirations in the region. Initially, no specific port was selected. British military planners favored Havana, but the Prime Minister Robert Walpole's ministry nixed the idea. However, once in the Caribbean, the tactical situation narrowed Admiral Vernon's choices. Ultimately, the target chosen was Cartagena, on the north coast of what is now Columbia.

The declaration of war against Spain was slow in coming as the Walpole government dithered about, trying to decide how to raise the troops needed, what the target should be, and the casus belli they would present to the rest of the world as justification for belligerence.

Jenkins delivers Fandino's message to Robert Walpole, along with his pickled ear.

It was eventually decided that the damages done to Capt. Jenkins and his crew (whether true or not) would do nicely to inflame the passions of the English public.

Of the myriad things that the government had to consider before declaring hostilities was how to best go about obtaining the men needed to man the expedition. Fighting a war on the other side of the world was no small task, and filling the ranks of the British army and navy was difficult at the best of times. Walpole's government would have to rely on the time-honored methods of the press gang, enlistment bounties, and using soldiers as seamen when afloat to fill the crews and rosters of ships and ground companies tasked with taking the fight to the enemy.

While Americans were recruited in the belief they were somehow more suited to the exertions of tropical warfare than soldiers from Great Britain's home islands, there was another reason for King George II to endorse the offer of raising colonial levies, put forth by Virginia's Alexander

This English caricature depicts Jenkins losing his ear (top left corner).

Spottswood and forwarded to the monarch by Walpole's ministry. King George II harbored reservations about a plan that saw perhaps a third of Britain's 28,000 land forces dispatched half a world away from home. The specter of a French, Spanish - or worse, a combined Franco-Spanish force - assaulting the British Isles, loomed large in his mind.

In London, Walpole's advisors worried that British regulars, accustomed as they were to the less taxing climes of Europe, would fair poorly if required to campaign for extended periods in the tropics. To remedy that, British planners decided to raise a levy of colonials from their American territories, men who they assumed had become better accustomed to the rigors of life in the Western Hemisphere. To that end, colonial governors in America were tasked with raising as many as 4,000 men to compliment a British army of regulars under Gen. Charles Lord Cathcart, dispatched from England aboard Vernon's navy transports. Virginia's Governor Alexander Spottswood, a longtime colonial administrator and leader who was well thought of throughout Britain's American colonies, was chosen to spearhead the effort. Spottswood would also lead the Americans as part of Cathcart's army.

Unfortunately, Lord Cathcart died. So did Spottswood, in June 1740. Overall command of British ground forces in the expedition devolved to Gen. Thomas Wentworth, while command of the American

Regiment fell to Spottswood's lieutenant governor, William Gooch. While his military rank was colonel, Gooch's status as a colonial governor made Gen. Wentworth less than thrilled to meet him.

Nevertheless, the American colonies responded with varying – but largely enthusiastic – degrees of eagerness for the adventure. Not all of the colonies contributed to the force being raised for British service, but most did. Reasons for joining the expedition varied. Some were impressed. Others joined in return for debt relief. Still others enlisted to share in the booty they expected to win after defeating the Spanish. Virginia was perhaps the most enthusiastic, likely because its call for levies zeroed in on the unemployed and landless as prime candidates for the draft. That those who enlisted would be entitled to land in the captured Spanish territories no doubt took some of the sting out of impressment.

Alexander Spottswood (above), and William Gooch (below).

In January 1740, orders went to the governors of Britain's American colonies to begin raising a force to compliment six regiments of Marines raised in the British Isles for the Vernon expedition. Not every colony contributed. Nova Scotia, South Carolina, and Georgia were exempt from the initial call for men. The remaining colonies – North Carolina, Massachusetts, Rhode Island, Connecticut, New York, New Jersey, Delaware, Pennsylvania, Maryland, and Virginia, all raised troops for the cause.

To get the men they needed, colonial governors resorted first to inducements, then later to less friendly forms of coercion. Only Pennsylvania's pacifist colonial assembly refused to grant the governor's request

for funds to pay enlistment bounties. Despite this, Pennsylvania had no trouble filling their quotas. In fact, while keeping the men in ranks after joining was sometimes difficult, getting them to enlist in the first place was relatively easy. The ranks were filled largely by men at the bottom of the socio-economic ladder – laborers, debtors, indentured servants. But finding men to join was the least of their problems. Col. William Blakeney, in New York to supervise recruitment efforts, reported that *"As to the American levies, they go briskly, even beyond what could be expected during high harvest and high wages."*

Despite the overwhelming willingness to serve in Gooch's regiment among colonial men, British officers found them somewhat less than what they could wish for. As an example, one of Wentworth's officers complained that the men enlisted from Maryland, Virginia, and North Carolina were *"mostly Irish (probably popists), or English convicts."*

Lawrence Washington

The Americans contributed four battalions of men to Wentworth's ground forces. The 1st Battalion was primarily Massachusetts men, along with elements from Rhode Island under a Captain Dunn. Other colonies were represented by levies under a Capt. Hepburn (S.C.), Capt. Walker (VA), and Capt. James Innes (N.C.). The 2nd Battalion was primarily New Englanders from New York, New Jersey, and Rhode Island, but with a sprinkling of Pennsylvanians under a Capt. Clarke. In 3rd Battalion, Pennsylvanians and men from Delaware were present in the largest numbers, although men from Massachusetts under Capt. Newberry also filled the 3rd's ranks. Lastly, 4th Battalion was made up of Marylanders, Virginians under Lawrence Washington, North Carolinians under Captains Colerain, Holton and Pratt, plus men from South Carolina under a Captain Gordon.

While records of white enlistments are scant beyond the names of the Americans' officers and a few other documents that mention service with Vernon, they are almost nonexistent for African Americans who were part of the expedition. The same is true for Native Americans who fought, but there is evidence that both were at least represented in the Cartagena campaign. One such record is a proclamation published by Maryland Governor Samuel Ogle in September 1740, seeking help in recovering *". . . William Burgess, a black man about fifty years old, six feet and an inch high, black hair, had on a brown cloth coat and other clothes . . ."*

American colonial governors had little trouble finding men willing to go on the Cartagena expedition, but support for their efforts from the British was somewhat poorly planned and slow in coming. Gen. Wentworth's deputy commander, Col. William Blakeney, was sent to the colonies with commissions for colonial officers, but did not have enough to meet the demand of the governors' recruitment efforts. Blakeney promised that those American officers willing to sail to Jamaica would be commissioned once they reached Vernon's forces, but his promise did not instill faith among the Americans. Colonial gentlemen who had raised companies, often out of their own pockets, were reluctant to assume further risk without a commission in hand. The result was that the British forfeited the services of a large number of men who refused to serve under anyone but their own officers.

Not all recruitment efforts were equal in the colonies. Different jurisdictions employed different means to fill their quotas for the expedition against the Spanish. In Virginia, the unemployed were conscripted to prevent the loss of precious white laborers. Maryland and Pennsylvania found themselves at the center of an uproar when indentured servants began enlisting to escape their bonds. Old, "worn out Negroes" were sent to fill ranks in Maryland. Pacifism in Quaker New Jersey hampered recruitment to the point that Governor Lewis Morris urged small debtors to enlist with the promise of immunity from prosecution. Things were better among the companies raised in New York and Rhode Island, who built their recruitments around existing militia units. These men, at least, had some nominal military training.

Lack of specie in the colonies was another impediment to recruitment. British paymasters were instructed to pay American troops in specie prior to their arrival in Jamaica, where they would be added to the regular British establishment under Vernon and Wentworth. The trouble was that a shortage of specie was a problem that existed for the Americans through-out the colonial era, and recruits were uneager to make their mark on en-listment papers when their signing bonus was paid in scrip. Paper currency in the colonies was notoriously subject to the vagaries of inflation and other limitations, making it unattractive to the men. North Carolina gover-nor Gabriel Johnston lamented the policy of paying in colonial scrip:

"I can now assure your grace that we have raised 400 men in this province who are just going to put to sea," Johnston wrote the Duke of Newcastle in October 1740. *"In those Northern Parts of the Colony adjoining to Virginia, we have got 100 men each, though some few desert-ed since they began to send them on board the transports at Cape Fear. I have good reason to believe we could have raised 200 more if it had been possible to negotiate the Bills of Exchange in this part of the Continent; but as that was impossible we were obliged to rest satisfied with four com-panies. I must in justice to the assembly of the Province inform your Grace that they were very zealous and unanimous in promoting this service. They have raised a subsidy of 1200 pounds as it is reckoned hereby on which the men have subsisted ever since August, and all the Transports are vict-ualed."*

Other problems persisted. The colonies themselves were expected to fund and provision their men until the Americans reached Vernon at Jamaica. That included transportation, which proved problematic for some colonies. Unlike regular British regiments, Gooch's Americans were not issued swords. This may have been because the general British impression of the American levies was not very flattering. Charles Knowles, who was on the expedition and who wrote an account of it later, said of the colo-nials that they were *"Blacksmiths, Tailors, Barbers, Shoemakers, and all the Banditry the colonies could afford."* Major General Wentworth initial-ly saw the Americans as fit for shipboard duty only.

Complicating the governors' efforts to pay for their levies until they could reach Vernon was the fact that political circumstances in the colonies made it impossible for them to issue an edict to secure the funds. The colonies were primarily agricultural, and as it has already been point-ed out, specie – hard money – was scarce. The colonial assemblies were populated with members who each represented a local constituency. The assemblies considered themselves miniature houses of commons, with all the rights, prerogatives and privileges that entailed. They were ex-tremely reluctant in most cases to raise the taxes of the people who had elected them, especially at the behest of a London government that to date had shown little concern for what was going on in the colonies. That the funds they were asked to raise would be spent on an expedition against a far away enemy that was no direct threat to the colonies themselves only deepened their reluctance.

Some assemblies grudgingly gave the governors the appropriations they wanted, but not without making the executive jump through a few hoops first. North Carolina's assembly heard Gov. Gabriel Johnston's request, but would only vote on the funds after the governor produced *"the original instructions signed by His Majesty, and other letters referred to in your Excellency's speech."* Even though the governor did not think the assembly had the right to make such a demand, Johnston complied. After inspecting the documents, the N.C. Assembly voted to issue "a certain amount of new bills" for the expedition. Johnston, despite having told the assembly that his orders did not include a royal consent to issuing new currency, agreed to the terms with the proviso that the money not be issued until he received further instructions from London. The assembly ignored Johnston's threat of a veto and issued the currency anyway. In doing so, the governor was forced to either assent to violating a standing prohibition

A contemporary illustration of the battle for Cartagena.

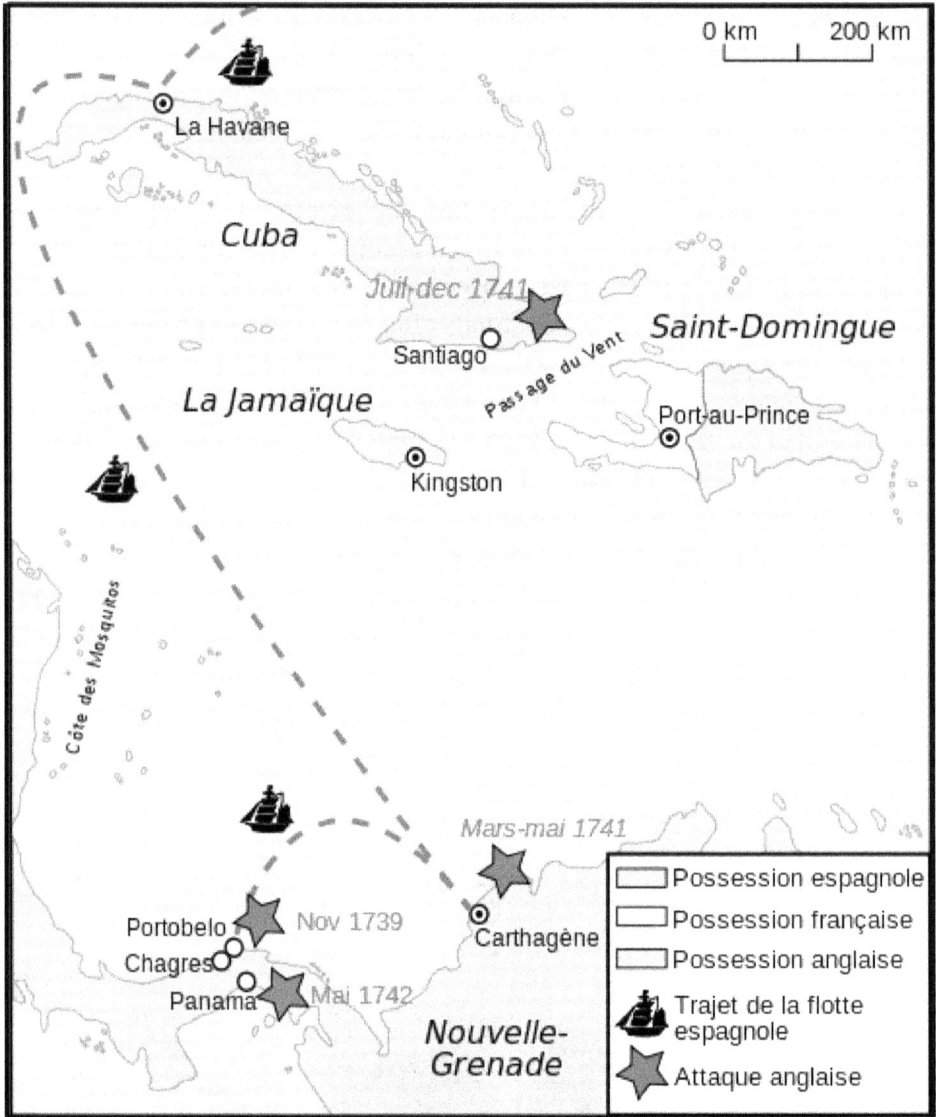

La Havane

Cuba

Juil-dec 1741

Santiago

Saint-Domingue

La Jamaïque

Passage du Vent

Port-au-Prince

Kingston

Côte des Mosquitos

Mars-mai 1741

Portobelo   Nov 1739

Chagres

Carthagène

Panama   Mai 1742

Nouvelle-
Grenade

0 km   200 km

Possession espagnole
Possession française
Possession anglaise
Trajet de la flotte
espagnole
Attaque anglaise

Operations of the Vernon expedition in the Caribbean.

regarding the issuing of paper money by the colonies, or not get the funds he needed to comply with London's orders to raise, provision, and transport troops for the Vernon expedition.

Obstacles though there were, the 4,000 men of Gooch's regiment were finally assembled and sailed to join regular British forces waiting with Vernon and Wentworth at Jamaica. Troops from Virginia, Maryland, Delaware and Pennsylvania sailed directly for the West Indies from their home colonies. Other northern colonies assembled their men at Hampton Roads on the Chesapeake Bay and embarked aboard transport ships there. The southern colonies sent men to Cape Fear to board ships for the journey into warmer Caribbean waters. As they boarded ships for Jamaica, they were a grumbling, disheveled, and mostly untrained force, on the brink of mutiny in some cases. These men, disparaged as they were by regular British soldiers and commanders, would make up forty percent of Britain's forces and be vital to Vernon's chances for success.

That success, when it came, was Pyrrhic at best. Geography at Cartagena and a stubborn defense by local Spanish forces conspired to keep British forces pinned on the beaches. The assault on the main Spanish bastion was a comedy of sad errors, where Wentworth's forces forgot to bring scaling ladders to breach the walls, and where colonials were caught in a terrible fire even before coming within distance of the fort. Disease killed thousands, and squabbling erupted between Vernon and Wentworth when the admiral refused to release colonials who had been drafted into ship's crews for ground action. British victories at Porto Bello and Chagres paled when considered next to the failure to take Cartagena. But perhaps the greatest loss to the British was the distrust of each other that was born in the disastrous campaign, between Great Britain and her American colonies.

Endnotes

[1] "Innes, James," *Dictionary of North Carolina Biography,* Vol. 3, William S. Powell, ed. Chapel Hill: University of North Carolina Press, 1988: 251-253. Innes commanded the Cape Fear company, one of four raised in North Carolina. The other three companies, from the Albemarle region, were commanded by officers named Pratt, Coltrain, and Holton. Innes also carried a letter of marque, allowing the troop transport to act as a privateer should they come across Spanish shipping.

[2] Albert Harkness, Jr. "Americanism and Jenkins' Ear." *The Mississippi Valley Historical Review*, Vol. 37, No. 1 (June 1950): 61-90, hereafter cited as Harkness. To meet the levies asked of them, some colonial governors offered those facing charges forgiveness if they joined the American Regiment.

[3] Harding, 17-18. This sense of Spanish impotence would come back to haunt the British expedition led by Vernon. Spanish failure to curb British encroachment prior to 1713 fostered an impression of Spain as something of a paper tiger in the minds of most Englishmen.

[4] Richard Harding. "America, The War of 1739-48 and the Development of British Global Power." Journal For Maritime Research, Vol. 6, No. 1 (February 2011): 1-20, hereafter cited as Harding, America. Much of the successes British merchants had in the Caribbean came from privateering, or Spain's opinion, piracy. Between 1739-1748, British priva-

teers would make at least 466 voyages into Spanish territory from North American or Caribbean ports, and capture some 829 enemy prizes.

[5] David Marley. *Wars of the Americas: A Chronology of Armed Conflict in the New World, 1492 to the Present*. Santa Barbara: ABC-CLIO, 1998: 250, hereafter cited as Marley; Harding, Richard. *Amphibious Warfare in the Eighteenth Century: The British Expedition to the West Indies, 1740-1742*. London: The Boydell Press, 1991: 3, hereafter cited as Harding. Though the spark for the war came with Capt. Robert Jenkins' unfortunate encounter off Cuba in 1731, the war would not begin in earnest until the Walpole government's trade negotiations with Spain reached an impasse in 1739.

[6] Marley, 250.

[7] Albert Harkness, Jr. "Americanism and Jenkins' Ear." *The Mississippi Valley Historical Review*, Vol. 37, No. 1 (June 1950) 61-90, hereafter cited as Harkness. Acting on bad intelligence that a French fleet lay anchored at Hispanola, Vernon sailed there in late January 1741. While there were no French to attack (France had allied with Spain), word did reach the British that Admiral de Torres' fleet had left Cartagena for Havana. This intelligence confirmed Cartagena as Vernon's target.

[8] Harding, 28. Manpower mattered greatly. Prevailing winds in the Caribbean are strong easterly to southeasterly. Once ships passed to leeward of the Antilles, it would be very difficult to tack back to windward. The weaker crews became, the more shorthanded they would become, and the harder it would be to simply navigate, much less engage in combat or combat support efforts. It was imperative that Vernon and the army's Lord Cathcart arrive with full complements of men.

[9] Ibid, 28, 33. Manning the British army was no easy task after relative peace for an England that had not fought a real war in more than a quarter century.

[10] "Spotswood , Alexander (1676–1740)," Gwenda Morgan in *Oxford Dictionary of National Biography*, eee ed. H. C. G. Matthew and Brian Harrison (Oxford: OUP, 2004); online ed., ed. Lawrence Goldman, January 2008,

• http://0-www.oxforddnb.com.uncclc.coast.uncwil.edu/view/article/26164 (accessed March 7, 2013); Higginbotham, Don. "The Early American Way of War: Reconnaissance and Appraisal." *The William and Mary Quarterly*, Third Series, Vol. 44, No. 2 (Apr., 1987): 230-273. Spottswood (sometimes spelled as Spottiswood or Spotswood) was no stranger to military action. He had been a lieutenant colonel in the British army, and was responsible for dispatching Lt. Robert Maynard to Ocracoke Inlet in 1718 to deal with the notorious pirate, Blackbeard. As to everyone thinking it was a good idea to use Americans in Vernon's forces, not everyone did. Prior to the Cartagena expedition, Americans had only been mustered into British service on a few limited occasions between 1690 and 1740. Prominently, Americans served in British actions against the French at Louisburg, Quebec and Montreal, and the Spanish at Port Royal.

[11] "Gooch, Sir William, first baronet (1681–1751)," Paul David Nelson in *Oxford Dictionary of National Biography*, eee ed. H. C. G. Matthew and Brian Harrison (Oxford: OUP, 2004); online ed., ed. Lawrence Goldman, January 2008, http://0-www.oxforddnb. com.uncclc.coast.uncwil.edu/view/article/62477 (accessed March 7, 2013). Gooch also had extensive military experience, having served Britain in the Low Countries during the War of Spanish Succession, and later during the Jacobite uprising. During the Cartagena campaign, Gooch would suffer wounds from a Spanish cannonball, and contract the fever that accounted for so many American and British deaths in the Caribbean operations.

[12] Lee Offen. *Gooch's Marine Regiment, 1740-1742: America's First Marines*. Jacksonville (FL): Veterans Publishing Systems, 2009: 8, hereafter cited as Offen. Apparently Wentworth worried over Gooch's rank as governor because civilian rank trumped military rank when it came to the colonials. Gooch wrote that, *"The General hearing and finding I was better received at Jamaica than himself* (by Jamaica's fellow governor, Edward Trelawny), *and being proud and stingy, tried all ways he could think of to let the people know, that though I was a Governor, yet he was the greater man, and indeed some orders he might have been spared, however, I submitted, and was all obedience, resolving that if military subordination was carried out to slavish subjection he should not tire of me."*

[13] Offen, 13, 14. The wording of Virginia's draft resolution: *"That it shall be lawful and may be lawful, to and for the justices of the peace in every county within this colony, or any three, or more of them, at any time before the first day of December next, within their several and respective counties, to raise and levy such able-bodied men as do not follow or exercise any lawful calling or employment, or have not some other lawful and sufficient support and maintenance, to serve his majesty, as soldiers, in the present war, against the Spaniards, in America."* – Laws of Virginia, May 1740.

[14] David Syrett, "The Raising of American Troops for Service in the West Indies during the War of Austrian Succession, 1740-1." *Historical Research*, Vol. 73, No. 180 (February 2000): 20-32; hereafter cited as Syrett. Although South Carolina did not officially raise men for the expedition some joined anyway, as troop rosters show a smattering of them in Gooch's 4th Battalion, under a Captain Gordon.

[15] Syrett, 25.

[16] Ibid, 26.

[17] Offen, 10-11. All of these officers were locally elected men, a dynamic that would impact the ability of the British to raise more levies later.

[18] Offen, 14, 15, 17. As far as Native Americans are concerned, there were at least thirty enlisted, as noted in this mention in a letter from Massachusetts and New Hampshire Governor Jonathan Belcher to British recruiting officer Col. William Blakeney in September 1740: *"30 odd of the company are Indians & very likely men...They are the King's natural born subjects, bred up in the English manner, are good shotsmen, and their having black hair & tawny faces don't at all disable them from being good soldiers."*

[19] Ibid, 26. As many as fifteen companies disbanded rather than trust the British to keep their word and commission their officers when they reached Jamaica: 6 from Massachusetts, 2 from Rhode Island, 5 from Connecticut, and 2 from North Carolina.

[20] Harding, 74.

[21] Offen, 31.

[22] Ibid, 12-13; Harding, 75, 66. To be fair, the expedition's commanders did not think highly of the men in their six British marine regiments, either. One description of them said they were, *"... raw new-raised undisciplined men, is a fact known to everyone, and the greatest part of the officers commanding them, either young Gentlemen, whose quality or interest entitled them to preferment, or abandoned wretches of the Town, whose prostitution had made them useful on some dirty occasion and by way of reward were provided for in the Army, but both of these sorts of Gentlemen had never seen any service, consequently knew not properly how to act or command."*

[23] Syrett, 27. The problem became bad enough that in April 1740, the governors were

authorized to draw funds from the accounts of the Navy Board in London to make good on recruiting bounties, as well as transport to Jamaica and victualling.

[24] Ibid, 29-30.

[25] Syrett, 30; Harding, *America*, 12. One North Carolinian, James Stafford, wrote of *"Sixty men who signed a round robin to Captain Robert Halton, one of the commanders of the North Carolina companies. The had been promised pay, bounty and clothes, but 'We are kept in such a manner we can bear it no longer, for Wee lye more like Hogs than Men . . . we are willing to serve his Majesty provided we have satisfaction and not if we must seek out for our selves, for night is so cold and our clothes so thin that we diser a Speedy Answer as witness our hands'."*

Running to Beat the Devil: Blockade Running and the Port at Wilmington
By Jack E. Fryar, Jr.

It was a quirk of geography that made the port at Wilmington, North Carolina such an integral part of the Confederacy's war effort during the blood-soaked years between 1861 and 1865. That does not negate the sheer audacity and heroism of the men who manned the sleek steamers carrying the goods so vital to the South's military and civilian survival during the Civil War. In that respect, if Richmond was the head of the Confederacy, then the blockade running port on the Cape Fear River and the three rail lines running from it were surely the heart and arteries it depended on for sustenance.

Despite the urgings of some Southerners, who exhibited remarkable foresight in advising that the South pay more attention to creating an infrastructure that would allow it to fend for itself should war with the North ever become a reality, most secessionists dismissed their warnings. The dominant thinking among the movers and shakers in the states below the Mason Dixon Line in those fiery days, before heated rhetoric was replaced by heated shot, was that cotton would be the instrument of the breakaway South's salvation. As the Industrial Revolution reached a fever pitch, turning the skies above British cities black with soot from factory smoke stacks, the demand for American cotton was incredibly high. Southerners were confident they could leverage the bounty of their fields into the arms and manufactured goods the Confederacy would need to fight a war. Not the least attractive aspect of this scenario was that the South could get what it wanted without having to make the capital investment required to build factories of their own. It was a flawed theory as it turns out, but in 1861 that had yet to be proved, and the need for ships and men to take Southern cotton out and bring the much needed manufactured goods in, fostered a time of danger and high adventure that was the ruin of some hardy entrepreneurs, but made millionaires of others.

The port at Wilmington was ground zero for much of the drama that was the hallmark of the days of blockade-running captains and the cordons of Union warships that tried to stop them. North Carolina's largest city[1] and principle port was uniquely suited to its role as a blockade running center. Situated twenty-eight miles up the Cape Fear River from the river's principle entrance at Old Inlet, Wilmington was the terminus of a system of riverine transportation that saw goods from inland farms and plantations floated down to the port aboard rafts, barges, and steamboats, to be loaded aboard coastal traders and transatlantic shipping for export to Northern and European markets. The Cape Fear River is the only such waterway in the state with direct access to the Atlantic Ocean, and stretches for 147 miles to the west-northwest, navigable all the way to Fayetteville. Ever since colonial days, the key to controlling North Carolina had been to control the Cape Fear River. When war broke out after Confederate guns shelled Major Robert Anderson's undermanned garrison in the harbor at Fort Sumter, South Carolina, Wilmington became a vital link in the block-

Wilmington riverfront at the time of the Civil War.

ade-running trade that author Stephen D. Wise has labeled "the lifeline of the Confederacy."[2]

The Blockade

As it became more and more apparent that hostilities were imminent, Union war planners[3] began preparing for the conflict that pundits on both sides assured the nation would be a short affair. The greatest strength of the Confederacy from a strategic standpoint may have been the advantage that having secure interior lines of communication would afford them. Southern planners prepared for a defensive war, in which Union troops would be forced to journey into Dixie to root out the heart and sinews of the rebellion. That meant Confederate troops would be fighting on their own land, close to their sources of material and moral support – a decided advantage in any military campaign. On the other hand, Union strategists like General Winfield Scott could read a map too, and knew that the real Achilles' Heel of the Southerners would be their lack of an industrial base to provide their armies with the things they needed to stay in the field.

To that end, Scott developed a plan to blockade Confederate seaports, choking off support for the Confederacy from the outside world. Before the war, the mostly agrarian South had a flourishing commercial relationship with manufacturers in Europe, who traded their products for cotton, the staple of Southern fields and farms.[4] Under the Scott proposal, Southern ports from Norfolk,

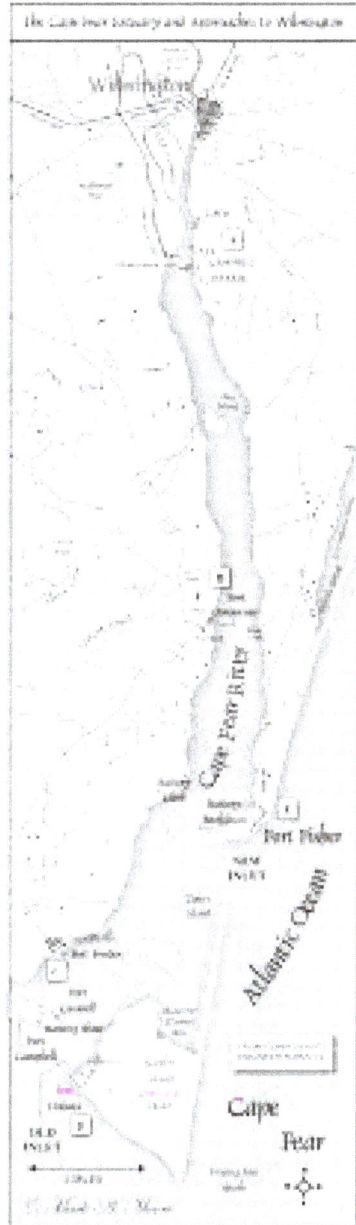

The Cape Fear River and its defenses in the Civil War, showing both entrances.

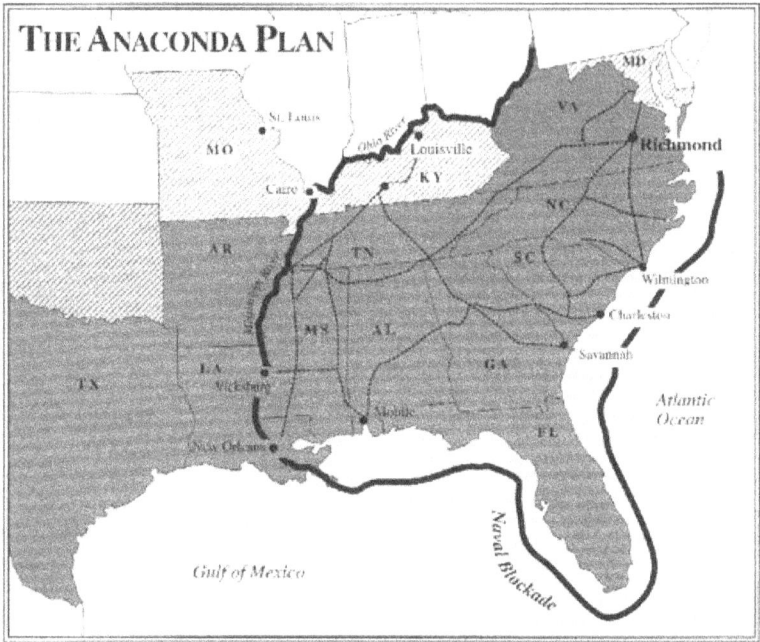

Winfield Scott's Anaconda Plan (top) was designed to strangle Confederate armies by cutting off imported manufactured goods from reachng them. The media was derisive of the plan, calling it "Scott's Great Snake" (below).

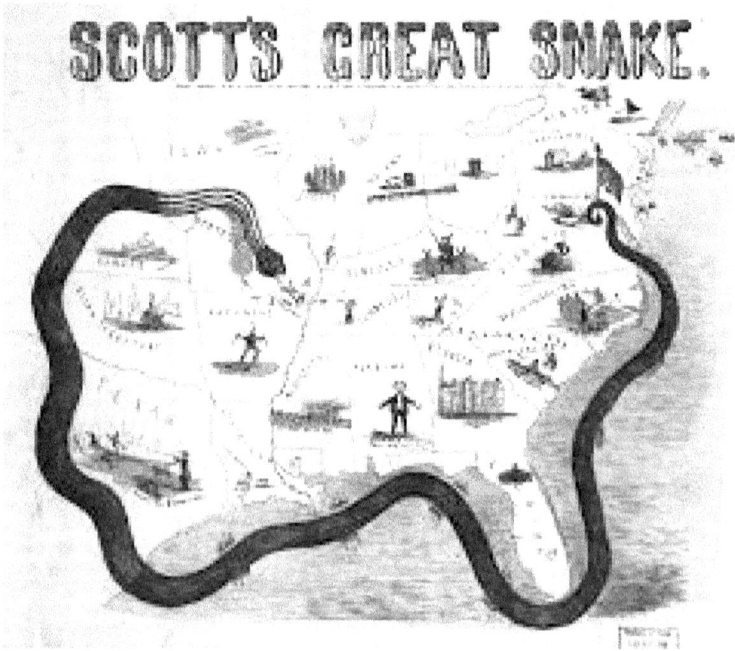

Virginia to Galveston, Texas, and up the Mississippi River would be shut down by warships of the United States Navy. Scott's theory was that if the entrepots of the Confederacy could be interdicted, then the Southern rebellion would whither on the vine. The theory was a sound one, except for a few niggling little details. Among the most prominent of them was the fact that the United States Navy was woefully inadequate to the task of blockading more than three thousand miles of Confederate coastline.[5] There, too, were concerns over how the blockade would be perceived by other powers that might look askance at the Lincoln administration's attempt to deprive them of a valuable trading partner. According to international law, for a blockade to be legal, it had to be effective. The Declaration of Paris of 1856 stated that a blockade had to have enough force on station to prevent access to the coast by the enemy.[6]

The concern was well founded. In Europe, Britain and France were confused as to what the Lincoln administration was doing with the blockade. Though the United States was not a signatory to the Declaration of Paris, it was widely accepted as the worldwide standard of how a blockade should be conducted. Under those rules, it was customary for a country to close its own ports in the case of an insurrection, but to blockade the ports of an enemy nation at war.[7] The Europeans could not decide which it was: either the South was in a state of insurrection (which meant the Lincoln administration should close the ports internally), or they were being blockaded (which could be construed to mean the Southern states were, indeed, a separate nation at war with the United States). In the latter case, trade with the Confederacy by neutral countries – and both France and England had declared their neutrality at the outbreak of hostilities in America – was legal under the Declaration of Paris.

For the more enterprising sorts on both sides of the Atlantic, the blockade announcement was greeted with enthusiasm. As Prohibition would prove decades later, goods usually see a spike in value once it becomes illegal to trade in them, and the blockade of the South during the Civil War had the same effect for those things carried into and out of Southern ports. Cotton, that staple of the Southern economy, sold for a comparative pittance in the Confederacy, but was valued many times higher once it hit markets in England.[8] Thomas Taylor, of the Anglo-Confederate Trading Company, asserted that his company's ship *Banshee* earned a profit of seven hundred percent on just eight successful trips through the blockade.[9] "Besides the inward freight of £50 a ton on the war material," he wrote, " I had earned by the tobacco ballast alone £7000, the freight for which had been paid at the rate of £70 a ton. But this was a trifle compared to the profit on the 500 odd bales of cotton we had on board, which was at least £50 per bale…No wonder I took kindly to my new calling…"[10] Those profits were enhanced after Charleston was effectively closed, when a cotton press was established across the Cape Fear River from Wilmington on the wharves of Eagles Island. By compressing, a bale of cotton could be reduced in size by two-thirds, allowing more to be loaded on a blockade-runner, thus increasing the earning potential of a single ship's cargo.[11]

The risks involved in getting those valuable bales from Point A along the Southern coast to Point B in Great Britain was such that a bold captain and crew could become wealthy men if their luck held. The world has never been short of those willing to test their luck for such rewards, and the Union blockade offered an unparalleled opportunity for such men between 1861 and 1865.[12] Others braved Union shot and shell out of a sense of duty, knowing that the fates of men on battlefields in Virginia, Maryland and Tennessee might depend on the steady flow of materials the blockade runners brought in to bolster Confederate arms.

On the Cape Fear and at other Southern ports, initial attempts to test the blockade with wooden sailing ships met with mediocre success. The days of wood-hulled ships spreading acres of canvas to the Trade Winds were coming to an end, in a time when James Webb's maritime steam engines were making iron-hulled warships faster and more mobile than the fastest clipper. Any successes they enjoyed at all were more a result of the U.S. Navy's haphazard blockade and sheer luck than anything else. Still, there was a profit motive involved for the crews of Union blockaders, too. Captured blockade-runners, once the ships and cargoes were sold by a United States prize court, could turn a nice bonus for the men who stood watch off Southern harbors.[13]

Once the navy's cordons off Southern ports began to have a bit more teeth to them,[14] it became obvious to even the most nostalgic observer that to beat the blockade, a new kind of ship would be required. By 1862 it was painfully obvious that the days of pitting just any old steamer against the Union blockade was a recipe for disaster, and to challenge it under sail was just plain laughable. To successfully run the blockade, light-drafted ships were the order of the day. Although screw propelled ships were used almost from the beginning, the dominant blockade-runner variety was the sidewheel steamer.

Shipyards in Liverpool and along Scotland's Clyde River were eager to meet the need, designing sleek, low-decked steamships powered by engines turning either side paddlewheels or single and double stern screws.[15] The Clyde steamers were especially prized ships, notable for their long iron hulls, narrow beams, powerful engines, and light drafts, all of which combined to give it tremendous speed and the ability to get into shallower harbors than other ships could.[16] Speed was of the essence for a blockade-runner, as it was her best defense against the guns of the Federal fleet trying to bring them to heel.[17] The average transit time between Wilmington and Nassau was fifty hours,[18] though some ships managed to beat that by a bit. Some ships also sported collapsible masts to accommodate sails that helped conserve valuable coal, for when the ships needed speed as they dashed into and out of blockaded ports. Others had collapsible smoke stacks, providing a trimmer silhouette for Yankee lookouts to spy against the sea's masking mists. The ships were painted a muted gray to better blend in with distant horizons, and carried no armaments, as piracy laws made armed resistance to a legal blockade grounds to treat the crews of offending ships as outside the protections of international maritime law.

Some blockade-runners used maritime law in a ruse to aid them in their enterprise. Sometimes a blockade-runner would hide its true purpose behind the flag of a neutral country, which under international law, should have offered it protection from search and seizure by Union warships. The *Bermuda* was one such ship that, in March 1862, was seized by the *USS Mercedita* off the Bahamas. Despite her captain's protests and ship's papers showing that the vessel was registered as British, a search uncovered evidence that the *Bermuda* had run the blockade into the Confederacy before, including instructions on how to beat the Union cordon at Charleston, S.C. The ship was taken to a Union port, where its capture was upheld by a Federal prize court.[19]

Manning the blockade-runners were a motley mix of Englishmen, Scots, Southerners, and others who thought the risks of being captured or killed in an encounter with Union naval vessels a fair tradeoff for the riches to be earned on a successful run.[20] Even Confederate States Navy crews carrying government cargoes were paid better than their fellows in the service, in recognition of the danger of the enterprise, and the importance of blockade-running to the Southern cause.[21] Some blockade-runner cap-

Blockade runners keep a watchful eye out for U.S. Navy warships cordining off the Southern coast at ports like Wilmington. Running the blockade required steely nerves and more than a little luck.

tains were officers of the Royal Navy who took leaves of absence in order to take advantage of the money to be made on just a few short runs across the Atlantic to Confederate ports like Wilmington. Others were Southerners who before the war had worked the coastal trade, ferrying cargoes and passengers along the American east coast, and who knew every nook and cranny of North Carolina's three hundred miles of coastline. Men with the special skills to negotiate tricky inlets and shoals around Southern ports earned premium pay as pilots who took over the ship's helm when a run through the Union cordon was imminent, and when the margins for error were razor thin. These Cape Fear pilots were prized crewmen aboard the blockade-running ships.[22]

One such pilot, Captain Thomas J. Lockwood, became a wealthy man from his exploits as a blockade-runner. Lockwood commanded several ships during the war, including the *Kate*, which delivered yellow fever to Wilmington in 1862. The wily captain braved the blockade in the ships *Theodora*, *Gordon*, and *Colonel Lamb* as well.[23]

Blockade-running was a dangerous trade, and the men who did it were perceived to be daredevils. In truth, virtually all of the advantages in their encounters with U.S. Navy ships lay with the blockade-runners. Speed (they were already under way when they came upon Federal ships blockading a port, while the Union vessels were either at anchor or just maintaining steerage to keep on station), and the element of surprise (the blockade-runner knew when they would make their dash for New or Old Inlet, while the naval vessels had to maintain a constant state of readiness to stop them – an alert level no one can keep up forever), put the odds in the blockade-runners' favor. Runners made their sprints for the Cape Fear at night, with little or no moon, often sailing past blockading Federals at virtual arms length, aiming for guiding lights placed by Confederates ashore to point them into the inlets' shipping channels.[24] Blockade running was dangerous, certainly, but on the whole a risk worth taking.

While John Fraser and Company was far and away the most successful of the firms engaged in blockade running, many of the competitors they inspired prospered, too. For instance, Charleston's Importing and Exporting Company of South Carolina recognized huge profits on the maiden voyage of the company's two ships, the *Edwin* and *Cecile*. Despite the schooner *Cecile*'s running aground and being lost on the April 1862 voyage, enough of her cargo was salvaged that, along with *Edwin*'s cargo, the company still paid a dividend of more than $92,000 to investors – after just one, semi-disastrous, voyage.[25]

Still, if the financial rewards were great for investors, so were the risks. The sponsors of the blockade-runner *Memphis*, loaded with Confederate munitions, ran aground in Charleston Harbor after successfully making it through a Union boarding off Nassau and beating the Union blockade off the South Carolina city. First, in a case of mistaken identity, the *Memphis* was shelled by Confederate troops at Fort Sumter. Then, when the sun came up, Federal warships picked up where the Southerners had left off. Surprisingly, not one shell hit her. The cargo was offloaded over the course of the day, and the *Memphis* floated off the bar. But a week later, on the return trip to Nassau, loaded with nearly 1500 bales of cotton, the blockade-runner was captured by the Union gunboat *Magnolia*. The *Memphis*' backers lost their entire investment.[26] Similar episodes played out on the Cape Fear too, with some men getting rich, others losing their shirts, and the waters around New and Old Inlets becoming littered with the carcasses of unsuccessful blockade-runners.

If Winfield Scott could look at a map and see the vulnerabilities of the Confederacy, the Southerners themselves could, too. It was obvious in Richmond that if the fledgling Confederate States were to depend on import and export to supply it with the things it needed to fight a war, then the places where that trade was centered would require defenses equal to the task of keeping the U.S. Navy at bay. When General William Henry Chase Whiting assumed command of the Cape Fear District after a less than smooth tour of duty in Virginia, he recognized immediately the advantages Nature had granted the port at Wilmington. Too far inland to be shelled by naval gunfire, and nearly thirty miles up from the two inlets that gave access to it via the Cape Fear River, Wilmington was an ideal port for blockade-runners. In addition to the traditional entryway at Old Inlet, the Cape Fear River had a second inlet four miles upstream at the tip of New Hanover County (what maps had called Federal Point, but which secessionists had renamed Confederate Point). There, a century earlier, a great storm that may or may not have been a hurricane opened an east-facing outlet to the Atlantic. Separating the two inlets was Frying Pan Shoals. That twenty-eight mile obstruction to navigation, running southeast off of today's Bald Head Island, had been creating problems for mariners since the sixteenth century. It was a great deal of the reason the southernmost region of the North Carolina coast was named Cape Fear in the first place.

Whiting, recognizing the natural defensive strength of the terrain along the coast and river, set about designing a series of forts and batteries that could add their round, bar, and heated shot to the array of obstacles placed in the way of the U.S. Navy by Mother Nature. The Confederate batteries defending the Cape Fear River and the port of Wilmington, the most imposing of which was the massive earthen fortification on Confederate Point dubbed Fort Fisher,[27] provided blockade-runners with a protective umbrella of three to five miles around each of the inlets. All a blockade-runner had to do was make it under the protection of those Confederate guns, and their safe arrival at Wilmington was all but assured. Whiting's defensive system included Fort Fisher and a gun battery on Zeke's Island to protect blockade-runners that opted for New Inlet,[28] while Forts Holmes, Caswell, and Battery Campbell flanked the Old Inlet entrance to the Cape Fear River. All told there were eleven major forts and batteries arrayed below Wilmington to protect the port town.

Distribution was also a key element of Wilmington's suitability as a blockade-running port. Three railroads extended to the north, south, and west from the port town in southeastern North Carolina, including the

Wilmington & Weldon Railroad, which had tracks running all the way to the Confederacy's capitol in Richmond. The Wilmington & Manchester took cargos to points south, while the Wilmington, Charlotte & Rutherford Railroad was the main artery of the distribution net from the port to points west.[29]

Initially the Federal blockade of the Cape Fear consisted of one lonely warship, *USS Daylight*, which took station off the cape in the summer of 1861. Blockade-runners found it less than intimidating.[30] The Union ships were poorly designed for the task of closing off the Cape Fear, and with only one ship available for the job, the *Daylight* was hopelessly outclassed.[31] A massive effort to build the number of ships on the roles of the U.S. Navy was undertaken, with agents for the Federal government building, buying and converting hulls as fast they could get them into Northern shipyards. It was in this way that the Union navy redressed the shortage of ships available for blockade duty. But for the short term, the ships of the U.S. Navy tasked with closing the ports of the Confederacy were simply too few for the job. In fact, some of them posed a bigger threat to their own crews than they did to the blockade-runners.[32]

Many times, captured blockade-runners were sent to Northern shipyards and refitted as warships, then sent back to help close off the very

A 1859 sketch of USS Daylight, for a time the lone warship blockading the Cpae Fear River.

ports they had been captured off of. The growing numbers of Union ships added off Southern coasts in this manner eventually had a telling effect on the success of blockade-runners in completing their journeys. At Cape Fear, the blockade assumed a defense in depth posture, with three pickets of Federal warships arrayed around New and Old Inlets at staggered distances. Shallow-draft gunboats patrolled nearest the breakers along the shore, while heavier ships stood guard in deeper water. None ventured too close to the forty-seven large bore cannon mounted in the traverses of Fort Fisher, or its sister forts elsewhere along the Cape Fear.

The other element of the equation that made Cape Fear the destination of choice for blockade-runners was its proximity to neutral ports at Nassau, Bahamas and St. George in Bermuda. Both island ports became centers for blockade-running, as British ships carrying manufactured goods off-loaded their cargoes to waiting runners, replacing the lost ballast with bales of Southern cotton.

Destinations

Cape Fear blockade-runners generally had three destinations when they weighed anchor, depending on their starting point. If outbound from Wilmington, North Carolina, their target would usually have been either St. George, Bermuda or Nassau in the Bahamas. Both were on British-held islands in the Caribbean, and thus outside the jurisdiction of the U.S. Navy. Their proximity to the Cape Fear also made them highly attractive to the captains who braved the blockade twice on each run.

The two island starting points were ideally situated for the blockade-running trade, and Nassau, in the words of British blockade-runner Thomas Taylor, was "par excellence" the best base for approaching Southern ports along the east coast,[33] including Wilmington. In addition to top-notch facilities for handling cargoes, the Bahamas island chain also stretched for a hundred miles or more through the Caribbean in the direction of the Confederate coast, offering blockade-runners just that much more protection from the U.S. Navy's blue water blockading squadron.[34]

If starting out for the run back to the Confederacy, the options were several: Charleston (S.C.), Savannah (GA), or Wilmington among them. But of the options open to them, the port at Wilmington was far and away the most attractive to blockade-runners – at least, by 1863.[35] It was the closest port from the Caribbean,[36] it had an unparalleled system of defenses to keep Federal blockaders at bay, and its rail lines made transferring

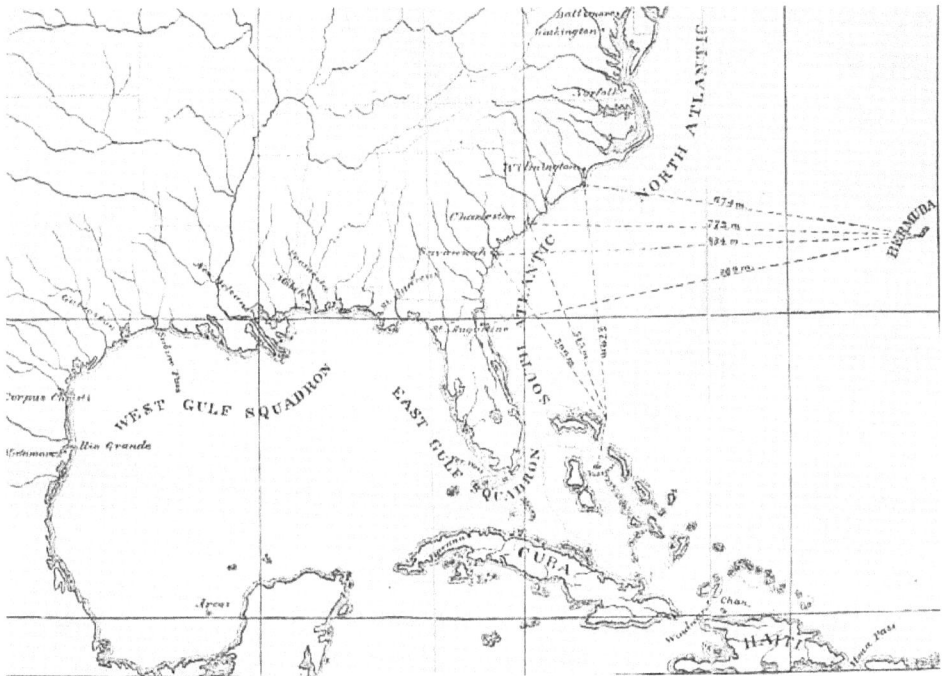

The port at Wilmington became a preferred destination for blockade runners.

the goods the blockade-runners carried much simpler than if they offload-ed at ports further south along the Confederate coast. But runners had to always be on the lookout for ships flying the ensign of the United States.[37]

Blockade-runner Thomas E. Taylor describes the attributes that made Wilmington a favorite port: "Though furthest from Nassau, it was nearest to headquarters at Richmond, and from its situation was very difficult to watch effectively. It was here, moreover, that my firm had established its agency as soon as they had resolved to take up the block-ade-running business. The town itself lies some sixteen miles up the Cape Fear River, which falls into the ocean at a point where the coast forms the sharp salient angle from which the river takes its name. Off its mouth lies a delta, known as Smith's Island, which not only emphasizes the obnox-ious formation of the coast but also divides the approach to the port into two widely separated channels, so that in order to guard the approach to it, a blockading force is compelled to divide into two squadrons.

"At one entrance of the river lies Fort Fisher, a work so powerful that the blockaders instead of lying in the estuary were obliged to form roughly a semicircle out of range of its guns, and the falling away of the coast on either side of the entrance further increased the extent of the ground they had to cover."

A favorite tactic was to steam north of the Cape Fear, then turn south and hug the shallows off the beach to limit exposure to blockading federals.

In general, manufactured goods from England and other European countries doing business with the Confederacy were shipped to Great Britain's ports in the Caribbean, where they would be exchanged for cotton brought from the South by the fast ships that challenged the Union blockade. Then those same blockade-runners would load the manufactured goods into their holds, put about, and begin the return trip to Wilmington.

Getting into port at Bermuda and Nassau was not always the end of the danger to the blockade-runners and their crews. Union warships maintained at least a token patrol along the shipping lanes surrounding the islands in an attempt to catch the blockade-runners as they left the "safe" waters of neutral territory and began the run back to the American coast. Union diplomats ashore supported this effort by doing what they could to interdict Confederate commerce, and supplying intelligence to the U.S. Navy regarding the comings and goings of the blockade-runners.

Getting into Wilmington was no cakewalk either. The Federal cordon off the Cape Fear coast consisted of three rings of warships that a blockade-runner had to penetrate to reach the safety of either New or Old Inlets. Thomas E. Taylor described one favorite means of accomplishing that goal: "There were of course many different plans of getting in, but at this time the favorite dodge was to run up some fifteen or twenty miles to the north of Cape Fear, so as to go around the northernmost of the blockaders, instead of dashing right through the inner squadron; then to creep down close to the surf till the river was reached."[38]

Wilmington: N.C.'s Civil War Melting Pot (or maybe cesspool)

Before, during and after the Civil War, Wilmington had the distinction of being North Carolina's largest town, and the coming of hostilities with the North made it even more so. The town population boomed during the war years, as the normal demographic of white citizens, free blacks and slaves exploded due to an influx of soldiers, sailors, speculators and assorted others brought to the banks of the Cape Fear River on war business or else seeking to profit from it.

During the war, the resources of the town were stretched to the breaking point. Food was scarce, and the residents were almost entirely dependent on the cargoes brought in by the fast, sleek blockade-runners that stacked the harbor along the Wilmington waterfront. The difficulty people had securing even the most common of goods made the arrival of the blockade-flaunting runners an event. "Wilmington was already sadly pinched and war-worn," Thomas Taylor wrote in his memoirs. "There was never too much to eat and drink there, and the commonest luxuries were almost things of the past; so when it became known that there was practically open house on board the *Banshee* (Taylor's blockade-running ship) friends flocked to her."

Decent citizens, or at least those who could afford to, abandoned Wilmington to the less than upstanding elements that seemed to take over the port and its environs. People like Dr. John Dillard Bellamy moved their families to country estates, away from the corrosive elements in town that made it unsafe (or at least, unsavory).[39] On almost a daily basis, newspapers of the day relate incidents of violence, vice, and lawlessness that made Wilmington resemble a Wild West cow town more than a genteel Southern metropolis.

Prostitution, in a time-honored tradition stretching back to the first military camps of ancient times, accompanied the influx of soldiers to the town. Murders fueled by alcohol in the many saloons of the Dry Pond and Paddy's Hollow sections of Wilmington were rampant, and general lawlessness overwhelmed the abilities of the local constabulary to prevent it.[40] Wilmington became an armed camp with so many Confederate soldiers within its boundaries, and the rough men who debarked from visiting blockade-runners added to a volatile mix that on several occasions burst into open flames threatening the public peace.[41]

The town was also a center of commerce. British and American companies in the shipping trades established offices in Wilmington to better administer their holdings engaged in the illicit trips to and from the North Carolina port on the Cape Fear River. This was especially true after Morris Island fell to Federals and allowed Union guns to blanket the entrance to Charleston Harbor in 1863. Most blockade-running firms shifted their operations to the North Carolina port town at that point.[42] At Wilmington, a blockade-runner could pick up and drop off cargoes, get needed repairs done at competing shipyards owned by Benjamin Beery[43] and James Cassidey, and offer an enjoyable bit of shore leave to jittery crews who many times had just braved a gauntlet of Union shot and shell. The town boasted a mile of warehouses, shipyards, and docking facilities along the waterfront and across the river at Eagles Island.[44]

Wilmington was especially attractive to Josiah Gorgas, who headed the Ordnance Bureau for the Confederacy. Gorgas established a depot there that took military supplies from blockade-runners and distributed them to other depots in Richmond and Augusta, Georgia. From there, the arms and munitions were sent to Southern armies fighting throughout the war's theaters of operations.[45]

A large proportion of the town's wartime population was made up of slaves, who frequently took advantage of the commotion that was a singular feature of Wilmington from 1861-1865 to make their escapes from the their chattel existences. Benjamin Gould led one such notable exodus from the foot of Orange Street in September 1862, when he and seven other slaves stole a boat and rowed the length of the Cape Fear River in one night, to be taken aboard the *USS Cambridge* of the squadron blockading the Cape Fear at Old Inlet.[46] Others resorted to becoming stowaways aboard blockade-runners leaving Wilmington for British ports, where slavery was outlawed.[47]

The Last Lifeline

Wilmington, thanks to the Cape Fear's unique geography and more pressing needs for Union resources elsewhere in the war effort, ultimately became the last open port of the Confederacy. Gen. Robert E. Lee plainly declared that his ability to keep his Army of Northern Virginia in the field depended entirely on the continued flow of blockade-runner borne cargoes through the port.[48]

That supply line was terminated when, after an aborted attempt to reduce Fort Fisher on Christmas Eve, 1864, Federal forces under the command of General Alfred Terry and Admiral David Dixon Porter returned in mid-January for a second go at what had come to be known as the "Malakof of the South." A little over a month after Fort Fisher fell on January 15, 1865, those same forces converged on Wilmington and ended the flow of war materials from the Cape Fear.

Blockade running ended at Cape Fear with the fall of Wilmington. Though some die hard captains continued to try beating Union cordons by pulling into other small, obscure ports along the Gulf Coast, the trade ceased to exist as a profitable enterprise after Wilmington was in the hands of Lincoln's bluecoats. Yet while it existed, blockade-running was a dangerous, profitable, and utterly necessary trade that facilitated Southern war efforts, made many men rich, made some men paupers and prisoners, and became the source for countless additions to the stories and legends of Wilmington and the Cape Fear.

Endnotes

[1] Carr, Dawson. *Gray Phantoms of the Cape Fear: Running the Civil War Blockade.* Winston-Salem: John F. Blair, Publisher, 1998, p. 128. According to the 1860 census, Wilmington's population totaled 9552, including 4400 free blacks and slaves.

[2] Stephen R. Wise. *Lifeline of the Confederacy: Blockade Running During the Civil War.* (Columbia: University of South Carolina Press, 1988).

[3] Robert M. Browning, Jr. *From Cape Charles to Cape Fear: The North Atlantic Blockading Squadron during the Civil War* (Tuscaloosa: University of Alabama Press, 1993), p. 8. Navy Secretary Gideon Welles directed the creation of a Blockade Strategy Board to devise the scheme of the Union effort to close Southern ports. The idea for the board originated with the superintendant of the United States Coast Survey, A.D. Bache, who had himself served in the Cape Fear sounding the river's entrances before the war.

[4] Chris E. Fonvielle, Jr. *The Wilmington Campaign: Last Rays of Departing Hope.* (Campbell (CA): Savas Publishing, 1997) p. 5. The Lincoln administration hoped interrupting the flow of goods from Europe would choke out the rebellion before it had a chance to blossom into a protracted conflict.

[5] Ibid, p. 6. Of the U.S. Navy's ninety ships in the spring of 1861, only forty-two of them were on active commission, and only twelve of those were actually in American waters. The rest were showing the flag on stations elsewhere around the globe. That force had grown to 671 ships by 1865.

[6] Ibid, p. 7. "Our 'effective' blockaded is a perfect farce," declared William Keeler of the *USS Florida* on station off Wilmington. "I believe there is scarcely a night passes but what there are some vessels of some kind run out or in." Keeler's complaint underscores the difficulty of the Union navy to mount an effective blockade.

[7] Dawson Carr. *Gray Phantoms of the Cape Fear: Running the Civil War Blockade,* (Winston-Salem: John F. Blair, Publisher, 1998), p. 10.

Ibid, p. 7. Cotton sold for three to eight cents a pound brought as much as eighty cents a pound in England. One trip for a blockade-runner loaded with one thousand bales of the white fiber could generate a profit of $250,000 for its owners and investors.

[8] Fonvielle, *The Wilmington Campaign: Last Rays of Departing Hope*, p. 7.

[9] Thomas E. Taylor. *Running the Blockade: A Personal Narrative of Adventures, Risks, and Escapes During the American Civil War*. (London: John Murray, 1912), p. 69.

[10] Carr, *Gray Phantoms of the Cape Fear*, p. 140.

[11] Fonvielle, *The Wilmington Campaign: Last Rays of Departing Hope*, p. 10. By the U.S. Navy's own estimation, the blockaders had captured 1,133 blockade-runners by the end of the war, and destroyed another 335 more. But the runners who made for the ports at Wilmington and Charleston, S.C. enjoyed an eighty-four percent success rate.

[12] Browning, *From Cape Charles to Cape Fear: The North Atlantic Blockading Squadron during the Civil War*, pp. 218-219. The crew of the *USS Florida*, after capturing the Nassau blockade-runner *Calypso*, split a purse of $37,000 among themselves.

[13] Fonvielle, *The Wilmington Campaign: Last Rays of Departing Hope*, p. 12. Those teeth started being more effective when the blockading fleet was reorganized into two commands: the Atlantic Blockading Squadron and the Gulf Blockading Squadron. These two larger commands subdivided into four smaller groups. It was the North Atlantic Blockading Squadron that was tasked with closing the port at Wilmington, N.C.

[14] Carr, *Gray Phantoms of the Cape Fear*, p. 101. In Liverpool, the firms of William C. Miller and Sons, John Laird and Sons, and Jones, Quiggin and Company were among those that did a brisk business laying keels for ships that serviced the needs of the South.

[15] Wise, *Lifeline of the Confederacy*, p. 108.

Ibid, p. 102. To that end, when twin-screw steamers were introduced, they found an eager market among the Confederate government and blockade-running firms. Twin screws allowed a ship more speed and maneuverability – including the ability to turn on a dime.

[16] Taylor. *Running the Blockade: A Personal Narrative of Adventures, Risks, and Escapes During the American Civil War*, p. 174.

[17] Wise, *Lifeline of the Confederacy*, p. 66.

[18] Carr, *Gray Phantoms of the Cape Fear*, p. 86. A seaman could make as much as $25 per day (on what were sometimes ten-day voyages). The captain of the vessel could earn $5000, the pilot from $3000 to $4000 (at least half paid in gold). In addition, the captains and officers were allowed to carry a few items of their own which they could sell for profit - for instance, a bale of cotton sold in Nassau, whose proceeds went to buying things in short supply in the Confederacy that could be sold in Wilmington on the return to town.

[19] Wise, *Lifeline of the Confederacy*, P. 98.

[20] Taylor. *Running the Blockade: A Personal Narrative of Adventures, Risks, and Escapes During the American Civil War*, p. 117. Taylor, making the run aboard the ship *Night Hawk* with a green captain at the helm, wrote, "What I would have given for our trusty Tom Burroughs."

[21] William Morrison Robinson, Jr. *The Confederate Privateers* (Columbia: University of South Carolina Press, 1990), p. 255.

[22] Wise, *Lifeline of the Confederacy*, p. 110.

[23] Wise, *Lifeline of the Confederacy*, p. 69.

[24] Ibid, pp. 71-72.

[25] Chris E. Fonvielle, Jr. *The Wilmington Campaign: Last Rays of Departing Hope*.

(Campbell (CA): Savas Publishing, 1997) p. 2. By 1863, Fort Fisher had grown from little more than a sand dune with a gun or two, to the most powerful seacoast fortification in the Confederacy.

[26] Claude V. Jackson, III. *The Big Book of the Cape Fear River* (Wilmington: Dram Tree Books, 2008), p. 56. New Inlet was formed by a "great storm" that may have been a hurricane in 1761, at the southern tip of Federal Point (just south of where Fort Fisher would be located a century later).

[27] Wise, *Lifeline of the Confederacy*, p. 16.

[28] Carr. *Gray Phantoms of the Cape Fear: Running the Civil War Blockade*, p. 9. Early in the blockade, Union warships managed to capture only one in every fourteen blockade-runners that challenged their cordon.

[29] Ibid, p. 22. On *Daylight*'s first day on station at New Inlet, they spotted a small craft making for open sea at Old Inlet. The federals took up the chase, making for the far end of Frying Pan Shoals to try and run the vessel down. But when a lookout glanced behind them and saw a bevy of ships dashing out of the recently abandoned New Inlet, they realized the futility of their mission.

[30] Carr. *Gray Phantoms of the Cape Fear: Running the Civil War Blockade*, p. 24. *USS Penobscot* was in such bad shape that her commanding officer pleaded to be allowed to travel back to Norfolk for repairs. The ship had gaps in the deck so large that when it rained, sand from scrubbing the planks mixed with the water to drizzle mud on the men below decks. Her one Dahlgren gun was completely unusable, the head almost was, and the galley had been condemned months earlier. As well, a grounding accident months before had left the ship dangerously unseaworthy in bad weather.

[31] Wise, *Lifeline of the Confederacy*, p. 95. St. George was considered less favorably than Nassau because it was more than a hundred miles farther from the port at Wilmington than the Bahamian port, and two hundred miles from Charleston (see note 32).

[32] Thomas E. Taylor. *Running the Blockade: A Personal Narrative of Adventures, Risks, and Escapes During the American Civil War*. (London: John Murray, 1912), p. 24. Territorial waters of the Bahamas afforded a blockade-runner neutral water passage up to within fifty miles of the American coast.

[33] Carr. *Gray Phantoms of the Cape Fear: Running the Civil War Blockade*. P. 15. Charleston, S.C. was the dominant east coast port for blockade-runners until the build-up of Federal ships made it too risky for ships to attempt.

[34] Fonvielle, *The Wilmington Campaign: Last Rays of Departing Hope*, p. 20. From Wilmington to Nassau: 570 miles; from Wilmington to Bermuda: 674 miles.

[35] Thomas E. Taylor. *Running the Blockade: A Personal Narrative of Adventures, Risks, and Escapes During the American Civil War*, pp. 44-46.

[36] Thomas E. Taylor. *Running the Blockade. A Personal Narrative of Adventures, Risks, and Escapes During the American Civil War*, pp. 49-50.

[37] Taylor. *Running the Blockade: A Personal Narrative of Adventures, Risks, and Escapes During the American Civil War*, p. 65.

[38] Fonvielle, *The Wilmington Campaign: Last Rays of Departing Hope*, pp. 18-19. "Wilmington is a perfect sink of iniquity," said one Confederate soldier. Another confessed he was "almost afraid to walk the streets from the passport office to quarters after 9 o'clock at night."

[39] Ibid, p. 19. On September 10, 1863, drunken soldiers from Texas assigned to John

Hood's division beat three local police officers almost to death in Paddy's Hollow, Wilmington's "red light district."

[40] Ibid, p. 19. To try to curb the possibility of trouble, Wilmington military and civic leaders passed rules restricting blockade-runner crews to their ships after sundown, but plenty of them managed to sneak off anyway.

[41] Wise, *Lifeline of the Confederacy*, p. 127.

[42] Claude V. Jackson, III. *The Big Book of the Cape Fear River* (Wilmington: Dram Tree Books, 2008), pp. 205-206. Benjamin and William Beery began producing ships for the Confederacy in 1861, at their shipyard (formerly the Cape Fear Marine Railway) that became known as the Confederate Shipyard. Their first job was converting the old steam tug *Mariner* into a privateer. They also built the ironclad *CSS North Carolina*, among other vessels.

[43] Fonvielle, *The Wilmington Campaign: Last Rays of Departing Hope*, pg. 4.

[44] Wise, *Lifeline of the Confederacy*, p. 128.

[45] William B. Gould IV. *Diary of a Contraband: The Civil War Passage of a Black Sailor* (Stanford: Stanford University Press, 2002), p. 15.

[46] Thomas E. Taylor. *Running the Blockade: A Personal Narrative of Adventures, Risks, and Escapes During the American Civil War*, p. 80. Taylor relates the story of one such stowaway discovered when the *Banshee* reached Nassau, an "unfortunate slave who had been standing wedged between two bales for at least forty-eight hours, and within three feet of whom I had unconsciously been sleeping on the cotton bales during the last two nights before putting to sea. He received a great ovation on our landing him at Nassau, though his freedom cost us $4000 on our return to Wilmington, this being what he was valued at."

[47] Ibid, p. 13. A single blockade-runner's shipment was sufficient to feed, clothe and arm an entire infantry regiment for one month. Because of the blockade-runners, no Confederate soldiers ever lost a fight because of a lack of armaments, ammo, or supplies.

Hardscrabble Lives: North Carolina's Sharecroppers Before and During the Great Depression
By Jack E. Fryar, Jr.

The end of the Civil War changed North Carolina. Gone were the large pools of enslaved labor that made the South's plantation economy viable. To replace it, landowners desperate to stave off ruin were forced to adopt new strategies in order to turn a profit. Plantations were sold off and subdivided. Poor farmers – both black and white – became tenants on other men's land, trading sweat equity for meager livings and leaky roofs. The precarious existence of North Carolina sharecroppers and tenant farmers was already little more than subsistence living in the decades between 1865 and 1929, but the coming of the Great Depression turned the lives of sharecropper families into a losing game that few could win. Only Franklin Delano Roosevelt's New Deal initiatives provided any sort of lifeline for North Carolinians trapped in the vicious poverty of sharecropping.

The end of the Civil War left large landowners bereft of the coerced labor that made large-scale farming economically feasible in the antebellum period. Given the wildly fluctuating prices of cotton (which, along with tobacco, was the dominant Southern crop), paying wage laborers to do the same tasks that slaves performed in years past was just not a workable solution. For a while, gang labor provided a reasonable facsimile of a labor force reminiscent of slave days, when large numbers of usually related freed blacks would contract with landowners to work plantation lands. But the work gang model foundered when competing farm owners began hiring away laborers from their current employers, leaving jobs half finished. Disenchantment with the work gang system grew out of dissatisfaction on the part of landowners with intra-season competition for laborers, and on the part of workers who were less than satisfied with the received fruits of their labors.[1] To curb this, Southern states began enacting black codes, or laws designed to prevent competition for labor.[2] But black codes ultimately proved ineffective in controlling labor mobility. By the turn of the century, farm workers were habitually moving from farm to farm.[3] A new system was needed to save Southern agriculture.

For a time gang labor replaced slaves in North Carolina's agrarian economy.

North Carolina Governor Thomas W. Bickett once described the crop-lien system as "the boll weevil of North Carolina," a sentiment echoed in a report generated by the N.C. Department of Agriculture in 1922.[4] In 1880, one in four farmers nationally were tenants on someone else's land. By 1922, that number had grown to two in five, and in North Carolina the ratio was even higher. The report of the N.C. Department of Agriculture asserted that while landlords and owner-operators suffered under the crop-lien and chattel system in place at the time, "…landless farmers (were) farming under this handicap in three times as great numbers as are the landed."[5]

Under the crop-lien system, landowners managed to create a labor model that closely mimicked slavery. One North Carolina contract from the Tar River area stipulated that workers would work from sun up to sun down, except on Sundays, and undertake no night work except as needed. Assemblies and visits from undesirable persons were forbidden (likely out of fear of union organizers). Workers were compensated with housing (in varying states of repair), permission to collect firewood, the right to keep one pig, a few chickens, and have a small personal garden. Bacon and cornmeal were provided based on the perceived worth of the laborer. Sixteen dollars a month was paid to the most productive, happy, deferential, and obedient worker. While the crop-lien system may not have been evil in and of itself, the exploitative nature of its implementation often made it so.[6]

The North Carolina state legislature passed the County Government Law and the Landlord and Tenant Acts of 1876 to codify the return of power to planters at the local level.[7] The laws allowed planters to use state and local law to insulate themselves from pressures to reform.[8] The laws ushered in a return to slavery in all but name. Landowners did not own the people who worked their fields, but they did control their wages, the houses they lived in, and the conditions they worked under. They controlled the workers' access to the necessities of life. In the event of non-compliance, they had the legal right to evict them from their homes and deprive them of their jobs.[9]

N.C. Governor Thomas W. Bickett

In North Carolina, tenant-plantations typically consisted of five tenants and their families, who worked an average of 570 acres.[10] Contracts between landowners and those who were hired to work their fields usually called for payment in shares of the crop (69%), or for standing wages (23%).[11] Planters sought to avoid the development of a labor market system, in which the demand for workers dictated wages. Black codes helped in this by limiting black voting rights, their ability to own property, or to be properly represented in the legal system. Debt peonage became a significant part of the economic side of Jim Crow, in which poor black tenant farmers had no recourse but to buy their necessities from landlords at inflated prices and with usurious interest rates.[12]

During Reconstruction and the years between 1880 and 1900, Southerners were slower to recover from the devastation of the war than other parts of the nation.[13] The percentage of owner-operated farms in the South decreased from sixty-four percent to fifty percent between 1880 and 1910. Two decades before the turn of the twentieth century, twelve percent of Southern farms were rented and twenty-four percent were sharecropped. By 1910, that number had risen to fifteen percent and thirty-five percent respectively.[14] The increase in farmers working land they did not own was a reflection of the lack of credit and employment options in the South. For many, farming was the only employment available to them. This led to the establishment of what has been termed the "agricultural ladder" system of farm economics, in which poor men started out working as wage laborers, tenants, or sharecroppers on the lands of wealthier men. In theory, as time progressed and they were able to climb the rungs of the ladder, these poor laborers would eventually come to be small landowners in their own right. The theory and the practice too often turned out to be very different things.

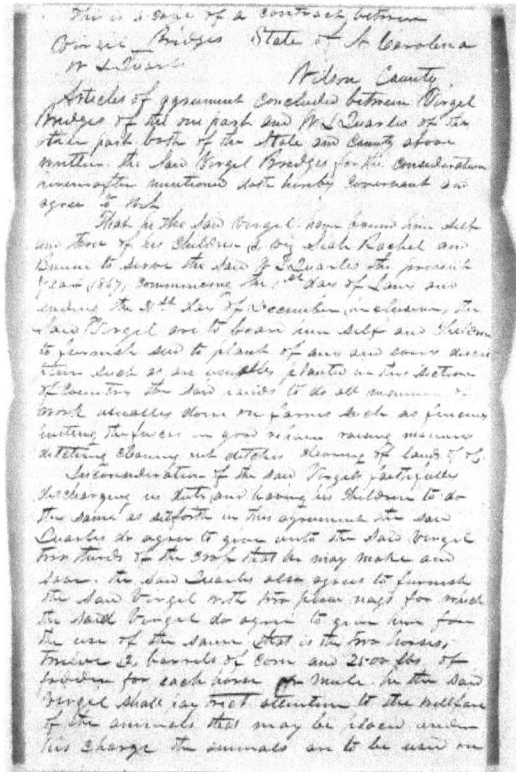

Sharecropping contracts like this one from Wilson County were one sided affairs that took advantage of poor N.C. farmers.

There were five rungs on the South's agricultural ladder. At the top of the ladder were the small and large landowners. At the bottom were wage laborers, men so poor the only asset they had was the sweat of their

The term "sharecropper" likely originated in the old naval stores industry built around the byproducts harvested from North Carolina's abundant longleaf pine trees.

brow. Wage laborers worked for landowners in return for a cash payday. Sharecroppers, a step above wage laborers, accounted for roughly fifteen percent of both black and white farmers in the South. The term sharecropper is likely linked to the turpentine industry of the American southeast that developed in the 1830s.[15] Legally, sharecroppers were wage workers paid with a share of the crop that they could sell for themselves at the best price they could find. Next came tenant farmers. Tenants came in two varieties: share tenants or cash tenants. Share tenants paid a portion of the crop yield to the landlord for use of the land (essentially the reverse of a sharecropper). Cash tenants rented land from the owner with a cash payment, and kept the yields of the land for themselves.[16]

Sharecropping expanded because the post-bellum South had few sources of credit that farmers with little or no collateral could call on to secure the funds needed to own and operate their own farms. Hard currency was scarce in the states of the old Confederacy, and banks and other lending institutions never really existed there in the first place. The depression of the cotton market retarded wages for laborers, too. Coupled with the lack of credit sources, sharecropping became a means to an end for Southern farmers. The common thread in North Carolina sharecropping contracts was the mutual interest of both the landowner and the cropper in the efficiency of the farming operation. Sharecropping offered workers a percentage of the crops they grew, and thus provided incentive to boost that production as much as possible. Because their profit depended on the crop yield, sharecroppers, in theory, were more productive than wage laborers.[17]

The 142nd Psalm laments, "In the path where I walk they have hidden a trap for me."[18] North Carolina sharecroppers might have thought the Biblical warning applied specifically to them. While the theory of the agricultural ladder seemed dandy, the practice suffered under the weight of an economy and society that could not provide the resources that participants needed to be successful. Most farmers worked lands too small to produce enough yield to allow them an adequate standard of living in a world that was based more and more on a commercial/capitalist model. The earnings they could make were simply not enough to provide the capital needed for larger operations, and sources of credit for borrowing did not exist either. The end of World War I saw the United States flooded with a host of doughboys that needed work that did not exist in the cities. The scarcity of factory work in urban centers resulted in a reverse migration back to rural climes. The root of the problem for farmers was that too many people sought a piece of a Southern agricultural pie that was already too small.[19]

To lessen the need for credit or assistance from outside sources, most sharecroppers and small farmers produced what they could for their

Soldiers returning from World War I complicated a labor market that already had too few jobs.

own consumption. In Gaston County, N.C., for instance, more than half the farmers there produced eighty-two percent of all the family food on the same farm they worked between 1913 and 1914. But sharecroppers still spent up to fifty percent of their meager incomes on store-bought food, evidence that just because sharecroppers were poor did not mean they desired modern conveniences any less than anyone else.[20]

The chief impediment to Southern farmers' ability to achieve some semblance of a modern lifestyle was the lack of capital. Money was available through three main sources: savings or earnings, borrowing, or via inheritance or marriage.[21] By the turn of the twentieth century, there were a million farmers in the South whose production was valued at less than $250 per year. For those people, their chief concern was not building a nest egg to grown the family farming concern. Their lives were consumed with trying to simply keep body and soul together.[22]

Securing credit was made even more difficult because North Carolina sharecroppers, like their brethren throughout the South, had little in the way of collateral to secure a loan. Sources of commercial and personal loans like banks were few and far between in the South, leaving only landowners and merchants as sources of capital for the farm families who worked the land. Sharecroppers had no choice but to borrow money for short-term living and operating expenses using their share of crops in the ground to secure the loan, at interest rates of twenty to thirty percent. Saving for a brighter future was simply not possible under such conditions. Between 1880 and the Great Depression, farming became family trades. When sons reached maturity, or daughters married, they moved off to farms of their own. By 1900, nearly forty percent of Southern farmers ran little more than subsistence operations, and black farm income was markedly less than that of whites.[23]

Perhaps the only thing worse than being a sharecropper in the South was being a black sharecropper there. For black sharecroppers like Georgia's Ned Cobb, seventy-five years of tilling the earth had been made infinitely more difficult by white arrogance, threats, abuse, and avarice. "*All* God's dangers ain't a white man," he told one interviewer, but then qualified the statement by allowing that a good many of them were. White landlords often treated black tenants and sharecroppers with a double standard, protecting them from local authorities, while at the same time trying to shortchange them at settlement time. "Every landlord I ever had dealings with tried to euchre me," Cobb declared. Cobb offered that treatment as explanation (and probably a lament) for why young people raised on Southern farms were often quick to quit the fields once they came of age.

"They has once in days past made crops under the white man's administration and didn't get nothing out of it," Cobb explained. "He don't want to farm today regardless to what he could make out there; he don't want to plow no mule – that was his bondage and he is turning away from it. He huntin' for a public job, leavin' the possession of the earth to the white man."[24]

While the years after 1880 saw more and more whites enter into sharecropping, in the plantation states blacks outnumbered white croppers by a margin of three to one for much of the early twentieth century. Both races depended on credit extended by the landowner for much of the crop year. Blacks and whites both were forced by necessity to shop in commissaries and stores owned by their landlords. When time came to settle up after the crop had been sold, blacks were totally at the mercy of the landowner, who calculated not just the crop costs, but also kept the books relating to monies owed for commissary purchases. Black croppers simply had to accept what they were told they owed. In this way, sharecropping was also a racial and class system, as well as an economic one.[25]

Sharecropping was infintely worse if you were Black.

The racial/class nature of sharecropping is evident in the preference most landowners had for black tenants. During the 1920s and 1930s, during the mass migration of African-Americans from the South to Northern urban centers, landowners became frustrated at the outflow of their preferred laborers. "A white tenant has his notions of running a farm and is less amenable to suggestions," said North Carolina landowner Henry Calhoon Weathers. "I can say…'Go hitch up a horse' when I want a horse hitched…to a Negro…and I can't to a white man. One white tenant…was such a know-it-all I soon had to get rid of him. He was a good farmer, it's true, but right or wrong the landlord should govern…Negroes are more loyal."[26]

Loyal or not, Southern blacks were not ignorant to the life that sharecropping led to. As sixty-two-year-old Jim Parker of North Carolina put it in 1939, "My daddy, after freedom, spent his life sharecroppin', movin' round from place to place, and died not ownin' a foot o' ground. I aimed to do better'n that, but it looks like I ain't made much improvement on his record. He eat and wore clothes; that's about where I am."[27]

Despite the racism of the South during the Jim Crow era, necessity forced a cooperation between the races in the rural countryside that was missing in urban centers. Sharecropping blacks and their white landlords all used the same general stores, doctors, gins, warehouses, roads, and recreation areas (lakes and other swimming holes, ball fields, etc.). The only places where integration was inviolate were schools, churches, social clubs, and cemeteries.[28]

The odd contradiction to that reality of racial cooperation are the hundreds of expressions of racial hostility spouted by every race and class in personal history interviews conducted by Federal Works Project writers in South Carolina between 1938-1939. Yet in North Carolina, such expressions of hostility were either absent or at least noticeably less venomous. For instance, in the 1930s white moonshiner and part-time Works Project Administration worker John Twiford, shared his mule, plow, and even jugs of corn squeezings with a black neighbor in eastern North Carolina. The interviewer who took Twiford's history described the two men as familiar in a chiding, witty way, men who drank from the same demijohn, disdaining racial etiquette.[29]

Even if relations between landlord and tenant in North Carolina were more cordial than that of their counterparts to the south, that does not mean the two classes did not have their differences. Landlords often disapproved of how tenants spent their meager incomes on things that, to the landlord, were not essentials. Automobiles purchased by sharecroppers particularly drew their ire, as it gave tenants a means to escape their rural isolation to shop at some place other than the landlord-owned general store. Landlords also felt that croppers should be spending more on work essentials like tools and fertilizer.[30]

In North Carolina, a 1922 study by the state department of agri-

Landowners often established their own general stores and encouraged sharecroppers to buy from there on credit against their share of the crop. It was another way of tying people to the land they worked.

culture found more than 117,000 farmers were landless. These families worked an average of just eighteen acres each, barely enough to make a living on even if weather cooperated and other factors worked in their favor.[31]

Such favorable conditions did not exist in North Carolina in 1922. Planting practices left land barren, bereft of nutrients because of the insistence on planting cotton and tobacco to the exclusion of almost anything else. In two of the three counties surveyed, ninety-nine percent of planted lands were given over to crops that exhausted rather than rehabilitated the soil. Edgecombe County, with the highest degree of tenancy, also had the highest percentage of land planted in exhaustive crops. Rehabilitating crops such as alfalfa, soybeans, cowpeas, rye, and hay were hard to find.[32]

The North Carolina sharecroppers surveyed were much poorer than the landlords whose fields they toiled in. The landless families, according to the 1922 survey, "live in poorer houses, they live under worse sanitary conditions, have poorer health, and lose more of their children by death than (land) owners do. They are more illiterate, fail to reach as high grades in school, take less papers and magazines, have fewer books in their homes, attend church and Sunday school less, have fewer home amusements, and attend community affairs less often."

Farmers in three North Carolina counties in three distinctly different geographical regions of the state were the subjects of the 1922 N.C. Department of Agriculture study.[33] Government workers interviewed 1,014 sharecroppers and their families, inventorying their lives in order to get a factual picture of the plight of poor farmers in the state. The findings were sobering:
• Only four percent of crops grown by black sharecroppers in eastern North Carolina were improvement crops that rejuvenated the soil.
• There was only one cow for every 138 tilled acres among white sharecroppers, and one cow for every 277 acres for black croppers in the Coastal Plains' Edgecombe County.
• Black croppers produced only 32.9 gallons of milk per year per family. That equals only seven tenths of a quart (or three tenths of a glass) per individual per day. Even at that, overall only nine percent of sharecropping families produced any milk at all.
• The cash income of white tenants and sharecroppers in mountainous

Sharecropping and tenant farming were occupations that the entire family participated in.

Madison County was less than ten cents per day per person.

• More than seventy-five percent of all farmers surveyed used short-term credit to conduct farming operations.

• The equity holdings of black families sharecropping in the Piedmont's Chatham County was just $36.

• Thirteen percent of all farm lands included in the survey were being worked by insolvent men.

A typical one-room sharecropper house.

• Two percent of all families surveyed were living in one-room houses. Extrapolating that number out to the rest of North Carolina's sharecropping population, that means more than 6,000 rural North Carolina families were living together in one-room houses of dubious and varying states of repair. For two-room houses, the number rose to 42,000, a total large enough to include a full fifth of every landless family in the state.

• None of the families surveyed, white or black, owned a bathtub or had indoor plumbing. None of the black farmers surveyed even had running water.

• Over thirty-one percent of the landless mothers and fathers surveyed were illiterate.

• Of those who did attend school, most managed to go only as high as third grade. Among black landless farmers, few even completed a whole year of first grade.[34]

The plight of these people barely keeping body and soul together on the margins of North Carolina society were part of a vicious cycle that demonstrated the failings of the agricultural ladder. Eighty-one percent of landowners surveyed in 1922 were the sons of landowners, while seventy percent of landless farmers shared the same status of their landless fathers. Only half the landed farmers had ever been landless. Even though almost twenty-eight percent of landowners had started at the bottom of the agricultural ladder, it was not uncommon for farmers to climb a rung or two, perhaps achieving the status of cash tenants, only to suffer some disaster that saw them fall back to the bottom again. Among tenants, some sixty percent of them started out as sharecroppers. For those who did manage to become small landowners, the journey took on average thirteen years of toil as croppers and tenants. Given that the average age of the North Carolina sharecroppers and tenants surveyed in 1922 was thirty-six, the likelihood of any of those farmers ever becoming owners was remote at best.[35]

Landowners seemed to hold all the cards when it came to farming in 1922 North Carolina. Although they accounted for a little less than half of those surveyed by the Department of Agriculture, they held almost ninety-three percent of all wealth, and an equal amount of all equity. Even though white families amounted to only seventy-three percent of families surveyed, they held ninety-two percent of wealth and ninety-four percent of all equity. Among Negro farmers surveyed, twenty-seven percent were tenants. For whites, that number was a bit smaller, at twenty-five percent. But among Negro croppers, fully twenty-two percent were insolvent, while that number was just three percent for white farmers.[36]

Like other places in the South, the biggest stumbling block to successfully climbing the agricultural ladder was the lack of credit. For most sharecroppers, credit sources were scarce aside from the merchants and landowners. In the three North Carolina counties surveyed, they were the sources of almost ninety-five percent of all credit issued. Banks accounted for an anemic two percent of credit lent to state farmers. Among the farmers surveyed in the state, the 1,014 families used a combined $185,000 in credit over the course of the year, or an average $182.40 per family. More than half that credit went to buy food, clothing, and home supplies. The rest went to buying stock, seed, fertilizer, and tools. Among the landless, sixty-two percent of their credit was used for living purposes, as opposed to almost forty-four percent among the landed. Such numbers indicate that among North Carolina's landless farmers, a higher percentage of borrowed money went for perishable and consumable goods rather than for production goods. With interest rates charged by non-bank lenders reaching as high as twenty-five percent (or thirty-four percent for black farmers), using crop shares to get out of debt was a virtual impossibility.[37]

Life for landless farmers in North Carolina, even before the Great Depression made things so much worse, was already a virtual subsistence existence. By every measureable metric sharecroppers, and to a lesser degree tenants, were the poorest constituents in the state. Statewide among sharecroppers, there were a hundred beds for every 199 people. Nearly all sharecropper homes staved off freezing winters with fireplaces. Those same homes were almost universally lit by oil lamps. They had no kitchens, or even refrigerators. Nearly twenty percent had no screens for windows or doors to keep disease-carrying insects outside or let cooling breezes in. More than half of all sharecropper homes were covered in tar paper, while 135 of those families surveyed lived in homes that used newspaper stuffed in gaps between boards to keep chilly breezes at bay. In nearly sixteen percent of the homes, yards drained towards the family well, contaminating drinking and bathing water. A quarter of the homes surveyed had privies, but only half of those had ever been cleaned out. Almost thirty percent of all homes surveyed dumped their used dishwater and garbage in the yard. To say life was hard for North Carolina share-croppers was a big understatement.[38]

Desperate times call for desperate measures, and the plight of tenants and sharecroppers of both races in the Depression-era South lead to an attempt at organization to spur reforms. The Sharecroppers and Tenant Farmer's Union (STFU) was the result. By 1936, the union boasted 31,000 members in Arkansas, Tennessee, Mississippi, Texas, Oklahoma, and North Carolina (though North Carolina only had one local).

A button of the Sharecroppers and Tenant Farmer's Union.

Such an organization was sorely needed. The STFU united poor whites, blacks, Mexicans, and Indians under the same banner. Where once landlords and planter elites could count on a racial divide to keep share-croppers and tenants from organizing to force concessions, the STFU helped laborers recognize that poor whites and blacks had more in common than the differences posed by the color of their skin. The STFU may have been the first organization to unite disparate races under one banner to pursue common interests in American labor history.[39]

White and black farmers of the STFU attend an outdoor meeting. Their finding common ground between them was a worst case scenario for Southern landowners and elites.

The STFU marked a big change in white attitudes. Before, white farmers resented having to compete for jobs that previously went to blacks. Lingering resentment of Negro rule during Reconstruction also soured white relations with blacks who, except for their skin, lived virtually identical lives as them. The bad times in rural North Carolina were made worse when the Great Depression saw jobless factory workers move back to the country to try farming for a living. The ensuing labor glut saw between eight and twelve thousand North Carolina sharecropping families displaced by 1934, people who had no crops to sell.

Under such conditions, racial biases began taking a back seat to mutual interest. It was from this that the STFU saw its genesis. "We live under the same sun, eat the same food, wear the same kind of clothing, work on the same land, raise the same crop for the same landlord who oppresses and cheats us both," said one old black North Carolina sharecropper. "The same chain that holds my people holds your people too… The landlord is always betwixt us, beatin' us and starvin' us and makin' us fight each other. There ain't but one way, that's for us to get together and stay together."[40]

The STFU sought better living conditions for sharecroppers and tenants, including decent homes and access to woodlands for the firewood needed to fend off harsh winters. They wanted portions of the land they worked to be set aside for garden plots to supplement the family diet, free schools with books and hot lunches, and decent contracts that paid higher wages, offered better hours, an end to evictions, and the right to sell their portion of the cotton crop to whoever they wanted at the best market prices they could find. None of which set well with landlords, who certainly did not want to undertake reforms that would take money from their pocket. Sending cropper children to school was seen as especially odious, because educated children were not likely to take their parents' places in the fields. White landlords viewed the STFU with fear and anger. They mobilized to combat the union with white supremacy and other terror tactics. These included sending armed thugs to STFU meetings, beatings, threatening families, increased evictions, and even murder.[41]

Shaw College student William Thomas Brown founded North Carolina's lone chapter of the STFU in 1936. Its membership was comprised initially of just six black tobacco farmers. Brown admitted reticence about approaching whites to join the union. "I wouldn't dare say anything to whites," he said, "because if you brought a white (to a meeting) you wouldn't know if he was an informer."[42]

The STFU failed to accomplish much in the grand scheme of things, outside of focusing attention on the plight of sharecroppers and tenants in the South. The union was undone by a number of factors, including the inability of poor farmers to take time away from their fields to attend meetings. Landowner-backed violence, the indifference of the Roosevelt administration at the Federal level, a weak financial base, and ultimately, the mechanization of cotton farming, all contributed to STFU's eventual disappearance. In North Carolina, Brown was unable to make more of an impact because of the lingering impact of Old South social mores and a lack of white organizers to broaden the membership base across racial lines.[43]

By the 1920s, it was apparent to even the most disinterested observer that the inequities of sharecropping and tenant farming were abominable. The Great Depression only exacerbated an already dismal way of life for thousands of people in rural North Carolina. But the agricultural ladder system was deeply entrenched in the Southern farming world. University of North Carolina sociologist Rupert B. Vance observed in 1929 that the system, whether equitable or not, was one that had been worked out by landowners and tenant in both custom and law. Financial interests, he argued, were at the root of the South's reliance on cotton. Farmers did not choose to grow cotton every year. Their creditors demanded it. There was no credit available for the seed and fertilizer needed to grow anything else. "Change will have to be engineered from above by bankers, landlords, and supply merchants," Vance surmised. Such reforms only came when Franklin Roosevelt's New Deal reshaped the American landscape.[44]

Franklin D. Roosevelt's New Deal brought some relief to sharecroppers through things like farm relief bills. Here Roosevelt signs such a bill into law in 1933.

The New Deal was intended to provide a safety net and optimism for the downtrodden American masses left destitute and drowning as a result of the Great Depression. If anyone fit that description, it would be North Carolina' sharecroppers and tenant farmers. Instead, the way New Deal programs were put into practice served only to reinforce the existing power structure in the South. New programs like the Agricultural Adjustment Act (AAA), designed to provide relief and a fair shake for poor farmers, were put in the hands of local elites who sat on committees overseeing its implementation. Those local power brokers, often the same men who were landlords to poor farmers, wielded that authority to steer monies intended for sharecroppers and tenants into their own pockets. Another noted North Carolina sociologist, Arthur Raper, declared that "practically all of the (AAA) money found its way into the hands of the landlord. One half of it belonged to him as rent, while the other half was used to reduce the tenants' indebtedness to him for furnishings."[45]

AAA policies hurt sharecroppers and tenants who suffered evictions when landowners took acreage out of production. The idea behind paying farmers to let lands lay fallow was to artificially boost cotton and tobacco prices by reducing the glut of the crops that depressed markets for them. But such payments went to the landowner, not the sharecroppers and tenants who actually tilled that land. Once a landowner accepted payment to take acreage out of production, any incentive he had to keep laborers on his land disappeared. Those who were allowed to stay were reduced to being wage laborers.

Landowners enjoyed huge windfalls at the expense of their laborers thanks to the perversion of AAA policies. At the same time, they protested Federal relief programs that took profits away from their stores during growing seasons. Yet when those growing seasons ended, landowners again became enthusiastic supporters of government relief because they did not want to support their tenants any longer than they had to. Apparently things changed from the growing season (when landowners claimed government relief would make already lazy tenants even more shiftless), to the offseason, when the landowner could milk no more profit from his workers.[46]

Some laborers found help by hiring out with other Federal employers such as the Civilian Conservation Corp, or in programs by the Works Progress Administration. Such programs under Roosevelt's New Deal put unemployed farmers and others back on the job, with

New Deal jobs with the Civilian Conservation Corps and the Works Progress Administration offered an alternative for many poor sharecroppers.

payrolls that offered at least as much as they stood to make as sharecroppers or tenants. Civic improvement projects such as Wilmington, N.C.'s Legion Stadium and Greenfield Lake benefitted from their labors.

Even more ambitious programs aimed specifically at poor farmers began cropping up in the countryside. Near Burgaw, N.C., roughly twenty miles northwest of Wilmington in Pender County, developer Hugh MacRae suggested to Federal officials that the Division of Subsistence Homesteads construct a planned community designed to provide homes and work for poor sharecropping and tenant farmers, bankrupt landowners, and unemployed ex-farmers. The government agreed, and Penderlea Homesteads became one of 135 such communities built by the U.S. government during the depths of the Great Depression to provide a lifeline to desperate citizens nationwide.[47]

Beginning in 1934, MacRae headed up the project on behalf of the U.S. Department of Interior. The developer's prior experience establishing farming communities in southeastern North Carolina made him eminently suitable to spearhead the effort to build Penderlea. Using designs by Boston city planner John Nolan, MacRae began building a community shaped like a horseshoe surrounding a central road on 4,700 acres of cut-over woodland. MacRae sold the land to the Federal government for $6.50 per acre. The ten acre community was intended to accommodate 300 people in a planned truck farm cooperative with its own fields and processing facilities.[48]

Families at Penderlea worked ten-acre plots that faced the main road, with small homes nearby. Wooded areas, ditches, or creeks that provided water sources bounded each homestead. Families lived in houses with running water and electricity. Each ten acres boasted a barn and a poultry house. There was also an A-type hog house, corn crib, and a combination wash and

Penderlea developer Hugh MacRae

smoke house. Homes ranged from four to six rooms, depending on the size of the family. An electric pump powered a reservoir that provided hot and cold water. The houses themselves were built on brick footings, with cedar shingle exteriors and tongue and groove pine interior walls and floors.

A school on a twenty-three acre campus, with a gymnasium, auditorium, cafeteria, library, and workshop, served the larger community. Plans included a vegetable grading shed, potato storage house, a cannery, grist and feed mill, a general store, social building, and furniture factory. Nearby Watha, Burgaw, and Wallace all had railheads served by hard surface roads to provide a means of getting Penderlea produce to market. By 1936, families began moving into the community. It was a far, far better life than any of the former sharecropping families had ever lived before.

Penderlea homes like this one offered poor families an alternative to the virtual slavery of sharecropping and tenant farming.

Government programs allowed former sharecroppers and tenants to work to own their Penderlea homesteads. By 1937, 112 families occupied houses in the development. Penderlea shifted to the Resettlement Administration that summer, and families continued to slowly find their way to Pender County to take up residence there. The success of the community was highlighted by a visit from First Lady Eleanor Roosevelt in August 1937. Penderlea, despite some growing pains over the next decade, existed with government support until 1949. The community succeeded in providing fresh starts for families who would never have had a chance at a decent life otherwise. Ninety-nine of the original Penderlea homes still stand at the site, along with the community center that was the nexus of the neighborhood.[49]

Sharecropping and tenant farming continued in the South long after World War II completed the job of recovery started by Franklin Delano Roosevelt and his Democratic allies in Congress. As late as the 1970s, there were still people tilling the soil on shares in the Carolinas, raising tobacco and other cash crops. While such people still had hard lives that often qualified as little more than subsistence living (some still did not have indoor plumbing until 1973 or later), they still lived better in most cases than their predecessors of the 1920s and 1930s.

There are many kinds of slavery. Abraham Lincoln may have done away with one form of it with his great proclamation in 1863, but the Jim Crow institutionalized by a South determined to cling to prerogatives and power from the antebellum era codified a system that was in many ways slavery in all but name. Certainly the landless poor, both black and white, who toiled from "can see to cain't" in cotton and tobacco fields owned by other men must have felt the burden of something that seemed a lot like slavery, or at least indentured servitude. They often lived in conditions that not even convicts were condemned to suffer, trying to earn their way in a system rigged to keep them in their place. North Carolina was but one Southern state that had to contend with large segments of its rural population that literally lived hand to mouth, their day-to-day existence far from guaranteed, with no safety net to catch those who lost their grip on that precarious stability. Relief came only when the depths of the Great Depression spurred the Roosevelt administration to create programs that helped pull a reeling nation up from the pit of despair.

Endnotes

[1] Joseph D. Reid, Jr. "Sharecropping As An Understandable Market Response: The Post-Bellum South." *The Journal of Economic History*, Vol. 43, No. 1 (Mar 1973): 109. Hereafter cited as Reid.

[2] Lee Alston. "Competition and Compensation of Sharecroppers by Race: A View From Plantations in the Early Twentieth Century." *Explorations in Economic History*, Vol. 38 (2001): 187. http://www.idealibrary.com (accessed 01 Sept 2014). Hereafter cited as Alston. For instance, in Alabama, an 1866 black code made it unlawful for "any person to interfere with, hire, employ, of entice away, of induce to leave the service of another, any laborer or servant who shall have stipulated or contracted, in writing, to serve for any given period."

[3] Alston, 188. Figures from the 1910 Federal Census showed that in the South Atlantic region, fifty-five percent of white and fifty-one percent of black farm workers had been on the same farm for less than one year.

[4] Carl C. Taylor and Carle Clark Zimmerman and Benjamin F. Brown, editors. *Economic and Social Conditions of North Carolina Farmers. Based on a Survey of 1000 North Carolina Farmers in Three Typical Counties of the State.* Raleigh, N.C.: State Department of Agriculture, 1922. http://docsouth.unc.edu/nc/ncfarmers/farmers.html (accessed 01 Sept 2014): 31. Hereafter cited as Taylor.

[5] Taylor, 5.

[6] William O'Neal. "The Emergence of the Crop-Lien System in North Carolina." East Carolina University prize-winning history paper. http://thescholarship.ecu.edu/handle/10342/3795?show=full (accessed 06 Sept 2014). Hereafter cited as O'Neal.

[7] O'Neal, 14.

[8] O'Neal, 11-12.

[9] O'Neal, 15.

[10] O'Neal, 16.

[1] Ralph Shlomowitz. "The Origins of Southern Sharecropping." *Agricultural History*, Vol. 53, No. 3 (July 1979): 563-569.

[12] O'Neal, 15-16.

[13] Reid, 106. Southern per capita income in 1880 was only fifty-one percent of the rest of

the country. By 1900, the growth in income had slowed even more.

[4] Martin A. Garrett and Zhenui Xu. "The Efficiency of Sharecropping: Evidence from the Postbellum South." *Southern Economic Journal*, Vol. 69, No. 3 (Jan. 2003): 579. Hereafter cited as Garrett.

[5] Marjorie Mendenhall Applewhite. "Sharecropper and Tenant in the Courts of North Carolina." *The North Carolina Historical Review*, Vol. 31, No. 2 (April 1954): 134. In the turpentine industry, a crop was a unit of measurement. Ten thousand boxes or faces (the cuts made in a longleaf pine tree to access the sap from which turpentine was distilled) equaled a crop. Originally a crop included roughly 5,000 trees (a number which rose to 9,000 later). "Croppers" tended their small forests on shares, splitting profits with the landowner.

[6] Alston, 182-184.

[7] Reid, 126; Garrett, 579, 592.

[8] Gilbert C. Fite. "The Agricultural Trap in the South." *Agricultural History*, Vol. 60, No. 4 (Autumn 1986): 38. Hereafter cited as Fite.

[9] Fite, 39-40. During the late nineteenth and early twentieth centuries, it was difficult for Southern farmers to begin farming, and once they did, to become successful operators. What money that was available for loans carried interest rates that made earning a profit all but impossible. Making enough to enjoy a modern standard of living was completely out of reach.

[20] Fite, 41-43.

[21] Fite, 43. Accumulations of capital were usually accomplished through savings and earnings, but the amount saved depended on income. While small landowners and tenants might manage to build some savings, for sharecroppers and wage laborers it was almost impossible.

[22] Fite, 44.

[23] Alston, 182; Fite, 45-49.

[24] Jack Temple Kirby. "Black and White in the Rural South, 1915-1954." *Agricultural History*, Vol. 58, No. 3 (July 1984): 411. Hereafter cited as Kirby.

[25] Kirby, 412-413.

[26] Kirby, 413. On the other hand, not all black tenants were invariably unhappy with their lot as sharecroppers. Records show more than a few who found their white landlords tolerant men who lived up to their obligations under contract fairly. A black sharecropper from the same area that Weathers lived said that "The men I've had crops with has always talked to me kind and treated me like I was a man…It ain't the landlords I'm complainin' about…It's sharecropping that's wrong."

[27] Kirby, 413.

[28] Kirby, 414.

[29] Kirby, 417, 420.

[30] Kirby, 420.

[31] Taylor, passim.

[32] Taylor, 5, 11, 12.

[33] Taylor, passim. The study was conducted in Edgecombe County in the Coastal Plains, Chatham County in the N.C. Piedmont, and Madison County in the mountainous western part of the state.

[34] Taylor, 6-7.

[35] Taylor, 36-38.

[36] Taylor, 34.

[37] Taylor, 30-31.

[38] Taylor, passim.

[39] Keith M. Griffin. "The Failure of an Interracial Southern Rhetoric: The Southern Tenant Farmer's Union in North Carolina." Paper presented at the Annual Meeting of the Carolinas Speech Communication Association. October 1982: 3. Hereafter cited as Griffin.

[40] Griffin, 6.

[41] Griffin, 7-11.

[42] Griffin, 12.

[43] Griffin, 9-13.

[44] Monica Richmond Gisolfi. "From Crop Lien to Contract Farming: The Roots of the Agribusiness in the American South, 1929-1930." *Agricultural History*, Vol. 80, No. 2 (Spring 2006): 170. Hereafter cited as Gisolfi.

[45] Gisolfi, 174. It was not just sharecroppers and tenant farmers who suffered under the elite administration of AAA assets by local elites. Small landowners endured forced acreage reductions that reduced the amount of cotton they had for subsistence. In contrast, large farmers and landowners raked in huge profits thanks to their positions on local AAA committees.

[46] Gisolfi, 174-175.

[47] "Facts About Penderlea Homestead." *Penderlea Homestead Museum.* http://www.penderleahomesteadmuseum.org/facts.html (accessed 16 October 2014). Hereafter cited as Penderlea.

[48] Penderlea. MacRae had previous experience developing farm communities. He was also the driving force behind Castle Hayne, St. Helena, and Van Eeden, all of which were built around truck farming.

[49] Penderlea, passim.

Fort Dobbs, near modern Statesville, N.C., was the colony's westernmost defense during the French & Indian War. (Photos courtesy of Fort Dobbs State Historic Site)

Fort Dobbs and the Fight for Empire
By Jack E. Fryar, Jr.

Hugh Waddell glanced over his shoulder at the log fort three hundred yards behind him, then turned to face the shadowed oak thicket to his front. He and the handful of men with him were on edge, as anyone might be if they suspected that people were lurking in those shadows waiting to kill them.

Waddell commanded North Carolina's westernmost defensive fortification on a frontier dangerously vulnerable to depredations by native warriors, egged on by Gallic instigators, in the ongoing war between England and France. He and the thirty men with him were charged with keeping those Cherokee war parties at bay, and providing a refuge for isolated farm families on what had become the front lines of the conflict.

Tension between the two strongest nations of Europe had been percolating since the late seventeenth century. London and Paris found themselves competitors for decades over issues of European politics and expansion.[1] That was especially true in the New World, where British and

French colonists from the Caribbean to Canada found themselves in a never-ending race to acquire territory at the expense of the other. In North America, British incursions into the Northwest Territory around the Great Lakes and the Ohio River were countered by French strikes against King George's domains along the North American east coast. Indian tribes often acted as proxies for both sides in the growing fight, and that was who Hugh Waddell and the men of Fort Dobbs faced on a crisp February day in 1760.[2]

The Fight for Empire in North Carolina

By the 1750s, the rivalry between France and Great Britain had spread to engulf the young colonies of North America, especially along the western frontiers where Europeans and their Indian allies fought a nasty conflict that had implications beyond just the wilderness where most of the battles were fought.

In the Carolinas, the war was always something happening over the horizon – more Virginia's problem than that of the colonies farther south. That changed when news of Gen. Edward Braddock's defeat

The defeat of British forces under Gen. Edward Braddock, who was mortally wounded in the clash, brought a sense of urgency to North Carolina's plans for defense.

reached Salisbury, N.C. on July 28, 1754. The Tar Heel contribution to the expedition consisted primarily of a lone company of 100 provincial troops under the command of Captain Edward Brice Dobbs, the son of North Carolina's royal governor, Arthur Dobbs. Governor Dobbs, an earnest and hard working Irishman who had assumed office only a short while before, immediately realized the implications of the French victory for his impoverished and unprotected colony. Two months later, he implored the colonial assembly to appropriate funds to change that.[3]

Dobbs implored the Assembly to authorize a generous contribution to the British war chest to fund the effort to oust French forces and to fortify North Carolina's own sadly unprepared coastline. The governor observed in his message to the Assembly that, "a proper sum cheerfully granted at once will accomplish what a great sum may not do hereafter…I therefore earnestly recommend it to you to grant as large a supply as this province can bear not only to defend your own frontier and sea coast but also to act in conjunction with our neighboring colonies."[4]

Hugh Waddell

Dobbs knew of the lack of currency in his colony, and had first hand experience of the Assembly's parsimony. When his son marched to join Braddock's campaign the North Carolina men, including a young Daniel Boone, carried a mix of English and Dutch arms. But the lack of specie in North Carolina resulted in Gov. Dobbs having to pay the men from his own pocket. After Braddock was killed, the Tar Heel company retreated to the relative safety of Fort Cumberland before nearly all of them deserted and made for home.[5]

The need for money to beef up North Carolina's defenses was urgent. Not long after Dobbs assumed office, he went on a tour of the colony to assess its readiness and needs. What Arthur Dobbs saw was disheartening at best, and alarming at worst. He wrote Virginia governor Robert Dinwiddie that he had been "…above four months in different parts of the

Province to observe our seacoast and western frontier in order to put them in a state of Defence, as far as this poor province can contribute at this critical juncture." Dobbs confided that he had ordered the construction of batteries at Ocracoke and at Fort Johnston, on the Cape Fear River. Even so, he complained to Dinwiddie that North Carolina still lacked enough powder, cannonballs, and artillery to mount much of a defense if the French and their allies should strike along the coast. Dobbs wrote to London that the colony had an "immediate occasion for Artillery and Bullets and Stores." He also asked authorities in London for "14 eighteen pounders, and 16 nine pounders, with 30 Swivel [guns] and as many Musquetoons" for Fort Johnston.[6]

N.C.'s Royal Governor Arthur Dobbs

In 1755 Dobbs again ventured away from the coast to locate likely places to establish forts in the North Carolina interior. A second priority was to explore the possibility of establishing alliances with the Indians along the western frontier. Dobbs understood the value of having allies among the tribes in the west, as an attack became increasingly more likely to materialize there than in the east. Dobbs liked what he saw along a tributary of the Yadkin River, near modern Statesville, N.C. To Dobbs' experienced eye, the site had much to recommend it. He described it has having "...an Eminence and good Springs, and fixed upon as the most central to assist the back settlers and be a retreat to them as it was beyond the well settled Country."[7]

The governor declared to Dinwiddie that he wanted to "put the frontier in the best State of Defence against Indian incursions." To that end, he devised to raise 100 men to serve in a frontier company. Command of the unit went to Wilmington's Captain Hugh Waddell, who led the escort for Dobbs' scout of the North Carolina backcountry. Dobbs went on to meet with members of the Anson and Rowan County militias. The governor instructed them to select fifty men from each to serve under Waddell as reinforcement to the fort in the event of an emergency. In the meantime, the men set to work building winter quarters.

Hugh Waddell was a good choice to command the western fort. Only James Innes had a better reputation as a military man in North Carolina. An Irishman like Governor Dobbs, Waddell served under Innes in the failed attempt to support a young George Washington's Virginia troops in 1754. He was also a family friend of the governor, who preceded Dobbs in coming to North Carolina.[8]

Braddock's defeat spurred the North Carolina Assembly to comply with Governor Dobbs' request for war funding. One traveler in the colony noted "A cold shuddering possessed every breast, and paleness covered nearly every face" he came across. The legislative body at New Bern voted an appropriation of £10,000 in paper bills to fund the raising of "3 Companies of 50 Men each" to serve for two years. Another £1000 was voted to fund the construction of Waddell's fort on the western frontier. The fort would come to be named in honor of the man who selected its site and championed its construction, Royal Governor Arthur Dobbs.

Work on Fort Johnston and Fort Dobbs was coming along as 1755 gave way to a new year. By January 1756 construction at the two installations was such that they might actually live up to their intended uses, but the governor still fretted that neither had yet to receive any artillery. Dobbs considered it good work that in the west, Hugh Waddell had so far managed to keep a lid on any simmering resentments the Indians might be harboring, and deflected any overtures by the French to enlist the Native Americans in their cause. Finding men willing to serve in the militia was difficult. Colonial law required that all men between the ages of 16 and 60 serve, but Dobbs lamented not finding many willing to meet their obligation. According to him, some men went to extreme lengths to avoid their duty, to include fleeing to the surrounding swamps, where they were "con-

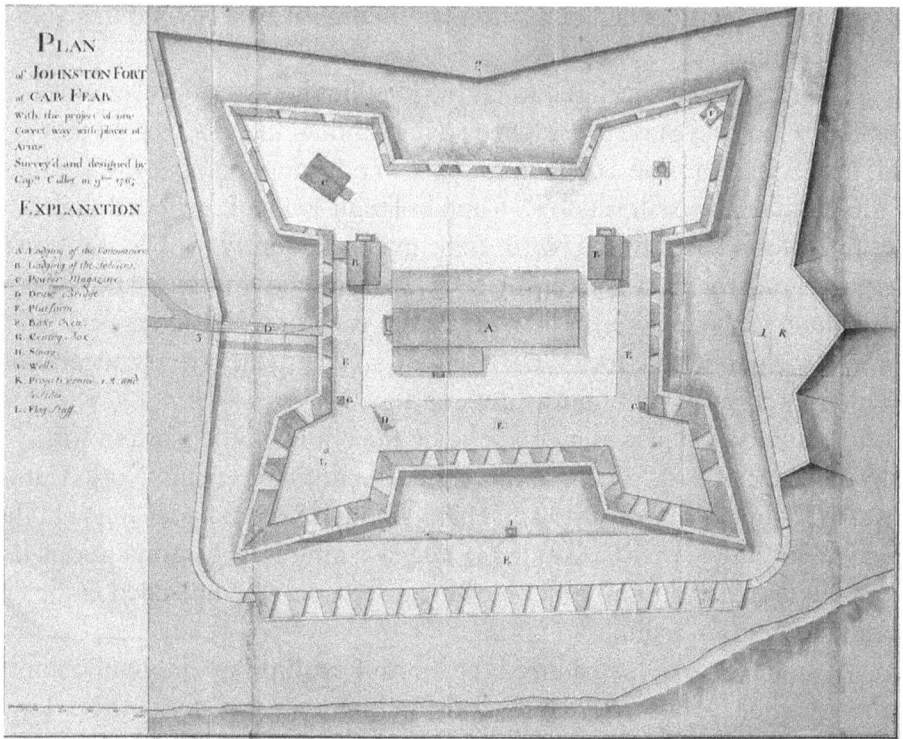

*Fort Johnston, situated at the mouth of the Cape Fear River, as imagined by its design-
ers. The fort never achieved the configuartion depicted above, but would serve under
three different flags until being retired from active service in 2004.*

cealed by their friends and Neighbors." The reluctance of many men to
serve in the militias required the raising of paid troops called provincials.[9]

It was the same at the other places where Dobbs was trying to
strengthen North Carolina's ability to defend itself. Those men who did
report for militia duty usually were unarmed. At Fort Johnston, Dobbs
reported to London that there was "neither ammunition, arms, nor cannon
except a few ship guns unfit for service." Batteries being erected at Core
Banks and Topsail Inlet suffered similar deficiencies. The latter was especially irksome to Dobbs, who saw the defenses around Ocracoke as the
key to successfully thwarting any French attack along the coast around the
Albemarle.[10]

The Warpath in the West

The war with the Cherokee did not develop from enmity that existed from the beginning of relations with white settlers. In 1756, a meeting

between the Indians and colonial officials resulted in the Cherokee agreeing to provide security for the Virginia frontier in return for the colonials' promise of two forts to be built by Virginia and South Carolina to protect Cherokee towns from attack by tribes in the pay of the French and their own natural enemies. The war party sent north ran into misfortune on the way to Virginia when they lost their supplies in a river crossing. The Cherokee were reduced to eating their own horses for food. When that ran out, they began taking what they needed from white farms along the way. The appropriations did nothing to endear the Indians to their white neighbors.[11]

With the loss of Fort Oswego, the French claimed control of the entire Ohio Valley. Cherokee loyalties began to shift in favor of the French because of the successes enjoyed by the Gallic forces and their Indian allies. Pro-French sentiments were greatest among the Overhills Cherokee, whose towns were closest to French influence. It was the French who persuaded the Cherokee that new forts being constructed along the frontier would be followed by British settlers encroaching on Indian lands. Not many Cherokee took the French warning serious at first, but as more and more whites moved into land that belonged to the Indians, they began to see the truth of the threat.[12]

Settlers and Cherokees did not start out as enemies.

Settlers on North Carolina's western frontier shared Governor Dobbs' anxiety about the colony's readiness for war. French control of the Ohio Valley left the southern colonies ripe for attack. In 1754 an Indian raid along the Broad River killed sixteen settlers and saw another ten taken captive. By the summer of 1756, roving bands of Indians had committed "several abuses and robberies" against colonists homesteading there. There was some indication that these "Strolling Parties of Indians" were Cherokee, who to that time had remained at least neutral regarding the war between the two European colonial powers. Dobbs suspected northern Indians in the employ of the French were egging Carolina Indians on to instigate a wider war. The governor ordered the two companies of militia attached to Fort Dobbs to begin patrols through the surrounding countryside in an effort to calm the fears of colonists who began imagining Indian war parties behind every bush. To give the militia real teeth with which to meet the threat, Dobbs had powder and shot transferred to Waddell from stores at Fort Johnston.[13]

John Campbell, 4th Lord Loudon

The fall of Fort Oswego that autumn led the North Carolina Assembly to take the threat to the colony's frontier more seriously. Another £4,000 was allocated to "erect a fort to protect and secure the Catawbas, and to maintain two companies to garrison that and another fort built last summer on the frontier" (meaning Fort Dobbs). In March of 1757, governors of the American colonies traveled to Philadelphia to devise a unified strategy for fighting the war. Lord Loudon, overall commander of British forces in the colonies, led the discussions that resulted in royal governors pledging to do their best to coax often recalcitrant assemblies into providing all they could for the war effort.

Dobbs had real doubts as to how much North Carolina's legislators would or could offer up, but he still promised 200 men to help South Carolina fend of a perceived French threat. He also committed to raise another 200 men for duty in North Carolina, split between coastal fortifications and Fort Dobbs.[14]

The Assembly dispatched Richard Caswell, Francis Brown, and Thomas Relf to inspect and report on the progress of defenses along the frontier and at Fort Dobbs. The two men liked what they saw. Their report described Fort Dobbs as "a good and Substantial Building" consisting of "an oblong square" measuring 53'x40', with "the Opposite angles Twenty-four feet and Twenty-two In height Twenty-four and a half feet." The thick walled blockhouse construction was made of horizontally laid oak logs that reached high enough to include three floors. Each floor had room for defenders to discharge "at one and the same time about one hundred Musketts." The exterior fortifications included a defensive ditch known as a fosse measuring less than two feet deep, but five feet wide. An abatis of felled trees with sharpened points completed the defensive preparations. Both inspectors found Fort Dobbs "beautifully scituated" with a garrison of 46 effective men and officers, all of whom appeared to be "well and in good spirits."[15]

Richard Caswell

Relations between the British and the Cherokee were friendly through 1757, and Fort Dobbs hosted a parley between them and other "northern Indians" that year. One of George Washington's officers got a first hand look at the fort as he escorted the Indian representatives there for the negotiations. Within the year, the Cherokee had soured on their friendship with the colonists after continued encroachment on Indian lands in southern colonies led to bad blood between the two camps. The deaths of dozens of Cherokee in Virginia also played a part in the Indians' change in sentiment. It is likely the ill will was fanned to flame with the help of French agents.[16]

Cherokee war parties raged across the western Carolina borderlands by 1759, prompting South Carolina's Governor William Henry Lyttleton to mount an expedition to put down the uprising. Lyttleton asked for help from North Carolina and Virginia, and Governor Dobbs dispatched instructions for the colony's militia to cooperate with any expedition carried out by their sister colony to the south. Further notices went out to North Carolina militia companies warning them to be prepared to mobilize if needed. At Fort Dobbs, Hugh Waddell received a promotion to colonel and orders to call out the militias of Anson, Rowan, and Orange Counties if needed, to "protect the Frontier inhabitants." The warning of impending hostilities would prove timely.[17]

Cherokee warriors were hitting British settlements in earnest by 1759.

The Attack

Lyttleton's expedition was both relatively bloodless and successful, at least at first. But any security it brought was short-lived. By 1760 Cherokee warriors rampaged across the southern frontiers once again. In February, Cherokee leaders planned a broad attack against settlers in both Carolinas and Tennessee. But before that major campaign began, warriors from Settico set their sights on destroying Fort Dobbs and its undermanned garrison.

On February 27, Col. Hugh Waddell recorded that a small Cherokee party had been spotted near Fort Dobbs. By the time a patrol had been dispatched to check into it, the Indians had disappeared. As night fell, the men of the fort described hearing "an uncommon Noise" down by a spring not far from where the provincials kept watch from within the log fort's thick walls. Waddell ordered a "Capt. Bailie" and eight men to accompany him outside to seek out what was causing the disturbance.[18]

The men crept along beyond the fosse and abatis that marked the outermost defenses of the fort. The woods were dark, shadows playing tricks on the mens' eyes as their palms dampened on the muskets they carried at the ready. Waddell brought the patrol to a halt and stared into the dark, trying to make out the forms of hidden enemies that he felt more than heard. They advanced a little further, now some 300 yards from the safety of Fort Dobbs' stout bulwark. Just when the colonists thought that they may have been imagining things, the threat materialized in the form of sixty or seventy screaming Indians rushing from concealment in the woods.

The Cherokee war party came on like a wave, slipping fluidly around and over fallen logs and trees. The howl erupting from their throats caused hair to stand up on the provincials' heads, and Waddell had to keep a tight rein on his men to prevent a headlong fight for safety. The small patrol was heavily outnumbered, and Waddell knew if they lost cohesion they would all be killed one by one. The only hope for any of them lay in maintaining the integrity of their ranks.

A sharp command from the colonel tamped down the urge to panic and brought the patrol into closed ranks. The Indians were very close now, close enough that the provincials could make out details of the warriors hurtling towards them. They could see the war clubs raised by muscled arms. They could make out faces painted in demonic patterns, and hear the pounding of their feet across the rapidly diminishing ground. The provincials stood there, should to shoulder, muskets raised, and waited for Waddell's command.

The Cherokee drew closer with each step. Thirty yards. Twenty. Ten. Waddell reminded his men to wait for his command, to swallow any impulse to panic they might feel. Still the war party came on, and the men in the ranks felt wetness on their brows that was out of place for a cool February night. According to Waddell's report on the attack, he waited until the majority of the attackers had discharged their own muskets. Then the colonel gave the order for his own men to fire, letting loose with a disciplined volley at "not further than 12 steps." The Indians were caught out, exposed just yards from the flaming muzzles of the provincial firelocks. They "had nothing to cover them as they were advancing either to tomahawk or make us Prisoners," Waddell recalled.[19]

The colonials' volley hit with telling effect. The men accompanying Waddell were all loaded with "a Bullet and 7 Buck shot," a load

Waddell's militiamen waited until Cherokee warriors were nearly upon them to fire.

that transformed a musket into something like a shotgun. As close as they were, the lead attackers went down in a heap. Those that followed behind were thrown into confusion. Waddell and his small patrol took advantage of the momentary respite to retreat back to Fort Dobbs. Inside the oak redoubt, the rest of the garrison stood to, the commotion beyond the perimeter having alerted them to the Cherokee assault. It was not until after the provincials beat back the attack that Waddell realized how close a thing his encounter with the war party had been. His musket bore testimony to that, having been shattered in the Cherokee's opening volley.[20]

The Tide Recedes

While Fort Dobbs withstood its first challenge when Waddell and company fended off the Cherokee attack of February, the war was not over. Within weeks of the attack, settlers along the Yadkin, Catawba, and Broad Rivers began a large-scale evacuation of frontier farms to the safety of either Fort Dobbs or the palisaded Moravian town of Bethabara. Soon at least half of Rowan County had abandoned their homes for more secure surroundings. Indian violence raged across western North Carolina for at least another year. The Cherokee opted to confine their attacks to lightly defended farms and settlements in the backcountry that witnessed atrocities on both sides. For instance, settler William Shaw had his feet amputated by the Cherokee in 1759, but at least he lived to tell the tale.

The men of Fort Dobbs skirmished with another band of Cherokee at the nearby Fourth Creek tributary in March 1760, near the home of Moses Potts. During the action, provincial Robert Campbell took "Two Shots in [his] back and the other Broke his Arm near his Shoulder and immediately [he] was tomahawked in Several Places & Scalp'd." The fight left seven provincials dead, buried by their comrades on the field where they died.

Great Britain was finally prodded to action in the aftermath of the attack on Fort Dobbs and the widespread destruction of settlements in the Carolina backcountry. Military commanders dispatched elements of the 1st and 77th Regiment of Foot, composed of Highlanders, to Charles Town in South Carolina. Their mission was to provide a professional military force with which to combat the Cherokee. By 1761, the war in the Carolinas was all but over. Later that year, Waddell's service ended when he and his men were finally ordered home from Fort Dobbs, North Carolina's only defensive installation on the western frontier.[21]

Endnotes

John R. Maas, *The French & Indian War in North Carolina* (Charleston, S.C.: The History Press, 2013), 13. Hereafter cited as Maas, *The French & Indian War in North Carolina.*

[2] Maas, *The French & Indian War in North Carolina*, 94.

[3] Desmond Clarke, *Arthur Dobbs, Esquire, 1689-1765: Surveyor General of Ireland, Proprietor and Governor of North Carolina* (London: The Bodley Head, 1957): 123-125. Hereafter cited as Clarke.

[4] Clarke, 125. This request was made during what be termed the honeymoon phase of Dobbs' administration, before relations between him and the Assembly took a turn for the worse.

[5] John R. Maas, The French & Indian War in North Carolina (Charleston, S.C.: The History Press, 2013): 34-42. Hereafter cited as Maas.

[6] Clarke, 124; Maas, 42. A musquetoon was a short-barrell musket capable of being used like a shotgun or with a single ball of ammunition.

[7] Maas, 42.

[8] Lawrence E. Lee, Indian Wars in North Carolina, 1663-1763 (Raleigh: N.C. Department of Archives & History, 1968): 64. Hereafter cited as Lee; Maas, 42-43.

[9] Lee, 67; Maas, 44. The amount allocated by the Assembly for the war effort was not very impressive compared to sums raised by other colonies, but it was about as much as North Carolina's barren coffers could contribute.

[10] Lee, 65; Maas, 44-45. Despite Dobbs' concerns to bolster coastal defenses, no enemy attack ever came along the coast.

[11] Lee, 68.

[2] Lee, 69-72.

[3] Lee, 65; Maas, 53-55. Gov. Dobbs dispatched then Captain Hugh Waddell and a company of men to patrol as far west as the Appalachian Mountains. The fears of the colonists in the backcountry were such that Moravian leaders ordered all farming suspended until they could complete the construction of a palisade around the settlement at Bethabara, where people could take refuge in the event of a full blown attack.

[4] Maas, 55-60.

[5] C.B. Alexander, "The Training of Richard Caswell," *The North Carolina Historical Review*, Vol. 23, No. 1 (Jan. 1946): 13-31. Hereafter cited as Alexander. Caswell was a good choice. He owned thousands of acres of land along the Neuse River in Johnston and Dobbs Counties by 1755, and three plantations in Orange County. Caswell would have been quite familiar with the frontier and its people. Maas, 62-63. No contemporary drawings of Fort Dobbs exist. Governor Dobbs may have designed it himself. Dobbs envisioned a defensive installation that could be defended with swivel guns.

[6] Maas, 84.

[7] Maas, 90.

[8] David Walbert, "Fort Dobbs and the French and Indian War in North Carolina," *Learn-NC*. http://learnnc.org/lp/editions/nchist-colonial/2046. The officer who accompanied Waddell on his sally out from the fort was Captain Andrew Bailey.

[9] Maas, 94.

[20] Maas, 95.

[21] Lee, 79; Maas, 96, 118.

The Sinking of the *John D. Gill*
By Jack E. Fryar. Jr.

A gnawing feeling in the pit of his stomach made Herbert Gardner, a 22-year-old member of the seven-man U.S. Navy gun crew assigned to the tanker *S.S. John D. Gill,* consider his options. On the night of March 12, 1942, Gardner and the rest of the crew aboard the 528-foot tanker, hauling gasoline and Texas crude oil to a refinery in Philadelphia, were all a bit on edge.

Not two days before, the ship had been ordered into the safety of the port at Charleston, S.C. German U-boats sighted off the Atlantic coast of the United States had been wreaking havoc on American shipping, as Hitler's wolfpacks sought to cripple the vital supply line keeping Great Britain afloat. The *John D. Gill* had picked up a shadow on its way north from the Gulf of Mexico, and navy officials had ordered the ship into the nearest friendly port just to be safe. That was all right with Gardner. German torpedoes were not something you wanted to mess with if you could help it.

Named after an executive of the Atlantic Refining Company of Philadelphia, part of the Atlantic-Ritchfield Corporation, the *John D. Gill* was just on her second voyage after her maiden cruise, but her crew already knew of the U-boat danger first hand. Just two weeks earlier, on February 27, the crew of the *Gill* had fished two lifeboats full of haggard survivors from the ore carrier *Marore* out of the cold Atlantic, after she

The oil tanker S.S. John D. Gill

was sunk by the Germans. Now Gardner and the rest of the men aboard the 11,641-ton tanker were testing their own luck in what mariners had begun calling Torpedo Junction, off the coast of North Carolina.

The captain was taking what precautions he could. Ever since the Germans began hunting off the coast of North America, starting with the New Year in 1942, it was a foolhardy ship that sailed a straight course. Straight courses made things entirely too easy for the submarines itching to plant a torpedo amidships of some defenseless merchantmen. And it wasn't like the U.S. Navy was in any position to offer much help. Admiral Ernest J. King, tasked with protecting the east coast of the United States with the newly created U.S. Tenth Fleet, had a paltry dozen ships to carry out his mission: four yard patrol boats, four subchasers, one Coast Guard Cutter, three "Eagle" boats left over from World War I, and 103 aircraft of various types – only five of which were combat ready. If the *John D. Gill* and other merchant ships like her were going to avoid the German subs, then they were going to have to assume most of the burden of protecting themselves.

It was a lesson learned the hard way. When the first five German U-boats arrived on station and began hunting along the American coast, they couldn't believe what they were seeing. It was painfully obvious that the United States homeland had not fully made the transition from peacetime to a war footing. Even after the trauma of Pearl Harbor, east coast cities still gleamed like jewels in the night with no light restrictions at all. The same thing was true of the many merchant vessels plying the waters off the east coast, steaming along in straight lines with lit decks and no radio discipline. In just ten days, German U-boats sank twenty-five ships, constituting a loss of more than 200,000 tons of shipping. In the month of January 1942, just five U-boats accounted for seventy percent of the Allied shipping sunk worldwide. By the time the *John D. Gill* rounded the Dry Tortugas and set course for Philadelphia, no one was ignoring the threat any longer.

It was hazy the night of March 12, calm seas slipping past with a quiet shushing sound. The haze dropped visibility down to just a mile, but if a U-boat was going to strike it would probably be from closer than that. Just eleven of the forty-nine-man crew was on duty as the ship zigzagged through the night. The rest were sleeping, or doing some of the myriad other things men find to occupy the time when aboard a ship at sea. But not far away, a wolf was waiting.

Erich Rostin, the captain of U-158, peered through the eyepiece of his periscope, sizing up the *John D. Gill*. Rostin figured the fat, new tanker had to be good for at least 10,000 tons –

U-158 Captain Erich Rostin

a nice addition to the already considerable tonnage his boat claimed as kills off the American coast. Just the day before, U-158 had claimed the *Caribsea* off the North Carolina Outer Banks, and Rostin was eager to add to his tonnage tally. Despite the zigzag pattern the merchantman was executing, it was simple to figure a firing solution for the torpedoes loaded in the sub's forward tubes. He looked at his chart, noting how the infamous Cape Fear jutted out into the Atlantic, the dangerous Frying Pan Shoals protruding another twenty-eight miles beyond Bald Head Island. Here the target ship would steer well clear of the obstacles that had given the cape its name. There would be plenty of water for the U-boat to maneuver in. Rostin made up his mind. He would

S.S. Caribsea, an earlier victim of U-158's torpedoes. She was sunk off the Outer Banks.

make his attack run while the merchantman was distracted with the tricky navigation required to get around Cape Fear.

In his sea cabin, Master Allen Tucker, the captain of the *S.S. John D. Gill*, glanced at the chronometer on the bulkhead – 2109 EWT. He felt the hull of the ship gently heel over to port as the helmsman guided the *Gill* along the next leg of its pre-planned zigzag course. It had been a nervous cruise since leaving Charleston. Other captains had related tales of ships burning in the night, and of pulling oil covered, half-dead men from flaming seas after U-boat attacks over the last two months. The last thing Tucker wanted was to see the same thing happen to his ship and men.

At 2110 EWT (10:10 p.m.), a faint line of phosphorescence split the water in a beeline aimed right at the *John D. Gill*. If anyone saw its approach, they didn't see it in time to sound an alarm. The torpedo fired by U-158 slammed into the tanker on the starboard side at the #7 tank, and exploded just below the mainmast. The blast threw sleeping men from their berths, and buckled the knees of others who were already standing at their stations. Every man aboard knew what had happened. They also knew that their lives might now be measured in minutes. A quick glance over the side answered any questions Tucker may have had as to whether or not his ship could survive the blow. Already the *John D. Gill* was listing, as black crude oil gushed from the ruptured plating amidships. Tucker gave the order to abandon ship. While men scrambled for life preservers and boat stations, the radio operator sent out a distress call, alerting authorities of the dangerous drama happening twenty-five miles southeast of the Cape Fear River.

On deck, men began executing the drill for abandoning ship, hurriedly donning cork life preservers and uncovering lifeboats attached to davits along the ship's rails. Someone threw a life preserver overboard (whether to a specific man, or just because someone might find themselves in the water without one, is unknown). That was a mistake of tragic proportions. Some life preservers of the time were equipped with a carbide flare that ignited when submersed in water. It was a safety precaution intended to show rescuers where a man might be even if he was unconscious and unable to help himself. But the waters around the *John D. Gill* were mixed with volatile oil and gasoline. When the flare on that life preserver lit, it ignited a blaze that consumed the ship and lit up the sky for miles.

Seaman Gary Potts was asleep when the torpedo hit, but he didn't stay that way. Potts immediately bolted out of his berth and made for the main deck, where a 5-51 breech loading cannon was located in a gun-tub on the starboard bow. The seaman was one of seven regular navy crewmen aboard, tasked with protecting the *John D. Gill* from submarine attack. Potts and everyone else knew the gun was more symbolic than practical. As Erich Rostin had just so ably demonstrated, most sub captains were unlikely to engage a merchantman in a surface action, when they could instead fire a torpedo while submerged, and avoid most of

German U-boat 158

the risk of taking damage. Potts and the rest of the gun crew knew this, too. Nevertheless, they dutifully ran for their action stations, hoping that maybe the sub would surface and give them a chance at a little payback for the death blow the Germans had dealt the *Gill*.

The men of the gun crew swept the barrel of their gun from side to side, looking for some sign of the enemy submarine. Around them boats hit the water and men jumped overboard to put distance between themselves and the wreck of the *John D. Gill,* as her decks dipped further and further towards the flaming water. The heat of the burning oil and gasoline singed the hair on their heads and arms, and the metal of the gun tub became blistering hot to the touch. Still the gun crew stayed at their post. Ensign Robert Hutchins, the ranking officer in the gun crew, finally ordered his men to abandon ship when the paint of the ammunition box began to pucker in the heat. Hutchins remembered the sight of his men jumping overboard into the burning sea.

"The flames got on top of us and we jumped over the side," he recalled five decades later. "I saw two of my boys go into those flames and I heard them scream as they died."

In the sea, one lifeboat managed to shove off from the floating torch that was the *John D. Gill*, but another capsized as it was being lowered. Two men spilled from the fouled boat and fell to their deaths on the ship's huge brass screws, still churning the water at the stern. Seaman Herbert Gardner joined a mess boy in shinnying down the falls to try and right the overturned boat. Somewhere in the effort, the mess boy lost his grip and fell into the water, never to be seen again. Gardner struggled to right the boat until his own strength gave out and he, too, plunged into flame-covered sea. He surfaced in a small pocket of water that hadn't been covered in flames yet, and saw a friend a short distance away. Gardner began stroking towards the man until he drew close and the friend warned him to stay away. Gardner's intention had been to buddy up with his crewmate, who had a life jacket on. But the wild look in the man's eyes as he told Gardner to stay away convinced him the man was near panic. Gardner decided to try and find some other means of staying alive. Moments later flames began to encircle him. The only way out was to dive beneath the burning oil and try to swim for clear water outside the ring of fire. He didn't quite make it. When he broke the surface, Gardner's hair caught fire. He dived under again, holding a quick breath inside singed lungs, and swam for his life. Gardner finally swam outside the flaming cordon surrounding the *Gill* and made it to a raft.

Gardner clung to the raft, finally able to breath in air that was not tainted with the stench of fire and fuel. Salt water stung his scorched flesh, and pain began to creep in as the adrenaline surge that had kept him alive began to ebb. He looked around him at the wretches who shared the raft with him – oil covered, bloodshot eyes reflecting the flames consuming their ship, unconscious moans slipping unnoticed from lips caked with brine and bile. Other eyes swept the sea looking for the unseen enemy responsible for their plight, recalling stories about desperate survivors of other U-boat sinkings being machine gunned in the water. They called this place Cape Fear, and on the night of March 12, 1942 there was plenty of fear to go around.

On the beach at Oak Island, the horizon shimmered with an orange glow marking the place where the *John D. Gill* was in her death throes. Men from the lifesaving station there launched their *Motor Lifeboat 4405* into the surf and threw the helm over to point the bow towards the burning ship. The U.S. Coast Guard Cutter *Agassiz*, along with *CGC 186* and the navy tug *Umpqua* joined the lifesaving crew in the race to rescue the survivors of the *John D. Gill* disaster. Arriving on scene at dawn, a flare drew rescuers to a life raft holding eleven burned and weary men. Later in the day the tanker *Robert H. Colley* stumbled upon the remaining lifeboat full of survivors, taking fifteen aboard. No others from the crew of forty-nine were found.

In Southport, residents stood on the riverfront and eyed the glowing sky where the *John D. Gill* was exploding in a fireworks show made sinister by the death that accompanied it. Nurse Josephine Hickman and other Red Cross volunteers prepared Arthur J. Dosher Memorial Hospital to receive the wounded *Gill* seamen – assuming any were saved. When *CGC 186* arrived at Southport with the first eleven rescued survivors, they were heartbreaking to behold. Among the dead was Catalino Tingzon, a messman from the Philippines who fell out of a lifeboat and could not be rescued. When a search of the Philippines could not turn up any family for the dead man, the people of Southport adopted him as one of their own and buried him in a local cemetery.

The night of terror ended when the *S.S. John D. Gill* finally slipped beneath the waves at nine o'clock on the morning of March 13, 1942. The scars it left on the survivors – on their bodies, in their minds, in the hearts of men who clung to life in a sea of fire, and in the memories of the people

The grave of Catalino Tingzon in the Southport cemetery.

who worked so hard to save them – were still fresh a half century later. Erich Rostin and the crew of U-158 suffered their own horrific moment of truth a few months later, when the German submarine that sunk the *John D. Gill* was itself sunk in the Bahamas with a loss of all hands. Today, a granite marker on the Southport riverfront remembers the night the war came home to the Cape Fear, and the Filipino crewman whose death so touched a town that they laid him to rest with their own.

Wilmington and the Spanish Lady
By Jack E. Fryar, Jr.

The quarantine ward at James Walker Memorial Hospital was stuffy, the heat from the radiators raising the temperature to a level that was uncomfortable for the doctors and nurses, but often not warm enough for the sick men and women filling the beds. There weren't too many empty beds left, either. Both James Walker Memorial and Harper's Sanatorium were awash with the sick and dying. When Johnny came marching home from the blood-filled trenches of Europe and the First World War, he wasn't alone. Spanish influenza came, too. Now Americans were falling to a foe deadlier than any wearing the Kaiser's uniform.

Wilmington was no stranger to epidemics. In 1862, yellow fever swept through North Carolina's largest city, cutting a swath worse than any onslaught by the Union army. Historically, the low-lying lands along the North Carolina coast were vulnerable to the maladies that beset the people living there. But the Spanish Influenza epidemic slashing through the United States in 1918 was something different. It seemed no community was safe, and that included those in the Tar Heel State.

The disease that would become a pandemic killer began in May 1918, in Spain. It soon swept through Europe, quickly rivaling the killing fields of World War I in the taking of lives. Civilians and soldiers both came down with the illness, in a time before flu vaccinations existed to moderate its impact. Many soldiers wounded in combat or rotating back

James Walker Memorial Hospital.

to the United States carried more home with them than just medals, war wounds and thousand-yard stares. Many of them were also infected with the Spanish flu virus, literally bringing a killer home with them.

Spanish flu was an especially virulent form of the flu virus, and it spread quickly among the crowded populations of the big cities in the northeastern United States. In the many military camps along the East Coast, more than 9,000 cases had been reported by the end of September. Once it was on American shores, it was only a matter of time until it made its way south. The first mention of the disease in Wilmington was a newspaper article relating that a number of crewmen aboard an Italian steamer at Norfolk had died from it. An American steamer in the same port reported another 52 cases among its crew. Only two days later, on September 20, thirty cases of the disease were reported in Wilmington.

Despite evidence that this was something unseen before in a city that had witnessed more than its share of epidemic-induced death, Wilmington residents didn't seem to take the threat seriously at first. Local health officials advised citizens to take precautions, but did nothing to convey the real seriousness of the danger. But fourteen short hours after the first reports of the disease in the city, the number of cases jumped from 30 to 100. With a population in the neighborhood of 32,000 – not counting those just passing through the city or working in the shipyards that were so vital to the war effort – Wilmington was ripe for the spread of the highly communicable disease.

At the Liberty Shipbuilding Company, managers became concerned when workers began falling ill. The yard was a vital part of the nation's war effort, turning out ships to ferry the men and materials needed to fight the war in Europe across the Atlantic Ocean. The Spanish flu epidemic quickly affected the shipyard's ability to keep up their schedule.

William A. Wright was the first victim of the flu in Wilmington, just 28 years old when he died on September 21. Three days later, police officer W.F. Craig became the second victim, and health officials reported the city had 500 new cases. Overnight, it seemed a new and unfamiliar pestilence was stalking the streets.

With so many cases reported, people began to be concerned. Parents refused to let their children attend school, as on average 100 new cases were reported each day. On September 28, public health officials were so alarmed that they ordered all places of public assembly to be closed until further notice. Churches, theaters, lodges, soda fountains – all fell under the ban in the interest of public safety. Police officers enforced the edict, though historian Bill Reaves relates that some Wilmington residents had run-ins with the law over whether or not pool halls and bars constituted places of public assembly.

One thousand cases were reported by September 27. Wilmington's 19 drugstores, 43 nurses, and 29 doctors soon found themselves swamped with patients at James Walker Memorial Hospital and at Dr. Charles T.

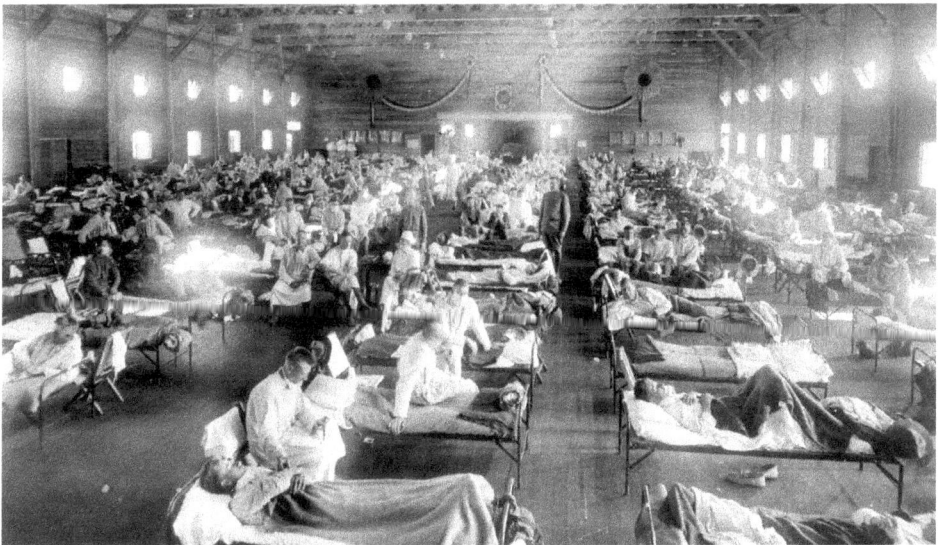

Hospitals across the country soon filled with the sick, and Wilmington was no different.

In 1918, public health officials instituted mask mandates to curb infection rates. Those who did not mask up were subject to jail time.

Harper's sanatorium. Making matters worse, by the time city councilman Benjamin Merritt died that day, only six physicians in the city were themselves well enough to tend to patients. Wilmington was in trouble.

A voluntary curfew went into effect on September 28, with all businesses except pharmacies and groceries asked to close their doors at 6:00 p.m. More telling as to how serious the situation had become was when, for the first time in the city's history, church gatherings were suspended. Only shipyards and railroads continued on their normal schedules, or at least as close to them as they could manage with more and more of the workforce becoming sick. Undertakers ran out of finished coffins and resorted to burying the rising numbers of dead in plain pine boxes. Parents wouldn't let their children play outside for fear of becoming infected.

The disease did its damage quickly. A person who seemed healthy could, a scant hour later, be reduced to suffering "weakness, aching, coughs, chills, and fever." People sat up with the ill in vigils that left them feeling helpless against the silent killer. Nothing seemed to work against it. All that could be done was to sit with the sick. If a victim made it, they made it. Too many didn't. Compounding the tragedy, the disease seemed to play no favorites. People across all demographics were stricken, and unlike in other epidemics, the young and strong were not immune to the disease. A surprisingly large number of those who ultimately died of the Spanish flu in Wilmington were between the ages of twenty and forty.

In an effort to bolster the woefully understaffed medical personnel fighting the disease, Mayor Parker Quince appointed a relief committee to visit homes and offer assistance to families stricken with the flu. Wearing face masks, these groups of two men and one woman went door to door seeking those who might be too ill to report to the hospitals on their own. Armed with quinine in the mistaken belief that the disease was caused by bacteria, these teams were granted permission to forcibly enter homes where no one answered the door in order to ferret out the sick. Aid teams also carried whiskey for use as an oral disinfectant, and codeine to succor the gravely ill. Mustard plasters were a favorite remedy for warding off the disease, but none of these measures seemed to have any favorable results. In the words of Dr. Robert Fales, "One either had the vitality and stamina to survive, or he didn't."

October brought the worst of the epidemic, with between 8,000 and 10,000 cases reported in New Hanover County. Existing hospitals were overwhelmed, with every available bed taken. Even the basement of James Walker Memorial was drafted to house flu victims. Around town, the overflow was taken into makeshift hospitals at Germania Hall and the Moose Hall. The Marine Hospital had opened on September 24, providing a place for military victims to be treated and freeing up beds for civilian use at the general hospitals, but they quickly filled again. The Carolina

Wilmington's new Marine Hospital had opened only a month earlier.

Shipbuilding Corporation opened and supplied a hospital at the corner of Fourth and Grace Streets for employees and their families, while Liberty Shipbuilding did the same in the Wood Building on Third and Walnut. Dr. John J. Blair, superintendent of New Hanover County Schools, opened up Tileston, Williston, Union and Wilmington High School as treatment centers. Citizen groups like the Housewives League, under the supervision of Mary Clifford Bennett, cooked thousands of gallons of broth for delivery to the stricken and their families. For black families, a similar kitchen was set up at the St. Stephen's Methodist Church parsonage.

The epidemic reached its peak in early October. Despite the fact that authorities in Wilmington were doing all they could to stem the tide of disease and death brought on by the epidemic, it just wasn't enough. Fearing for their own populations, Lumberton, Charlotte, and Fayetteville all passed quarantine ordinances preventing anyone from having contact with people in Wilmington. Rumors abounded that the disease was German sabotage (infected Germans were said to have been landed from submarines), that "influenza germs" were in aspirin shipments, and that Health Department officials were concealing the true magnitude of the death toll.

When Wilmington made a formal request for help from the federal government, it was quick in coming. Dr. Charles Stiles of the U.S. Public Health Service, traveled to the city to take charge.

As doctors and nurses from other cities in the Carolinas began making their way to Wilmington to help the beleaguered city, Dr. Stiles centralized the management of the epidemic. To do so sometimes required drastic measures. County Health officials were authorized to send health officers into homes and take the sick to hospitals whether they wanted to go or not. Doctors and nurses coming to town were quickly drafted into service under Stiles' authority. Any nurse who offered private service faced arrest and expulsion from the Red Cross.

As quickly as it came, the cloud of pestilence seemed to pass. By October 10, Dr. Stiles was confident enough that the city was on the road to recovery that he was considering releasing two of the physicians sent to Wilmington for service elsewhere. Between 100 and 120 people died of the "Spanish Lady," as the disease was called, with literally thousands more who were afflicted with the disease that survived. As the crisis passed in Wilmington, it was just beginning in other North Carolina cities and towns. Before the epidemic ended nationally, more than a half million Americans would be dead. Globally, the Spanish flu would bring suffering to 700 million infected victims, and kill 20 million. In contrast, only 53,402 Americans died as a result of combat in what, to that point, was the deadliest war in history.

Wilmington has a long history of suffering the ravages of periodic epidemics and plagues. Yellow fever, malaria, smallpox, and flu – all have laid low the people who live by the brown waters of the Cape Fear River. In a new century where new threats to our health seem to crop up every day (Covid, SARS, avian flu, etc.), it is only a matter of time before the city once again suffers at the hands of some illness. It has happened before.

Captain Benjamin Beery

Good Ships and True:
Shipbuiding on the Cape Fear River
By Jack E. Fryar, Jr.

The blockade runner was racing for the mouth of New Inlet and the protection offered by the huge guns of Fort Fisher on the night of May 6, 1864. Aboard the *U.S.S. Britannia*, Acting Volunteer Lieutenant Sam Huse maneuvered his warship to bring her guns to bear on the fast ship called the *Annie*, as the smuggler tried to deliver a cargo of much-needed supplies to the Confederate port at Wilmington. Around Huse, the U.S. warships *Tuscarora*, *Nansemond*, *Howquah*, *Mount Vernon*, *Kansas* and *Niphon* tried to do the same.

As the *Annie* streaked into the shallow waters of the inlet that was created by a hurricane in the 1760's, Huse witnessed a near collision between the blockade runner and something that looked remarkably like a floatlng house with sloping sides. Rumor in the federal fleet said that the two rebel ironclads being built at Wilmington were on the move. Now Huse realized with a start that the rumors were correct. The floating house was the *C.S.S. Raleigh*, and she was coming out to engage the fleet. As the Union naval officer watched, the sinister looking ship came straight for him and his ship.

Huse immediately fired several rockets to light the night and make the other ships of the blockading squadron aware of the threat. At the same

Confederate iron-clad CSS Raleigh, built on the Cape Fear River at Wilmington, sallied forth to duel with Federal blockaders. The fight was a draw, but provided great fun for the men at Fort Fisher.

time, the *Britannia*'s gunners answered the ironclad's challenge with a round from their 30-pound Parrot cannon. To their alarm, the round had no effect. Huse snapped out a command, and the *Britannia*'s helmsman put the wheel over as hard as it would go. As the ship's paddle wheels dug into the water to gain headway, her gunners let loose with a shot from the 24-pounder cannon at the stern. It had no effect on the ironclad, either. Huse's ship reeled from one heading to another, dodging this way and that to avoid the return fire they knew was coming. They didn't have long to wait.

The *Raleigh*'s first shot smashed the binnacle lights at the helm, while the next just missed the starboard paddle box. To Huse, the shot's tumbling sound reminded him of nothing smaller than a 100-pound Parrot shot. After what must have seemed like an interminable period of time, dashing crazily from side to side in a wild zigzag pattern to dodge the rebel fire, the faster Union ship finally outran the *Raleigh*. Sam Huse let go of a breath he had not noticed he was holding as the ironclad turned to find other targets.

That next target turned out to be the *U.S.S. Nansemond*, whose crew did not know they were a target until someone spotted the *Raleigh* bearing down on them as if to ram. Acting Ensign J.H. Porter, quickly threw the helm over and the *Nansemond* heeled sharply to starboard. The two ships exchanged shots, both to no effect. Now the *Raleigh* was about five hundred yards away, and the *Nansemond*'s sister ships were too far off to lend their support in the fight against the armored juggernaut. Porter decided to follow *Britannia*'s example, choosing retreat over being shredded by the *Raleigh*'s seemingly impregnable guns.

By one a.m. it was so dark that both sides suspended hostilities until dawn brought enough light to resume the contest. At 4:25 a.m. lookouts aboard the *U.S.S. Howquah* sighted the *Raleigh* and the ship went to battle stations. The Union gunners fired several shots from their own 30-pounders as the *Howquah* headed out to sea, putting distance between her and the ironclad. They were just as discouraged as their fellow gunners aboard the *Britannia* and *Nansemond* were, when their shots glanced off *Raleigh*'s sloping hull "like peas."

Other ships of the blockading squadron joined the fight with the daylight, and by early morning the federals were making a determined effort to sink the *Raleigh*. The U.S. warships *Mount Vernon*, *Fahkee*, *Niphon* and *Kansas* joined the fray, some of them firing huge shells from 100 and 150-pounder cannons and IX-inch guns. *Raleigh* shrugged them off like so many fleas.

Aboard the *Raleigh*, Flag Officer W.F. Lynch and the ironclad's commander, J. Pembroke Jones, determined that with more Union ships entering the fight and the tide falling, they had done all the damage they could. Jones ordered the *Raleigh* back into New Inlet as Col. William Lamb ordered the guns of Fort Fisher fired in salute. But on the way back into the shallow inlet, the *Raleigh* ran aground on the shoals known as "the Rip." Stuck hard in the falling tide, the Confederates worked feverishly to lighten the load on the ship. Like all armor-clad warships, *C.S.S. Raleigh* was very heavy, and when the water level in the

J. Pembroke Jones, CSN

inlet fell far enough, that weight would break her back like a child's toy. Despite their best efforts, the crew was unable to get the heavy guns and ammunition off in time. *Raleigh*'s back broke with a sickening snap when the water could no longer support her weight. The marvelous weapon that held such potential for the Confederates defending the port at Wilmington was now just one more shipwreck in waters that hold hundreds of others.

C.S.S. Raleigh was built at the Cassidey Shipyard, one of two in Wilmington during the Civil War that built ships of varying sizes for the Confederate States Navy and other customers. Along with brothers Benjamin and W.L. Beery, whose shipyard on Eagles Island predated the war, F.A.L. Cassidey's yard at the foot of Church Street did a booming business during the war. Not only did they build ships such as the ironclads *C.S.S. Raleigh* and *C.S.S. North Carolina*, but they were also responsible for the construction or conversion of many other types of ships. Among these was a submarine that was scuttled before ever seeing service as the Union army advanced across Eagles Island in 1865, and the gunboat *Yadkin*, which did see service on the Cape Fear River. Benjamin Beery also converted a tug, the *Mariner*, into a privateer mounting one sixteen-pound cannon manned by a crew of thirty, which he commanded himself. The shipyards on either side of the Wilmington waterfront also serviced blockade runners who needed repairs after braving the Union fleet trying to shut off access to the Cape Fear River.

Of the two ironclads built at Wilmington, only the *Raleigh* saw service against the enemy fleet. The *North Carolina*, built at the Beery yard just north of where the modern Cape Fear Memorial Bridge spans the brown waters today, was deemed to have too low a draft to be used in the rough waters of the Atlantic. Instead, she was confined to patrolling the Cape Fear River. Left tied to the dock in Smithville (modern Southport), toredo worms infested her hull. She sank at her mooring without ever having fired a shot in anger.

The Beery brothers began their careers as shipbuilders twenty years before the Civil War, when Benjamin went into business with his father at their yard at Harrison's Saw Mill in 1842. By 1852 Beery's father had left the partnership, and Benjamin bought the Eagles Island land they had worked at and went into business for himself. Berry's Commercial Mill and Shipyard became a mainstay of the Wilmington maritime industry, boasting a steam mill and maritime railway, and a blacksmith shop and rigging loft in addition to the shipyard itself. Beery's business was capable of a full line of maritime construction and ship repair, with a work force numbering as many as 200 employees.

The Cassidey yard survived the war and did business on the Wilmington waterfront for more than forty years, well into the twentieth century. Benjamin Beery's yard on Eagles Island did not. During the war, the Beery yard did so much business with the Confederate government that it earned the name "the Navy Yard." When Union soldiers under the command of John M. Schofield began crossing Eagles Island from Brunswick County early in 1865, Beery saw the writing on the wall: Wilmington could not stand. Rather than see the tools, docks and works of the yard fall into enemy hands, Benjmain Beery set his own shipyard on fire. Beery survived the war and continued in the maritime business, operating in partnership with a man named Sink to salvage the many shipwrecks to be found in the waters of the Cape Fear. By 1882 Beery was once again in business for himself, building boats and ships at a new yard at the foot of Castle Street in Wilmington. He continued to do so until disappearing from all records in 1894.

Wilmington's history of shipbuilding goes back even further than the Beery and Cassidey yards. In 1524, Lucas de Ayllòn, a wealthy Spaniard from Hispaniola, lost a ship while exploring the waters off of Cape Fear. Records of the voyage tell that the men used timber from Bald Head Island and the surrounding area to construct a replacement ship before the journey continued, though more recent scholarship casts doubt on the claim. James Sprunt relates that the first sailing ship built at Wilmington was the *Eliza and Susan*, built by John McIlhenny at his shipyard at the foot of Queen Street in 1833. The ship was named for McIlhenny's two daughters. Josh Toomer did the construction, using live oak from Bald Head Island and Lockwood's Folly in Brunswick County.

Eagles Island's shipyard site lay dormant after the war, until Wilmington Iron Works used it to construct two four-masted schooners of 238 feet long in 1916. The big ships had a capacity of 2,000 tons, and required more than a million and a half feet of North Carolina long leaf pine, Oregon pine and Louisiana oak to build. They may have been the largest wooden ships ever built on the Cape Fear, and took one hundred ship carpenters four years to build. Christened the *Happaug* and *Commach*, only one would enjoy a lengthy service life. Owned by a wealthy New York business man, the *Commach* was sunk by a German U-boat on its maiden voyage.

With steamships doing business on the Cape Fear River after the war, ferrying cargo and passengers from the interior to the port at Wilmington, there was plenty of other business to keep Wilmington Iron Works busy. With a full range of machine and boiler making shops, pattern shops, and a foundry, the company operated first on Front Street between Market and Dock Streets. They later moved a block down to the foot of Orange Street.

Liberty Ships being constructed along the Cape Fear River.

In 1917, Swiss immigrant August Eppler, who at the time lived at Eighth and Dock Streets, devised plans for what he termed a "jitney" submarine. The sub would have been powered by two crewmen operating an engine that ran on batteries or oil. It could carry four torpedoes and be capable of high speed evolutions. No records exist of the sub ever having been built, but the plans seemed sound to marine construction experts of the day.

When America rose to the challenge of two World Wars in the twentieth century, warships and merchant ships were constructed on the Cape Fear. At a site on the east side of the river just south of the Cape Fear Memorial Bridge in 1918, the Liberty Shipyard built a new kind of ship, with hulls made of concrete. Stretching for 1400 feet along the Cape Fear River (although the company actually owned 3,500 feet of river frontage), the shipyard met wartime demands by quickly building ships designed to carry men and supplies to Europe to face down the Kaiser's hopes of domination. The first was christened the *Cape Fear*, a 3,500 –ton behemoth measuring 281 feet long, 46 feet wide, and 39 feet from keel to deck. After World War I, the yard closed for a short time until Newport Shipbuilding took it over to construct concrete tanker ships and seven river steamers for the U.S. government.

Opposite and just south of the Liberty Shipyard, the Carolina Shipbuilding Corporation operated a yard to build steel ships during

World War I. Boston's George A. Fuller Company ran the yard for the government until 1919, when Fuller took it over completely. Ships built here averaged 9,600 tons, and operated with steam propulsion plants. The property was located at the extreme southern end of the property occupied now by the N.C. State Ports at Wilmington.

In World War II, North Carolina Shipbuilding Corporation turned out Liberty ships that became the lifeline that Great Britain depended on to survive. The *Zebulon B. Vance* was the first, but 125 more would follow before the war ended. At its peak, the shipyard employed more than 20,000 men and women, who were able to build a Liberty ship from start to finish in just thirty days. After the war, the site gradually morphed into the current N.C. State Port on the Cape Fear River.

There have been others over the years who used the Cape Fear River to design, build, and launch the vessels for war and peace that are so much a part of southeastern North Carolina's past. Though much of the grand marine construction has passed us by for now, modern boat builders still uphold that heritage at plants building pleasure craft on the Brunswick County side of the brown water. It is a heritage that stretches back to our earliest days, rich in history and innovation.

The **Zebulon B. Vance** *makes way with the help of river tugs after launch.*

Robley D. Evans

Robley D. Evans Account of the Fall of Fort Fisher
By Rear Admiral Robley D. Evans,
from his memoir *A Sailor's Log*

The First Fort Fisher Campaign

dmiral Porter assumed command in November, and at once began assembling a powerful fleet. Every precaution was made for active service. Boilers and machinery were overhauled, magazines, shell rooms, and storerooms replenished, and constant target practice was had with all guns. By the end of November the largest fleet ever seen under the American flag was assembled in Hampton Roads, all classes, from the largest monitor to the small gunboat, being represented. Our destination was a secret, carefully guarded; but we surmised from what was taking place that some important move was contemplated, and in this we were not mistaken. It was evident from the daily target practice that the admiral meant we should hit something when the time for action came, and the landing of the men on the beach for drill was an indication of possible shore service.

The *Ticonderoga*, anchored near us, was firing at target one morning, and making such good practice that we were all watching her with great interest, when one of her pivot guns, a large-caliber Parrott, was fired. There was a terrific report, as if the shell had burst at the muzzle of the gun, a great cloud of smoke, and then something struck close to her, making a great splash in the water. At the same time, or shortly afterward, the shot she had fired fell near the target. About two feet of the muzzle of the gun had blown off, straight up in the air, and come down within twenty feet of the ship. It was the most curious of the many accidents we had then and afterward with the Parrott rifles. This particular gun, though two feet shorter than it was intended to be, was continued in service, and did good work.

Early in December the troopships arrived - thirteen thousand men under General B.F. Butler – and still our destination was a secret.

About this time I received a letter by flag of truce from my brother, who was serving as a captain of scouts on General Lee's staff, in which he said, "We will give you a warm reception at Fort Fisher when you get there!" – showing that our intended move was not so much of a secret to the rebels as it was to us. The information must have been sent from Washington, as no one on the fleet, outside the admiral's immediate official family, knew anything about it. When I showed the letter to Commodore Schenck, which I was required to do by regulations, he seemed much surprised, and sent me with it at once to Admiral Porter, who was very indignant when he had read it. For myself, I thought my brother had only made a good guess; there were only a few important places on the Southern coast remaining in the hands of the rebels, and, as our preparations surely indicated an important move, he guessed, and guessed correctly, that we were after the most important of the lot.

Toward the middle of December all our preparations had been completed, and we put to sea under sealed orders. It was a grand sight as we passed Cape Henry; all the water as far as anyone could see was covered with ships, and among them the flower of the navy. Commodore James Findlay Schenck commanded the third division of the fleet, and flew his flag on the *Powhatan*. The fleet was formed in three columns, the transports and storeships in the centre.

After passing Cape Henry we experienced beautiful weather, and got around Hatteras in almost a dead calm, much to the delight of the troops, who were dreadfully crowded on the troopships. On December 22nd the fleet, having parted company with the transports, anchored in column thirteen miles off the mouth of the Cape Fear River, and then, of course, we knew what we had in hand. That afternoon it came on hard to blow from southeast, and when the sun went down the sight was a grand and threatening one. The seven monitors at the head of the columns held on well at their anchors, but would disappear entirely from sight as the heavy seas swept over them. The ships soon began to drag, and all hands were kept on deck during the entire night, ready to do what was possible in case of collision. When daylight came the monitors were still in place, but the rest of the fleet was scattered over a space of sixteen miles, and nowhere could we make out a single transport. At sundown of the 23rd the fleet was again anchored in good condition, none the worse for the shaking up it had had; but still we wondered what had become of the transports, as none of them showed up. It turned out later that they wre safely anchored well inshore of us, waiting for the stragglers, who had been blown out of place in the gale, to come up.

Before leaving Fortress Monroe, General Butler had proposed a "powder boat," by the explosion of which he hoped to seriously injure the forts on Federal Point, including Fort Fisher. Indeed, he was confident that he would dismount most of the guns and level the works. An old steamer, the *Georgiana* (editor's note – Evans' recollection fails him here, as the ship was actually the *U.S.S. Louisianna*), had been loaded with several hundred tons of powder, and turned over to the navy to explode at the proper spot. A crew of volunteers, commanded by Captain A.C. Rhind, had her in charge, and on the evening of December 24th took her in for the final act in her career. No man in the navy believed for a moment that she would do much harm, but none of us anticipated how little injury would come from the explosion.

At eleven o'clock that night Admiral Porter steamed about the fleet in his flagship, the side-wheeled steamer *Malvern*, and made signal: "Powder boat will blow up at 1:30 a.m. Be prepared to get under way, and stand in to engage the fort!" After that there was no sleep for any one; we stood and watched and waited as the hours slowly dragged by. Half pas one came, and no explosion, and we were fearful of some mishap; but just as the bells struck two o'clock It came. At first a gentle vibration, then the masts and spars shook as if they would come down about our ears; and then came the low rumble like distant thunder, while the sky to the westward was lighted up for a few seconds, and then great masses of powder smoke hung over the land like thunder clouds. The powder boat had blown up surely, and as the fleet rapidly formed for battle there was great curiosity everywhere to see what the effect had been.

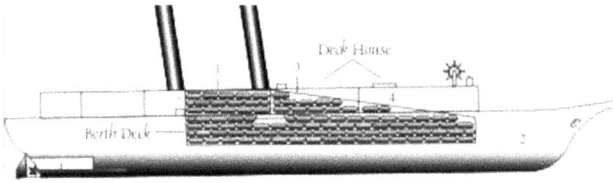

The Powder Vessel - Starboard Cutaway

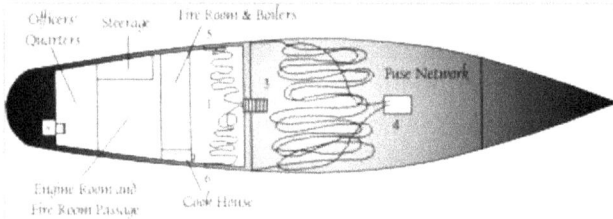

The Powder Vessel - Top View

U.S.S. Louisiana, *outfitted as a powder ship, was to be sacrificed in hopes of forcing a breach at Fort Fisher. Gen. Benjamin Butler's scheme ultimately proved to be more fizzle than pop.*

At daylight we were heading in for the fort, and almost in range, when we saw General Butler's flagship coming at full speed, heading straight at Fort Fisher, which looked to us very grim and strong, and totally uninjured. Everything was very quiet until the general got fairly within range, when there was a flash from the fort and a prolonged roar, and all the guns on that face of the fort opened on his ship. If he had any notion that he could land unopposed he was quickly undeceived, and the way that ship turned and got offshore spoke well for the energy of her fireroom force! The last we saw of her she was running east as fast as her engines could carry her. The powder boat had proved a failure , and the general was grievously disappointed. A rebel newspaper reported that a Yankee gunboat had blown up on the beach and all hands lost.

The fleet stood on in columns, the monitors leading until in position, when the leader anchored; and then the rest anchored in succession as they reached their places. It was a beautiful evolution and beautifully performed. As soon as the monitors came in range, all the guns that would bear opened furiously; and as the range was only seven hundred yards, the hits were frequent. The rebels seemed to conclude very quickly that they could do nothing with the ironclads, so they held their fire for the wooden ships. Then the *Minnesota* took her place, and as her anchor went down her batteries opened, first a broadside from the spar deck, and then her gun-deck broadside roared its Christmas greeting. At the same moment all the rebel guns replied, and the ship was completely enveloped in the smoke from her own guns and the bursting rebel shells. For a moment it looked as if she must be disabled, but then her guns began to speak out with a welcome sound, and we knew she was all right. The *Wabash* and the *Colorado* followed the *Minnesota*, and quickly dropped into their places, opening as they did so with their tremendous batteries. In rapid succession each vessel of the fleet passed them on the off side, firing through the intervals between them, and thus the battle line was formed. At times the shower of shells coming over the vessels engaged gave us a foretaste of what was in store for us, but the losses were wonderfully few.

Just as the *Powhatan* dropped her anchors an incident occurred which caused much bitter comment afterward. The *Brooklyn*, the next ship to us in line, was commanded by Captain James Alden, whose conduct at the battle of Mobile Bay had not met the approval of Admiral Farragut. In taking his position in line he held his fire until his anchor was down, when he fired a broadside very smartly, which brought from the admiral the signal, "Well done, *Brooklyn*!" the only signal of commendation made during the fight. The general feeling was that it was a theatrical performance, and that the signal did injustice to many veteran officers who had handled their ships with consummate skill. However, the signal undoubtedly went far to removing the stigma of Mobile Bay, and the friends of Captain Alden rejoiced over it.

We had been up, many of us, all night, and our only breakfast had been coffee and hard-tack. As we approached our position Commodore Schenck sent me aloft with a pair of glasses to locate, if possible, some guns that were annoying him. It was a raw, cold morning, and I had on a short, double-breasted coat, in the pockets of which I had stowed several pieces of hard-tack. When I had taken my place in the mizzen rigging, just below the top, I put the corner of a hard-tack in my mouth, and was holding it between my teeth while I took a look through the glasses for the guns. I caught them at once, and saw gunners train one of them around until I could only see the muzzle of it, which interested me, because I knew it was pointing directly at us. There was a puff of smoke, something like a lamp-post crossed the field of the glass, and a moment after the rigging was cut four feet below me, and I swung into the mast. I at once thought of my hard-tack, but it was gone, and I never found even a crumb of it. I am sure that I swallowed it whole. When I had reported what I had made out of the battery I was directed to lay down from aloft to my station, which was in charge of the after division guns; but I hesitated to do so, because my knees were shaking, and I was afraid the men would see it. However, I had to come down, and as soon as I reached the deck I stood and looked at my legs, and was greatly relieved to find that they did not show the nervous tremor that worried me so. I soon forgot about it as I became interested and warmed up to my work.

We had only eighteen inches of water under us when we finally anchored and began firing rapidly in obedience to the signal from the admiral. There was wreck of a blockade runner between us and the battery at which we were to fire, and it was soon evident that this had been used as a target and the range was well known. One or two shots were fired in line with it, each one coming closer to us, and then they struck us with a ten-inch shot. Four more followed, each one striking nearly in the same place, on the bends forward of the starboard wheel, and going through on to the berthing deck. Then for some reason the shot and shells began going over us, striking water thirty or forty feet away. Probably the gunners on shore could not see the splash of these shots, and thought they were striking us. If they had not changed their range when they did they would have sunk us in an hour. As it was, we hauled out at sundown pretty well hammered, and leaking so that we had to shift all our guns to port in order to stop the shot holes.

We had damaged the fort to the extent of dismounting some of the guns and burning the barracks and officers' quarters. When the whole line was fairly engaged the sight was magnificent, and never to be forgotten by those who saw it. No fort had ever before been subjected to such a fire, and the garrison could only make a feeble response; most of them were driven into the bombproofs, where they remained until we hauled off for the night. The heaviest losses on our side had been caused by the bursting of the one-hundred pound Parrott rifles; thirty-five or forty men had been killed or wounded in this way.

The transports in the meantime were got together, and while a slow, steady fire was kept up on the forts by the monitors and a portion of the fleet, the rest of us devoted our energies to getting the troops on shore. The weather was favourable for the purpose, and in one day and night we landed General Butler and his thirteen thousand soldiers with their ammunition and stores. Then for two days more we hammered away at the fort , expecting every hour to see them carried by the army; but we were not to have that pleasure. Some officers and men did get very near the fort, but, without making effort, the general decided that the works had not been seriously damaged as defensive works, and were too strong to be carried by assault. He therefore asked that we re-embark his men, which we did, and he sailed for the North. So ended the first attack on Fort Fisher, which had promised so much to the national cause.

The Second Assault on Fort Fisher

Admiral Porter was not willing to give up so easily, and on his representations, concurred in by General Grant, the second expedition was organized. The fleet was ordered to Beaufort, North Carolina, and such vessels as could do so entered harbour; the rest anchored outside, and all hands worked day and night coaling and filling up with ammunition and stores. Any one who has served on that coast in the winter months will know the difficulties with which we had to contend; to those who have not, no adequate idea can be given. Gales of wind were of almost constant occurrence, and, as we were in the open sea, the vessels rolled so that frequently we had to use lifelines on our decks to prevent the men from being washed overboard. On many occasions vessels had to slip their cables and go to sea to ride out the storms.

Adm. David Dixon Porter

Notwithstanding all this, in two weeks we were ready to try it again, and this time success seemed to be in the air. That gallant soldier, General Alfred Terry, was in command of the army contingent; his men were enthusiastic and anxious for the fight, and he and Admiral Porter were working in harmony – a fact of itself promising the very best results. It was agreed between the commanders that a naval brigade should be landed to assist the army in the assault, by attacking the sea face of the fort, while the army went in on the northwest angle. Volunteers were called for from the navy for this service, and it was gratifying to see the

Union warships fired over 19,000 shells at Fort Fisher during the bombardment.

officers and men come forward, almost in a body, for a job they knew would be a desperate one. So many volunteered that finally a detail had to be made from each ship, and there were many sorely disappointed ones when the names were published.

It was my good fortune to be officer of the deck when the order came on board directing the movement, and so I had my name put first on the list of those who volunteered. At this time there were four classmates aboard – Harris, Kellogg, Morris, and Evans. All volunteered, and as only two could go, we agreed that Harris and Kellogg, being in the first section of the class, should have one chance between them, and Morris and I being in the second section, should have the other chance. Harris won his chance on the toss of a penny; but I, being a Virginian and having no particular family ties, insisted that I should go rather than Morris, who came from New York and would be sadly missed if he were killed. To all of this Morris naturally objected, and we seemed a long way from any conclusion, when he suggested that we leave the selection to Lieutenant-Commander George Bache, who was to command the men from *Powhatan*, which was done, and Bache selected me.

January 13th found us again in front of Fort Fisher, and this time we came to stay. The fleet opened on the fort, and kept up a constant and accurate fire. We soon found a great difference in the garrison from the one we had fought in the first attack. They stood up and fought their guns most gallantly, and would not be driven into the bombproofs. A division of gunboats was sent close in to cover the landing of troops, which was done by the boats of the fleet in a sea heavy enough to make care necessary.

I was in charge of the commodore's barge, a very handsome, large, able boat, fit to carry thirty-five or forty men. We made the first landing with over two hundred boats, and the sight was a notable one as we pulled in, an occasional shell splashing among us, and the bullets spluttering on the surface of the water.

As soon as the order was given to land we went for the beach at full speed, and, after passing the first breakers, turned our boats and backed them in until our passengers could land almost with dry feet but to get them out of the boats at the right moment was almost impossible. They would wait too long, and as a result most of them were rolled up on the beach by the surf, soaking wet. But once on shore it was glorious to see how they knew their business and the way they did it. As soon as they got their feet they spread out in a skirmish line, and the rifles began to crack. When I came in with the second load those on shore had captured some cattle, and were skinning them, and did not seem the least bit worried by the fire of the skirmishers, only three or four hundred yards away. Before dark we had all the men landed, and enough ammunition and stores to make them safe and comfortable in case it should come on to blow. During the night we completed the landing of stores and supplies and some thirty-pound Parrott guns, which were immediately put in position facing General Bragg, who was coming from the direction of Wilmington to re-enforce the garrison of Fort Fisher. The bombardment was kept up during the 14th, while the army got into position for the assault, which had been fixed for the afternoon of the 15th.

The premonitions that men have before going into battle are very curious and interesting, particularly when they come true. We had on board the *Powhatan* a fine young seaman named Flannigan, who came from Philadelphia. On the night of the 14th of January he came to my room with a small box in his hand, and said to me, "Mr. Evans, will you be kind enough to take charge of this box for me – it has some little trinkets in it – and give it to my sister in Philadelphia?" I asked him why he didn't deliver it himself, to which he replied, "I am going ashore with you to-morrow, and will be killed." I told him how many bullets it required to kill a man in action, and in other ways tried to shake his conviction, but it was no use – he stuck to it. He showed no nervousness over it, but seemed to regard it as a matter of course. I took the box and, after making a proper memorandum, put it away among my things. On the afternoon of the next day, when we were charging the fort and just as we came under fire, at about eight hundred yards, I saw Flannigan reel out to one side and drop, the first man hit, with a bullet through his heart. I stepped quickly to his side and asked if he were badly hurt; the only reply was a smile as he looked up into my face and rolled over dead. The box was delivered as he requested, and I afterward assisted in getting a pension for his sister.

January 15th proved a beautiful day for our work, clear and warm enough, with a smooth beach for our landing. At early daylight the whole fleet opened on the fort, and poured shells in on it at a fearful rate. After a hasty dinner at noon the signal was made at one o'clock, "Land naval brigade." In a few minutes we were off, cheered by our shipmates, and pulling for shore, where we landed unopposed and without serious accident, about one mile and a half from the northeast angle of Fort Fisher. On the way ashore some evilly disposed person fired a shot at us, which struck the stroke oar of my boat, cut it in two, and sent the handle spinning across my stomach with such force that I thought I was broken in two. On landing we were quickly formed in three divisions, with the marine battalion in the lead.

Lt. Kidder Breese led the charge of the naval column.

During the forenoon a force of firemen had landed under Lieutenant Preston to dig rifle pits, well to the front, and these were to be occupied by the marines, who were to keep down the rebel fire until the sailors, armed with cutlass and revolver, reached the parapet. When the divisions were formed, we advanced until we reached a point about twelve hundred yards from the fort, where we waited the signal to charge, which was to be the blowing of the steam whistle on the flagship, repeated by other vessels of the fleet. All the guns that we could see had been dismounted or disabled in the bombardment, but after we landed there was one large rifle that opened on us and did some damage. The shells generally struck short of us, and would then ricochet down the level beach, jumping along for all the world like rabbits. To avoid this shell fire the divisions had been marched by the flank to take advantage of what shelter the slope of the beach offered. It thus happened that the three divisions forged up abreast of each other, and we charged in this formation – three columns abreast, the marines leading. While we were waiting for the army to report ready, our men had a good rest, and seemed to be in excellent spirits. The rebels were firing at us slowly, but doing no damage to speak of. Curious little puffs of sand showed where the Enfield rifle balls were striking, but they only hit a man now and then by accident.

At three o'clock the order to charge was given, and we started for our long run of twelve hundred yards over the loose sand. The fleet kept up a hot fire until we approached within about six hundred yards of the fort, and then ceased firing. The rebels seemed to understand our signals, and almost before the last gun was fired had manned the parapets and opened on us with twenty-six hundred muskets. The army had not yet assaulted, so the whole garrison concentrated its fire on us. Under the shower of bullets the marines broke before reaching the rifle pits that had been dug for them, and did not appear again as an organization in the assault. Most of the men and many of the officers mixed in with the column of sailors, and went on with them. About five hundred yards from the fort the head of the column suddenly stopped, and, as if by magic, the whole mass of men went down like a row of falling bricks; in a second every man was flat his stomach. The officers called on the men, and they responded instantly, starting forward as fast as they could go. At about three hundred yards they again went down, this time under the effect of canister added to the rifle fire. Again we rallied them, and once more

U.S. sailors and marines charge to assault the one place at Fort Fisher where both land and seaface guns could be brought to bear.

started to the front under a perfect hail of lead, with men dropping rapidly in every direction. We were now so close that we could hear the voices of the rebels, and what they said need not be written here. The officers were pulling their caps down over their eyes, for it was almost impossible to look at the deadly flashing blue line of the parapet, and we all felt that in a few minutes more we should get our cutlasses to work and make up for the fearful loss we had suffered.

At this moment I saw Colonel Lamb, the Confederate commander, gallantly standing out on the parapet and calling to his men to get up and shoot he Yankees. I considered him within range of revolver, so took a deliberate shot at him. As I fired, a bullet ripped through the front of my coat across my breast, turning me completely around. I felt a burning sensation, like a hot iron, over my heart, and saw something red coming out of the hole in my coat which I took for blood. I knew, of course, that if a bullet had gone through this part of my body I was done for; but that was no place to stop, so I went on at the head of my company. As we approached the remains of the stockade I was aware that one particular sharpshooter was

Col. William Lamb, CSA

shooting at me, and when we were a hundred yards away he hit me in the left leg, about three inches below the knee. The force of the blow was so great that I landed on my face in the sand. I got a silk handkerchief out of my pocket, and with the kind assistance of my classmate, Hoban Sands, soon stopped the blood, and again went to the front as fast as I could.

About this time the men were stumbling over wires which they cut with their knives – they proved to be wires to the torpedoes over which we had charged, but they failed to explode. My left leg seemed asleep, but I was able to use it. The stockade, or what remained of it, was very near, and I determined to lead my company by the flank through a break in it, and then charge over the angle of the fort, which now looked very difficult to climb. I managed to get through the stockade with seven others, when my sharpshooter friend sent a bullet through my right knee, and I realized that my chance of going was settled. I tried to stand up, but it was no use; my legs would not hold me, and besides this I was bleeding dreadfully, and I knew that was a matter which had to be looked to. I heard someone say, "They are retreating!" and looking back I saw our men breaking from the rear of the columns, leaving no one to steady the men in behind; and it was in this way that we were defeated, by the men breaking from the rear. Two minutes more and we should have been on the parapet, and then – nobody can even guess what would have happened, but surely a dreadful loss of life. As the men retreated down the beach they were gathered up and put into the trenches opposite Bragg, and there served until after the fort was captured. Of the eight of us who went inside the stockade all were shot down; one, the colour bearer of my company, was halfway up the parapet when he received his death wound.

When I received the wound in my right knee I began at once to try to stop the flow of blood. I used for the purpose one of the half dozen silk handkerchiefs with which I had provided myself, but I was so tired and weak from loss of blood that I was some time doing the trick. In the meantime my sharpshooter friend, about thirty-five yards away, continued to shoot at me, at the same time addressing me in very forcible but uncomplimentary language. At the fifth shot, I think it was, he hit me again, taking off the end of one of my toes, tearing off the sole of my shoe, and wrenching my ankle dreadfully. I thought the bullet had gone through my ankle, the pain was so intense. For some reason, I don't know why, this shot made me unreasonable angry, and, rolling over in the sand so as to face my antagonist, I addressed a few brief remarks to him; and then, just as some one handed him a freshly loaded musket, I fired, aiming at his breast. I knew all the time that I should kill him if I shot at him, but had not intended to do so until he shot me in the toe. My bullet went a little high, striking the poor chap in the throat and passing out at the back of his neck. He staggered around, after dropping his gun, and finally pitched over the parapet and rolled down near me, where he lay dead. I could see his feet as they projected over a pile of sand, and from their position knew that he had fought his last fight. Near me was lying the cockswain of my boat, Campbell by name, who had a canister ball through his lungs, and was evidently bleeding to death. When he saw the result of my shot he said, "Mr. Evans, let me crawl over there and give that _____ _____ another shot." He was dead before I could tell him that the poor fellow did not require any further attention from us.

One of the marines from the *Powhatan*, a splendid fellow named Wasmouth, came through the stockade, quickly gathered me up under one arm, and before the sharpshooters could hit him laid me down in a place of comparative safety; but a moment afterward the fleet opened fire again, and the shells from the *New Ironsides* and the monitors began falling dangerously near us. Occasionally one would strike short and, exploding, send great chunks of mud and pieces of log flying in all directions. Wasmouth again picked me up, and, after carrying me about fifty yards, dropped me into a pit made by a large shell. Here I was entirely protected from the rebel fire, and several times called to him to take cover, but he said each time, "The bullet has not been made that will kill me." I was very drowsy and almost asleep when I heard a peculiar thud of a bullet, and looking up, found poor Wasmouth with his hand to his neck, turning round and round, and the blood spurting out in a steady stream. The bullet had gone through his neck, cutting the jugular, and in a few minutes he dropped in the edge of the surf and bled to death. He certainly was an honor to his uniform.

Just as our men began to break, the army made their charge, and were able to make a lodgment on the northwest portion of the works before the rebels, who had taken us for the main assaulting column, saw them. When they discovered them, however, they went at them with a savage yell, and for seven hours fought them desperately, the same bombproof in several cases being captured and recaptured five or six times. A number of sharpshooters remained on the sea face and northeast angle, and shot at every moving thing. No doubt this was owing to the fact that quite a number of marines were scattered about the beach wherever they could find cover, keeping up a steady fire.

After Wasmouth was killed I soon fell asleep, and when I awoke it was some time before I could recall my surroundings. The tide had come in, and the hole in which I was lying was nearly full of water, which had about covered me and was trickling into my ears. I could see a monitor firing, and apparently very near, and the thought came to me that I could swim off to her if I only had a bit of plank or driftwood, but this I could not get. It was plain enough that I should soon be drowned like a rat in a hole unless I managed to get out somehow. Dead and wounded men were lying about in ghastly piles, but no one to lend me a helping hand. By this time I could not use my legs in any way, and when I dug my hands into the sides of my prison and tried to pull myself out the sand gave way and left me still lying in the water. Finally, I made a strong effort, and rolled myself sideways out of the hole. When I got out I saw a marine a short distance away, nicely covered by a pile of sand, and firing deliberately at the fort. I called to him to pull me in behind his pile of sand, but he declined, on the ground that the rebel fire was too sharp for him to expose himself. I persuaded him with my revolver to change his mind, and in two seconds he had me in a place of safety – that is to say, safe by a small margin, for when he fired, the rebel bullets would snip the sand within a few inches of our heads. If the marine had known that my revolver was soaking wet, and could not possibly be fired, I suppose I should have been buried the next morning, as many other poor fellows were. As soon as I could reach some cartridges from a dead sailor lying near me I loaded my revolver, thinking it might be useful before the job was finished.

When I was jerked in behind this pile of sand, I landed across the body of the only coward I ever saw in the naval service. At first I was not conscious that there was a man under me, so completely had he worked himself into the sand; he was actually below the surface of the ground. The monitors were firing over us, and as a shell came roaring by he pulled his knees up to his chin, which hurt me, as it jostled my broken legs. I said, "Hello! Are you wounded?" "No sir," he replied; "I am afraid to move." "All right then," I said; "keep quiet, and don't hurt my legs again!" The next shell that came over he did the same thing, and the next, notwithstanding my repeated cautions. So I tapped him between the eyes with the butt of my revolver, and he was quiet after that. The poor creature was so scared that he would lie still and cry as the shells flew over us. As I said before, he was the only coward I ever saw in the naval service.

From my new position I could see the army slowly fighting its way from one gun to another, and it was a magnificent sight. They knew their business thoroughly, these gallant fellows from the Army of the Potomac, and in the end, at ten o'clock that night, won a victory that will live as long as heroic deeds are recorded. I can recall to this day the splendid courage of General Curtis, leading his brigade; he seemed to stand head and shoulders above those around him; and while I looked at him he went down, but was soon on his feet, only to go down a second time, shot in the eye. As darkness approached and the cold began to be felt, our men seemed to fight with more desperate determination, and the advance was more rapid. The Confederates were doing, and had done, all that human courage could do, but they were wearing out, and the arrival of a fresh brigade on our side discouraged them.

The scene on the beach at this time was a pitiful one – dead and wounded officers and men as far as the eye could see. As a rule, they lay quiet on the sand and took their punishment like the brave lads they were, but occasionally the thirst brought on by loss of blood was more than they could bear, and a sound-wave would drift along, "Water, water, water!" and then all would be quiet again. It was one of the worst of the awful features of war. Just as the sun went down, and it did seem to go very slowly that afternoon, I saw an officer coming up the beach dressed in an overcoat and wearing side arms. As he approached me I recognized Dr. Longstreet, and begged him to lie down, as the bullets were singing around his head. He took a canteen off a dead marine and gave me a swallow of sand and water, and did the same for another wounded man. Then, turning his face toward me, he said, "We will have you all off the beach to-night," and was moving on to the front, when a bullet struck him in the forehead. He sprang several feet in the air, fell at full length on his back, and lay quite still and dead. His resignation had been accepted a week before, and as soon as the fight was done he was going home to Norfolk to be married.

After the death of Dr. Longstreet I saw another man coming toward me; but he was taking advantage of all the cover he could get, and arrived without accident. He was a fireman from the gunboat *Chicopee*, and said he had come after me, but had only a coal-shovel with which to aid me. He said if I could sit in the coal-shovel he could drag me off! The twilight was deepening, and it seemed improbable that a sharpshooter could hit either of us, so I managed to get seated on the shovel, and the fireman, with both hands behind him on the handle, started to pull me off, but had only gone a few steps when a bullet struck him, passing through both arms below the elbows. That ended my trip on the coal-shovel, and I spent the time until dark making my friend as comfortable as possible. Then I heard some one calling my name, and in a few minutes two men came who said Captain Cushing had sent them to bring me off. They had only their hands, but they used them most willingly and tenderly. One would put me on his back and carry me, while the other held me on. When the first one was tired, the two would change places; and thus I was carried, shot through both legs, a distance of a mile and a half.

The outfit for the care and comfort of the wounded consisted of a large fire made of cracker boxes and driftwood, a fair supply of very bad whiskey, and a number of able and intelligent medical officers. To the vicinity of the blazing fire I, among a large number of wounded men, was carried, stretched out on a plank with my head on a cracker box, where I enjoyed the warmth, which was very grateful in the chill of the January evening. My clothing was saturated with blood and salt water, and thoroughly filled with sand. My wounds were in the same condition. A rebel gunboat in the bayou back of the fort was using our fire as a target, and finally succeeded in landing a shell fairly in the middle of it, much to our discomfort. When the shell exploded several men were killed, and the fire blown about over the rest of us. The doctor finally got to me, and after cutting off my trousers and drawers well up on my thighs, split them down the sides and threw them into the fire. Then he ran a probe, first through one hole, then the other, said I was badly wounded, gave me a stiff glass of grog, and passed on to the next man, leaving me practically naked. A brother officer, seeing my condition, took the cape off his overcoat and wrapped it about my legs, and this, with the assistance of the grog, soon made me very comfortable.

About half past nine that night Captain Breese, who commanded the brigade, succeeded in getting a lifeboat in through the heavy surf breaking on the beach, and at once wounded officers were tumbled into her, while the crew stood in the water holding her head on the seas. My turn came at last, and two friends landed me I the boat with my legs hanging over the stern; then the crew jumped in, the cockswain sat down calmly on my knees, gave the men the word, and out we went through the surf in beautiful style. The boat was from the gunboat *Nereus*, Captain Howell commanding, and to her we were taken. We found her rolling in a trough of the sea, but the officer of the deck had all preparations made, and we were quickly hoisted up to the davits, and willing hands soon transferred us to the deck. Just as they were putting me on a cot, before taking me below, I saw a signal torch on the parapet of the fort calling the flagship, and a moment later I read this signal: "The fort is OUR-" and then everything broke loose! Nobody waited for the completion of the signal; all hands knew what the last letter would be. There was a great burst of rockets and blue lights, and the men manning the rigging cheered as the guns roared with saluting charges. Long after I was comfortably swung I the wardroom I could hear the fleet rejoicing over the downfall of the great rebel stronghold.

The officers of the *Nereus*, from the captain down, spent the night doing all in their power to make us comfortable. We had a good supply of whiskey and a pitcher of morphine and water, and they gave us plenty of both. Shortly after daylight signal was made to transfer all wounded men on board to the *Santiago de Cuba*, and for vessels having dead on board to hoist colours at half-mast. I shall never forget the sight that greeted me when I was carried on deck to be put in a boat. The fleet lay just in the position in which it had fought the day before, and it seemed to me that every ship had her flag at half-mast lazily flapping in the drizzling rain. The weather was cold and raw, and all our wounds were stiff and sore, and every movement of those helping us caused indescribable suffering. In the excitement of the charge, getting wounded was fun, but we had a different problem to solve, and it required real nerve to face it.

The General Goes Down To Georgia
By Jack E. Fryar, Jr.

L ieutenant Colonel Young observed the three ordered columns of redcoats, marching six abreast, approaching across the savannah in precise columns. They peeled off to the left and right upon reaching a point a mere one hundred fifty yards from the place where the men of the Wilmington militia stood. The tightly packed British soldiers were a far cry from the kilted Highlanders Young had faced in the brief but fierce fight three years earlier at the battle of Moores Creek. Then, the Scots had broken under a hellish fire from the assembled militias of Richard Caswell and Alexander Lillington. The bayonets glittering atop the Brown Bess muskets carried by the British regulars he faced now suggested these men were cut from different cloth.

A short distance away, with the men from Edenton, Brigadier General John Ashe calmly paced and watched the British enemy assembling. It had been scant minutes since the alarm had sounded, the drums in the American camp sending men running for the stands of muskets close by their tents. Even though the North Carolinians had marched 400 miles to join Benjamin Lincoln's southern army, their arrival was not the end of their journey. Lincoln immediately ordered the Tar Heels from Wilmington, New Bern, Halifax and Edenton to march another

130 miles south, to join General Williamson's soldiers facing the British at Augusta, Georgia. Young hoped Ashe was up to the task facing him.

Young was not being unreasonable. John Ashe had also been at Moores Creek, as a captain commanding a company of Wilmington militiamen. He had performed well then, but it had been three years since that February day in 1776. This was John Ashe's first military action since, and this time the enemy was not Highlander farmers and backwoods malcontents. This time, the foe was well-equipped professionals of the strongest army in the world.

Weary as they were, the North Carolina commanders understood why Lincoln hurried them south. In the battle at Kettle Creek in mid-February, patriot forces had dealt a significant blow to loyalist ambitions in Georgia. In the fight that took place near a muddy stream in Wilkes County, Andrew Pickens and 350 men from South Carolina and Georgia had surprised the pickets of loyalist commander James Boyd. Despite the Tories' efforts to slow the attack from hasty fighting positions behind boulders and trees, Pickens' men refused to quit. Boyd was killed when a Whig ball smashed into

BrigGen. John Ashe

him. His second in command, a major named Spurgeon, just barely managed to get 450 loyalist troops across the creek and retreat to the safety of British-held Savannah. The numbers of loyalists killed ranged from 19 to 70, and a number of others were captured. The end result was that Tory forces in Georgia were reeling, and Benjamin Lincoln wanted to smash them once and for all. The blade he would wield in that effort was the North Carolina troops under General John Ashe.

Ashe was no newcomer to the Whig cause. Born at Grovely Plantation in Brunswick County, North Carolina in 1720, he was not unlike many of those who would become known to later generations as the Founding Fathers. Ashe was from a prominent family with the wealth to give him an education and the finer things in life. He served as Speaker of North Carolina's colonial assembly from 1762 to 1765. His first taste of a soldier's life came with his service under the British flag during the French & Indian War nearly two decades earlier. But like others of his class, he cast his lot with those who would have independence for the American colonies. To that end, Ashe joined other Cape Fear men including Cornelius Harnett and Robert Howe in opposition to the Stamp Act, marching on Royal Governor William Tryon's house at Russellborough to demand the act not be enforced. The same three patriots also marched at the head of a force of roughly 500 men who sacked Fort Johnston, at the mouth of the Cape Fear River, in the wake of the Battle of Moores Creek. After raising and equipping a militia regiment out of his own pocket, Ashe was promoted to Brigadier General, and sent to reinforce patriot forces under Lincoln, who were defending Charleston, South Carolina in 1778.

LtCol. Archibald Campbell

Arriving in Lincoln's camp at Purrysburg, on the South Carolina – Georgia border, Ashe was almost immediately given orders to continue south, with the objective of recapturing Augusta, which had fallen to British forces under Lieutenant Colonel Archibald Campbell. In an attempt to raise loyalist support from the Georgia interior, British commander Augustin Prevost had allowed a force of roughly 1,400 troops to advance on Augusta. British allies indicated a substantial number of men loyal to the crown were waiting there for a show of support from the British army to rise up and join the King's standard. Despite being harassed by a small force of Georgia Continentals under Brigadier General Samuel Elbert, Campbell arrived at Augusta in good order.

General Andrew Williamson withdrew his force of South Carolina and Georgia militia from Augusta at Campbell's approach. The British took the town after a brief skirmish with a rearguard force, left behind when the Whigs retreated. Williamson pulled his men back to just over the South Carolina border, to build his strength and keep tabs on British movements.

While Campbell held Augusta, it was a precarious occupation. Understrength as he was, the Scottish officer was unaware of Boyd's defeat at Kettle Creek when news of Ashe's impending arrival prompted him to pull out of the city. Combined with the rebel forces already in the area, Campbell realized he would be facing a force twice the size of his own once Ashe arrived. Until he could be reinforced, Campbell opted to avoid a fight with a numerically superior enemy. The British packed up and marched south, winding up at their outpost at Ebenezer. Not long afterwards, Campbell boarded ship for home, after turning over command to Lieutenant Colonel Mark Prevost.

Despite being short of rations, and dog tired from a virtually uninterrupted forced march of hundreds of miles from North Carolina to the Savannah River, John Ashe was confident. His 1,700 men had been augmented by local troops and now numbered around 2,400. When the British pulled out of Augusta, Ashe was ordered to follow them. At Briar Creek, fifteen miles north of Ebenezer, the Americans made camp along the road to Savannah, not far from Miller Bridge.

The creek itself was a tributary of the Savannah River, and the burned out Miller Bridge was the main means of crossing it. By positioning himself where he did, John Ashe was situated to control access to the Georgia low country from the piedmont. In doing so, he could prevent British reinforcements from loyalists in the interior, and cut off supplies the British desperately needed. To the east, swamps and the Savannah River anchored one flank. Brier Creek itself anchored the south and southwestern approaches. With 200 cavalry attached to his force, Benjamin Lincoln considered Ashe adequately manned and equipped to rebuff a British attempt against him.

In Savannah, General Augustin Prevost realized the danger posed by Ashe's force. With his son, Mark, now in command of Campbell's men, the British commander decided to put a plan into motion that he hoped would eliminate the threat. Formulated while Campbell was still in command, the plan called for one element of the British force to make a demonstration to the Americans' front, while another marched around the rebels to attack their flank. Lieutenant Colonel Prevost marched his 900 men fifteen miles to Paris Bridge on March 1, 1779, while a decoy force of 500 men of the 71st Regiment left Ebenezer and stopped at Bucks Bridge, just three miles from the Americans. If all went well, the closer force at Bucks Bridge would prevent Ashe from noticing Prevost's flanking attack from the north until it was too late.

When Prevost arrived at Paris Mill, he found the Americans had destroyed the bridge. The British tried to reconstruct it, but there were no materials on hand to rebuild a bridge sturdy enough to handle the load of a troop crossing. The British built a pontoon bridge instead, but the construction wasn't complete until later that evening. It wasn't until March 3, 1779 that all of Prevost's men and cannon were able to get across the creek. All that time the British were vulnerable to American scouts, who could have discovered them while they labored to ford the creek. It was good fortune for Prevost that they did not.

Gen. Augustine Prevost

In the American camp, John Ashe felt like he was playing catch up. He arrived at the Savannah River on February 27, but then was called away to a commander's conference with Lincoln. It fell to subordinates to construct the American camp. This they did despite being woefully short of entrenching tools or artillery. On the plus side, Ashe was reinforced by a couple hundred South Carolina cavalry, some Georgia Continentals under Samuel Elbert, and Anthony Lytle's North Carolina light infantry. On the negative side, there was little any of them could do to secure the camp without the tools to construct earthworks or without cannon to defend it.

Upon returning to Brier Creek, Ashe considered reports that the enemy had been on the move. Cavalry scouts were dispatched to locate the British and look into rumors that they had been sighted near Paris Bridge. The question of what the cavalry found, or what Ashe knew of it, would become central to what happened later. Whatever happened, by the time the rest of the cavalry made it back into the American camp later that evening, Ashe did not send out more scouts due to fatigue on the part of both the soldiers and their mounts.

The following afternoon brought an unpleasant surprise for the Americans. A rider raced into the camp, excitedly shouting that the British were no more than eight miles away. Prevost had completed his fording of Brier Creek, and was now marching on Ashe's force from the northwest. Drummers beat a tattoo that sent men scrambling for stands of arms stacked outside tents. Cavalrymen rushed to get saddles on their horses. In the command tent, John Ashe called for his officers to deploy the troops. One of those orders recalled Lytle's light infantry from positions a mile away from the main encampment.

Despite some confusion as to where they were supposed to go, Ashe calmly put his 900 men into line. Although roughly 1,300 troops were under his command, Lytle's and Ross' light horse was deployed elsewhere. Ashe had issued orders recalling them, but until they could return, John Ashe had only two thirds that number to face the approaching redcoats. Despite the confusion, the Americans were soon deployed with the Edenton militia on the right, Elbert's Georgia Continentals in the center, and New Bern's militia on the left. A second line of battle consisted of the men from Wilmington on the left and the Halifax militiamen on the right. Ashe's position formed a wedge between Brier Creek on the left, and the swamps feeding the Savannah River on the right. It should have been a good position, with water guarding his both his flanks. But while the troops on the left were virtually on the banks of the creek, on the right there was a gap of about a half a mile that Ashe was unaware of.

Once the Americans had swung into line, their ammunition was issued. Ill equipped as they were, most of the men had no cartridge boxes to keep the precious paper wrapped powder and balls safe and protected until they were needed. Men stashed them under their arms, or tied in hunting shirts. In the haste to get the ammunition out, many of the militiamen were issued the wrong caliber of ammo for their weapons. While the cartridges were still being handed out, the first of the scarlet-clad columns appeared in front of them.

At 150 yards, the British deployed with Baird's light infantry on the left, the 71st regiment in the center, and Tory militia from the Carolinas on the right. The three columns melded into one line with a precision that the Americans' own deployments had been sorely lacking.

BATTLE OF BRIER CREEK - MARCH 3, 1779

BRITISH LINE

Right - Sir James Baird's Infantry.

Center - 2nd. Battalion 71st. Reg. - Lt. Col. Prevost.

Left - 150 Cavalry.

Extreme Left - 50 Rifle Men Placed In Ambuscade To Protect Left Flank.

Reserve In Rear - 3 Companies Florida Grenadiers And A Troop Of Dragoons.

AMERICAN LINE

Right - Under General Young With N.C. Militia.

Center - Under General Bryant With N.C. Militia.

Left - General Elbert And Lt. Col. John McIntosh With 60 Continentals And 150 Ga. Militia.

Rear At Bridge Site - Col. Perkins With Light Infantry And One Brass Four Pounder.

Map labels:

- LT. COL. PREVOST REACHED HERE MARCH 2, 1779
- BRITISH LINE
- AMERICAN LINE CAMP OF GEN. ASHE MADE FEB. 28, 1779
- PARIS MILL
- BRIDGE DESTROYED BY MARBURY
- FREEMAN'S OLD BRIDGE (DESTROYED)
- REDOUBTS.
- GENERAL AUGUSTINE PREVOST HEADQUARTERS
- OLD AUGUSTA ROAD

- GEN. PREVOST'S HORSE AND LIGHT INFANTRY MET COL. LEONARD MARBURY'S DRAGOONS HERE, MARCH 2nd AND CUT THEM OFF FROM ASHE'S MAIN TROOPS AFTER DEFEATING THEM.
- PART OF COL. MARBURY'S HORSE TROOPS ESCAPED BY CROSSING HERE MARCH 2nd.
- BURTON'S FERRY. COL. SMITH STATIONED HERE WITH MUCH OF THE BAGGAGE OF GENERAL ASHE'S.
- MATHEW'S BLUFF. GEN. GRIFFITH RUTHERFORD WITH 800 MEN WAS CROSSING HERE AT TIME OF BATTLE, TO REINFORCE GEN. ASHE.
- LIGHT INFANTRY PROTECTING REAR OF ASHE'S ARMY.
- MAJOR ROSS WITH 300 CAVALRY FACED McPHERSON HERE MORNING OF 3rd. BUT DID NOT ENGAGE HIM OR REPORT HIS PRESENCE.
- MAJOR McPHERSON WITH 1st BATTALION OF 71st REGIMENT BRITISH TROOPS TOOK POSITION HERE AS DECOY 3-1-79.
- BLACK SWAMP, S.C. WHERE GENERALS LINCOLN, MOULTRIE, ASHE AND RUTHERFORD MET MONDAY, MARCH 1st, 1779 TO PLAN GEORGIA CAMPAIGN.
- HUDSON'S FERRY
- GEN. ANDREW WILLIAMSON WITH 1200 MEN ON WAY TO JOIN ASHE
- ROUTE OF LT. COL. PREVOST - MARCH 2, 1779

COMPILED BY CLYDE D. HOLLINGSWORTH 1953

Clyde D. Hollingsworth's map of the Battle of Briar Creek, Georgia (shown sideways for size and clarity).

245 The Coastal Chronicles Vol. III

Small artillery punctuated the main British line, while Prevost's grenadiers and dragoons formed a reserve to the rear. Prevost opened the dance with a volley of musket fire that obscured the British line in the gray veil of powder smoke.

While the redcoats offered up the first volley of the day, like was often the case, the shots flew high, doing the Americans little damage. Elbert's Georgians and the militia from Edenton returned the favor with an ineffectual volley of their own. Elbert's men fired two or three times more before saving their ammunition until the redcoats were in closer range. To get within range, Elbert took it upon himself to advance his men until they were just thirty yards from the British. Now both sides were well within the effective range of their weapons they held, and a brisk fire began between the Georgians and Baird's Highlanders.

Elbert's men had drifted to the left when they marched forward to engage the enemy. In doing so they put themselves between the British and the line of fire of the New Bern regiment, who had to maneuver to the left to engage the redcoats without hitting their own men. Meanwhile, British cavalry menaced the American right, forcing the Edenton militia to angle in that direction to meet the threat. The result of the two moves was that Ashe's understrength Americans now had a gap between the two elements of the American army. The Highlanders saw it and immediately rushed forward to exploit it.

As British bayonets flashed in the afternoon light, the militia units wilted. Few of the Americans had bayonets of their own to meet the British rush, so engaging in close combat with redcoats, who were wielding foot-long points of steel on the end of their muskets, was a fool's notion. Only Elbert's Continentals held their ground. John Ashe wheeled his horse and raced for the rear to try and rally his disintegrating command. Only a small portion of the Wilmington militia under Col. Young stayed, and that only because they were maneuvering to prevent a flank attack. Some of the units fired two or three rounds more, but soon the whole lot was in headlong retreat.

General Elbert found himself in dire straits. As the British surrounded them, their thanks for holding their ground was to see the British savage their ranks from the rear. A British ball struck Elbert. Further fighting became futile, and Elbert ordered his men to lay down their arms, as blood streamed down his sides.

Lieutenant Colonel Prevost reported 150 Americans killed, and more perished trying to escape across Brier Creek. Ashe lost 227 men as prisoners, and more who abandoned their roles as soldiers to run for home.

Later, a court-martial would absolve John Ashe of the charge of cowardice, but it didn't absolve him in the eyes of his men. To be fair, Ashe was thrown into a fight for which he was woefully under equipped an under prepared. The worn-out troops he took in to the fight at Brier Creek could not have been a match for fresh, well equipped and trained redcoats. Be that as it may, the American defeat at Brier Creek, which many persisted in seeing as John Ashe's fault, put Georgia squarely back under the control of the British.

Not long after, John Ashe returned to his native Brunswick County. When Major James H. Craig's redcoats occupied the city as pat of Cornwallis' campaign of 1781, Ashe hid in the nearby swamps to avoid capture. He was betrayed by one of his slaves and taken into British custody. Thrown into the same roofless jail that would claim the life of Cornelius Harnett, John Ashe became deathly ill, too. He contracted smallpox and was paroled by Major Craig to prevent the disease from becoming epidemic in the occupied city. John Ashe passed away from his illness on October 24, 1781, not long after his release.

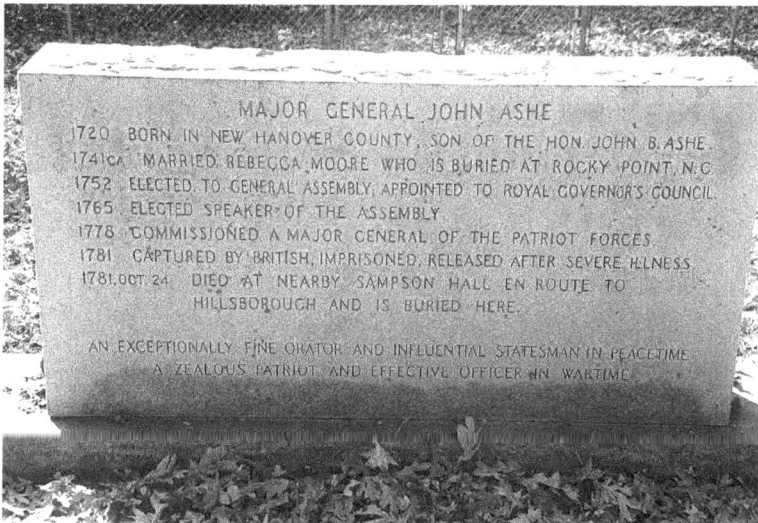

MAJOR GENERAL JOHN ASHE
1720 BORN IN NEW HANOVER COUNTY, SON OF THE HON. JOHN B. ASHE
1741ca MARRIED REBECCA MOORE WHO IS BURIED AT ROCKY POINT, N.C.
1752 ELECTED TO GENERAL ASSEMBLY, APPOINTED TO ROYAL GOVERNOR'S COUNCIL
1765 ELECTED SPEAKER OF THE ASSEMBLY
1778 COMMISSIONED A MAJOR GENERAL OF THE PATRIOT FORCES
1781 CAPTURED BY BRITISH, IMPRISONED, RELEASED AFTER SEVERE ILLNESS
1781.OCT. 24 DIED AT NEARBY SAMPSON HALL EN ROUTE TO
HILLSBOROUGH AND IS BURIED HERE.

AN EXCEPTIONALLY FINE ORATOR AND INFLUENTIAL STATESMAN IN PEACETIME
A ZEALOUS PATRIOT AND EFFECTIVE OFFICER IN WARTIME

About the Author...

Jack E. Fryar, Jr.

...is a life-long resident of southeastern North Carolina. He has been a professional writer and publisher since 1994. In 2000, Jack founded Dram Tree Books, a small publishing house whose titles tell the story of North and South Carolina and the Carolina coast. He has authored or edited twenty-eight volumes of North Carolina and Cape Fear history, and is a frequent lecturer for historic groups in the region. Jack is also the editor and publisher of the digital magazine, *Carolina Chronicles* (www. carolinachroniclesmagazine.weebly.com), covering the history of North and South Carolina. His historical specialty is the Cape Fear and colonial North Carolina, particularly during the seventeenth century. Jack has served as a United States Marine, worked as a broadcaster, freelance magazine writer, night club bouncer, sports announcer, book store manager, publisher's representative, high school history teacher, and book designer. He holds Masters degrees in History and Teaching from the University of North Carolina at Wilmington.

www.ingramcontent.com/pod-product-compliance
Lightning Source LLC
Chambersburg PA
CBHW052035090426

42739CB00010B/1914